The Great Ideas of Philosophy, 2nd Edition
Part I

Professor Daniel N. Robinson

THE TEACHING COMPANY ®

PUBLISHED BY:

THE TEACHING COMPANY
4151 Lafayette Center Drive, Suite 100
Chantilly, Virginia 20151-1232
1-800-TEACH-12
Fax—703-378-3819
www.teach12.com

ISBN 1-56585-983-9

Daniel N. Robinson, Ph.D.

Philosophy Faculty, Oxford University
Distinguished Professor, Emeritus, Georgetown University

Daniel Robinson is Distinguished Professor, Emeritus, Georgetown University, where he taught from 1971 to 2001. He is a member of the philosophy faculty of Oxford University and former Adjunct Professor of Psychology at Columbia University. Although his doctorate was earned in neuropsychology (1965, City University of New York), his scholarly books and articles have established him as an authority in the history and philosophy of psychology, history of ideas, philosophy of mind, and kindred subjects.

Dr. Robinson's books include *The Enlightened Machine: An Analytical Introduction to Neuropsychology* (Columbia, 1980), *Psychology and Law* (Oxford, 1980), *Philosophy of Psychology* (Columbia, 1985), *Aristotle's Psychology* (1989), *An Intellectual History of Psychology* (3rd edition, Wisconsin, 1995), and *Wild Beasts and Idle Humours: The Insanity Defense from Antiquity to the Present* (Harvard, 1996). He has served as principal consultant to PBS for the award-winning series *The Brain* and the subsequent nine-part series *The Mind*. He is past president of two divisions of the American Psychological Association: the Division of the History of Psychology and the Division of Theoretical and Philosophical Psychology. Dr. Robinson also serves on the Board of Scholars of Princeton's James Madison Program in American Ideals and Institutions, is a member of the American Philosophical Association, and is a Fellow of the American Psychological Association.

Table of Contents
The Great Ideas of Philosophy, 2nd Edition
Part I

The Great Ideas of Philosophy, 2nd Edition

Scope:

This course of 60 lectures is intended to introduce the student to main currents and issues in philosophical thought from the founding of the subject in ancient Greece to more contemporary studies. The lectures are organized around three abiding problems: the problem of knowledge (epistemology and metaphysics), the problem of conduct (ethics and moral philosophy), and the problem of governance (political science and law). Each of these has by now evolved into a specialized subject treated rigorously in professional texts and journals. But even in these more technical projections, the problems remain largely as they were when the schools of Plato and Aristotle dealt with them and imposed on them the features they still retain.

More than a series of lectures on the great philosophers, this course is designed to acquaint the student with broader cultural and historical conditions that favored or opposed a given philosophical perspective. Attention is paid to the influence that scientific developments had on the very conception of philosophy and on the scientific rejection of "metaphysics" that took place when the "two cultures" began to take separate paths.

Needless to say, the vast terrain that philosophy seeks to cover extends far beyond what can be explored in 60 lectures—or in 200 lectures! Entire areas of active scholarship have been ignored. But still other areas have been more carefully examined than is customary in an introductory course: philosophy of law, philosophy and aesthetics, evolutionary and psychoanalytic theory. The hope and expectation is that, informed by these lectures, the interested student will press on, will fashion a fuller curriculum of study, and will return to these lectures for the more general framework within which the specialized knowledge ultimately must find a place.

Lecture One

From the Upanishads to Homer

Scope:

In the myth of Theseus and the Minotaur, Theseus, having killed the Minotaur, is able to escape from the labyrinth only because Ariadne had given him a golden cord by which he can retrace his steps. Myths are an endless source of metaphor, and the cord of Ariadne is an apt metaphor for history: We solve a problem or a puzzle by retracing the steps that got us where we are. In these 60 lectures on philosophy from remote antiquity to the 21st century, history will be our guide.

Central to the history of philosophy are three overarching problems. For the sake of economy, these may be dubbed the *problem of knowledge*, the *problem of conduct*, and the *problem of governance*. The first of these would be developed within the fields now called epistemology and metaphysics. The second is the domain of ethics and moral philosophy. The third is the province of political science and jurisprudence. But these developed realms of reflective inquiry were slow to reveal themselves to human intelligence.

Beginning in *mimesis*, in dance and ritual that encode and explain the world, the questions become more insistent, and as a whole, communities begin to ponder the nature of things. The dance is augmented by song and poetry, by epic tales so vivid that children never forget the main characters and their extraordinary experiences and exploits and that pose, in different terms, the fundamental questions: What is the world? What should I do? How are our lives to be ordered? Between 800 and 600 B.C., such accounts proliferated. Both the Hindu Upanishads and Homer's famous epics are rich in what may be called pre-philosophical reflections on the human condition and the point and purpose of life. Such works are the background "folk" wisdom of an age; philosophy is a refinement or a rejection of the claims of the dancer and the bard.

Outline

I. We are about to embark on an intellectual journey of 60 lectures devoted to great ideas in philosophy, covering a period of time from remote antiquity to the present century. Our guide will be the history of ideas.

   A. We begin with myth, which seeks to answer perplexing questions but does so in such a way as to create and preserve a kind of civic coherence. The mythology of a people is the basis on which they recognize themselves as a people and have a coherent relationship, not only to each other but with their own past.

   B. To some extent, philosophy is disruptive in this regard. The enterprise is not an essentially civic one. It does not begin with a settled position on political and moral matters, then seek ways to enshrine the settled view. Rather, the mission is a broadly epistemological one. The search, as we shall discover, is the search for truth.

   C. Nonetheless, the questions that mythology must set out to answer are not unlike the questions that philosophy sets out to answer. We can identify three overarching issues that consume much of the subject matter of philosophy: the *problem of knowledge*, the *problem of conduct*, and the *problem of governance*.

      1. The problem of knowledge is straightforward. How is it that we come to know anything? On what basis do we undertake to frame and seek answers to questions? Long before the appearance of philosophy, people facing the challenges of daily life were required to seek knowledge, if only practical knowledge. In philosophy, the problem reaches beyond the practical and the everyday to more general and abstract realms.

2. The problem of conduct is nothing less than the problem of deciding how one's life should be lived. How should I conduct myself in such a way that my life is a satisfying one? How will I be able to act in a way that maximizes pleasure and minimizes pain? What sort of person should I strive to be? What's the nature of the relationships I have to others?

3. Were there no basis on which to plan or conduct a course of life, there would be no real "problem" to be solved politically. The problem of governance arises in light of conflicts at the level of conduct. On what basis does a people come to understand itself as a people? What is the basis on which modes of leadership are chosen? What is the basis on which leaders are resisted, revolutions staged, radical upheaval fomented?

D. Long before the appearance of philosophy, issues of this sort were engaged, often heroically, by persons and by entire communities. Indeed, philosophy comes about at a late stage in the development of this daily encounter with the problems of knowledge, conduct, and governance.

II. The Upanishads are a brilliant example of the vast body of morality tales that appeared in many settled communities between 800 and 600 B.C.

A. The etymology of the word *Upanishad* carries the action of "sitting next to," as in "sitting next to the master." The Hindu Upanishads pose philosophical questions, but the answers are mythic.

B. The questions posed by the Upanishads are the abiding ones: Where do we come from? How do we explain the fact that some things live and other things don't? How did this great earth come about, and what are we to make of the objects in the sea and sky? What kind of life should I be living? Why is there so much evil in the world?

C. Central to the Upanishads is the notion that the universe itself, and everything in it, exists in virtue of some fundamental power or force or fire, a kind of cosmic soul, *Atman*, which because of its presence, gives reality to things and to us.

    1. We share something fundamentally in common with the universe itself. We have the breath of fire within us. We have soul within us. It is an imperishable feature of our very nature. Everything that there is participates in the cosmic *Atman*.

    2. There is a sense that there is something fundamentally identical between the life of the person and the life of the cosmos, that one is the microcosmic expression of the macrocosm.

D. These teachings come to equate *Atman* not only with fire and life and creativity but also with *Brahma*, a form of knowledge, knowledge as the manifestation of the spirit. The quest for knowledge then becomes quite a natural undertaking for those invested with *Atman*, and *Brahma* becomes the search that renders life meaningful.

E. All comes from the soul (*Atman*), even space itself. Creation is attributed to an imperishable and heavenly person, *Purusha*, who though breathless, gives breath. Again, what is *Brahma*? It is breath; it is thought; it is enlightenment. Thus, it is the macrocosm within the microcosm, which is oneself—both the self and the cosmos endowed with *Atman*.

F. Through the Upanishads, we have the beliefs of an ancient culture, a distinctly *Eastern* culture; however, nearly all civilized people adopt the Hindu teachings on ethical grounds. The Buddha's teachings include rules against killing and theft, against any form of moral degradation, against cruelty and deception. Nonetheless, the teachings do not stand as philosophy.

III. Moving from East to West, we can make certain comparisons between the Upanishads and the famous epics of the blind poet Homer, composed circa 750 B.C.

    A. What moves the Homeric actors is not precepts coming from above but something arising inside themselves. Diomedes, for example, is said to be overcome by *lyssa*, the blind rage of the wolf.

    B. The gods in Homer are enlarged versions of the hero, in fact, often have sired or mothered the hero. What divides humanity and divinity is mortality; otherwise, they have much in common, including little power over destiny itself.

    C. There is something terribly immediate and awesomely human and real in the Homeric epics. We find ourselves on every page. There are no final answers to the questions of why things happen. Why, for example, does the Trojan War take place? Is it the anger of the gods? The pride of men?

    D. *Iliad* and *Odyssey* are entirely open-textured at the levels we call epistemology, ethics, and political science.

        1. The problem of knowledge is underscored in the epics in the form of delusional dreams, gods imitating mortals, hallucinatory experiences.

        2. The origin of conduct is illustrated repeatedly by our vulnerability to our own passions, our loss of rational control.

        3. The problem of governance in this war of princes and kings is written in blood and gore, where the Destinies are more powerful than the rule of law.

    E. The Upanishads would merge us with the eternal cosmic soul, but *Iliad* and *Odyssey* assert that we are beings of this earth. Throughout the epics, the focus is on the problems of earth, on the beginning and middle and end of human life, the need for a conservative approach to life, the recognition that we are part rational and part passionate, and that there is an internal conflict taking place within us.

F. One character given to us in Homer, described as the most pathetic of all, the person in the worst imaginable situation, is the heartless, lawless, stateless man.

    1. What Homer is claiming here is quite different from the Upanishads, which promotes a kind of introspective and, indeed, isolating form of contemplative life.

    2. Homer tells us that nothing is worse than to be outside the civic order of things, to be separated from the laws and customs and habitats of one's people.

    3. The human condition calls for life within a settled community, a *polis* in which one participates and from which one draws lessons for life.

G. A final note about Homer is that everywhere in the epics, nature is the guide. In philosophy, at least in its earliest stages, we will also see nature as a guide. How apt, in this connection, that one of the great philosophers of the 20th century, Ludwig Wittgenstein, would say of his own mission as a philosopher that he attempted nothing more than "to show the fly the way out of the bottle."

Recommended Reading:

Hume, R. E., trans. *The Thirteen Principal Upanishads*. Oxford, 1971.

Homer. *The Iliad*. R. Lattimore, trans. Chicago, 1951.

Robinson, D. N. *Aristotle's Psychology*. Columbia, 1989, chapter 1.

Questions to Consider:

1. Summarize the implications that follow when the soul of the cosmos is assumed to be within the person, in contrast to the sharp Homeric division between the human and the divine.

2. The Upanishads feature a search for wisdom; Homer's epics, for heroic achievement. Describe how both may be regarded as "perfectionist" in their aims but in quite different ways.

Lecture One—Transcript

From the Upanishads to Homer

This current series of 60 lectures is actually the second edition of the original *Great Ideas in Philosophy* prepared nearly a decade ago. Now, philosophy being the subject it is, I would not say that comparably great ideas have come along in the recent decade, but there are good reasons for a second edition, in any case.

First, I myself have had some additional thoughts and even second thoughts that might improve the original lectures. Some of these are conceptual; some are at the level of detail. I allow myself the hopeful belief that the emendations and additions will make the revised lectures better than the originals were.

More important than this, though, in the original 50 lectures—committed as they were to that part of the history of ideas in which philosophical issues are dominant—far too little attention was paid to specialty subjects, and to some recent progress in our understanding of the traditional problems. Hence, 10 new lectures.

Well, that much said, let me cut out, now, the prefatory remarks at this point, and get to the course of lectures themselves.

When Sir Arthur Evans excavated the great court at Knossos on the island of Crete, the court of King Minos, he discovered extraordinary mural paintings featuring young athletes, brave Greek boys, hurtling over large bulls in tasks at once ritualistic and dangerous. Now, in his war with Athens, King Minos of Crete exacted as annual tribute seven young boys and seven girls as sacrifices to the Minotaur. Theseus was to be one of these sacrificial victims.

If Theseus was to find and kill the Minotaur, thereby liberating Athens from this macabre burden, he would have to negotiate a complex maze, the labyrinth, so cleverly fashioned by Daedalus. So vexing was the task that no one who ever entered this maze was able to find his way out. However, Ariadne, the princess daughter of King Minos, fell in love with Theseus and gave him a ball of string, a golden cord, which he could use to find his way back out of the labyrinth that had led him initially to the Minotaur. Now, once within the labyrinth, Theseus confronts and kills the Minotaur, thus becoming a fabled hero to the Athenians.

Of course, all mythology is laden with metaphor. Surely, the cord provided by Ariadne is something of the metaphor of history itself. You find your way out of a bind, you find your way out of great perplexity, by retracing the steps that led to the difficulties in the first place.

Now, we are about to embark on a journey into an intellectual labyrinth of 60 lectures devoted to great ideas in philosophy, covering a period of time from remote antiquity to the present century, and I am going to need something of Ariadne's cord to do this. The guide here really will have to be the history of ideas, the great ideas in philosophy, a history that is not cumulative in the sense that scientific knowledge is cumulative.

Rather, intellectual history presents us with a set of ideas that, building on precedents, on past mistakes, past understandings, lead us, perhaps, toward the light of progress.

Well, science develops in the sense of ever more general laws and ever more reliable data, but the developments in philosophy are chiefly in the form of greater clarity, an ever more refined sense of just what makes the problem problematic. If ignorance is not thereby totally overcome, at least it is exposed.

Now, what about these great myths, the myth of Theseus liberating Athens? Theseus is a great hero in the ancient world of the Athenians. They saw him as something of the founder of Athenian independence during the time of King Minos, which is circa 1400 or 1500 B.C.

However, Theseus's was to be a troubled life. First of all, he had Medea as a stepmother and, as if that were not portentous enough, he came to believe that he actually should have a daughter of Zeus as his wife. Thus, he abandons fair Ariadne on the island of Naxos and, in ancient Greek mythology, there are generally grave consequences following displays of bad character. Thus, Theseus solves one great problem, but his success leads to still other problems, all this underscoring what it means to be mortal.

Well, myths seek to answer questions, but they raise at least one question for each one they seem to settle. Witness: If boys and girls are sent to Crete as sacrifices, the question that naturally arises is well, the Minotaur, if a bull, isn't a meat-eater. What, then? Well, bulls do not eat children!

Ah, well, the Minotaur is not a bull. It is a kind of beast. It's a kind of monster. It's half human, half bull, and, of course, the human part answers the question of why these sacrifices would be consumed by something otherwise so bull-like.

Why is it that young children were sent to the island of Crete, then? Well, King Minos had lost a son, and as a result of his deep grieving and resentment, at least according to one myth, he exacted this penalty on the Athenians. "Oh, I see, but then how is it that no one was ever able to get out of that labyrinth until Theseus? After all, does 'love conquer all,' and is Ariadne's treason against her father what dooms her to abandonment by Theseus?"

Here is a folklore, useful to capture the attention of the child, and cultivate a certain attitude toward actions and feelings, toward values and goals. The myth answers perplexing questions, but it answers them in a special kind of way. It answers them in such a way as to create and preserve a kind of civic coherence.

Now, to some extent, philosophy is disruptive in just this regard. The enterprise is not an essentially civic one. It does not begin with a settled position on political and moral matters, then seeking ways to enshrine the settled view. Rather, the mission is a broadly epistemological one. The search, as we shall discover, is the search for truth, or at least for such illumination as to allow us to see the biases and half-truths that have led from one blind alley to another in the labyrinth of thought. Wherever the mission might lead us philosophically, we are morally obliged to go, and, as I say, this does not always have the effect of cementing civic bonds or enshrining cultural values. It should not be surprising that, throughout the ages, philosophers have often found themselves in deep trouble.

Nonetheless, the questions that mythology must set out to answer are not unlike the questions that philosophy sets out to answer, and at the risk of being economical to the point of libel, I would say there are three overarching questions that consume much, if not all, of the subject matter of philosophy; three central problem areas.

There is first the problem of knowledge, then, the problem of conduct, and finally, the problem of governance in the political sense. How are we to understand these problems? Why are they set down in this order? Well, let's begin with the problem of knowledge.

The problem of knowledge is a straightforward problem. How is it we come to know anything, or assume that we do? On what basis do we undertake to frame, and then seek answers to questions?

Now, long before the appearance of philosophy, people facing the challenges of daily life were required by the very reality of the case to seek knowledge, if only utterly but necessary practical knowledge. The less one knows, the more frightening and uncertain is one's world; it remains so even in ages that regard themselves as highly informed, so the search for knowledge is not a narrow "academic" enterprise, but a pressing one, in a world that is unpredictable and dangerous, one that has lethal consequences when not dealt with correctly.

The problem of knowledge is co-extensive not only with human life, then; it is co-extensive with the life of the entire animal economy. Creatures must know things in order to survive. Some are fitted out instinctually to know what they have to know, but for those of us, mere *Homo sapiens*, we more or less have to work many of these things out as best we can and as we go along.

However, as ubiquitous as the problem of knowledge is, it will take on fundamentally different characteristics with the advent of philosophical modes of understanding. The problem will reach beyond the practical and the everyday, to more general and abstract realms, which nonetheless, are thought to be ever surer guides than the mere, unreflecting folkways of an unreflecting mind.

The problem of conduct is nothing less than the problem of deciding how one's life should be lived. We are able to address this problem only on the assumption that there is some sort of reliable knowledge available to us as regards the sorts of lives that are possible, and the general consequences of adopting one form over another. If only implicitly, then, one takes a position on essentially ethical matters only after having already taken a position on—what? On "what one knows."

Now, were there no basis on which to plan or conduct a course of life, no basis upon which to choose one form of life over another, there probably would be no real "problem" to be solved politically. The problem of governance arises in light of conflicts at the level of conduct, conflicts at the level of those core precepts that incline persons to act in certain ways. Every community, every known human enclave of any appreciable size, includes leaders, kings, chiefs, tyrants, presidents, senators. Now, what's the basis upon which modes of leadership are chosen? What's the basis upon which leaders are resisted, revolutions staged, radical upheavals fomented? What's the basis upon which territorial boundaries are established, and honored? What's the basis upon which a people comes to understand itself as a *people* in virtue of the form of government or form of leadership, or laws that it possesses?

These are the essential questions. What is it I am able to know? How should I live my life? What are the political realities and options facing me? Is this the sort of *polis*, is this the sort of community, is this the sort of tribe capable of sustaining, nurturing, and otherwise furthering what human beings take to be their best interests—those best interests often specified in the form of myth and tradition?

Now, long before the appearance of philosophy as such, issues of this sort were engaged, often heroically, by persons and by entire communities, as they are to this minute. Indeed, philosophy comes about at a very late stage in the development of this engagement, in the development of this daily encounter with the problem of knowledge, the problem of conduct, and the problem of governance.

Let's consider the period from 800 to 600 B.C., in which there are so many remarkable developments throughout the populated world, developments in the Celtic world, in the Nile Valley, including, centrally, the Hebrew prophets, in India, and the Mediterranean; developments that are pre-philosophical, but obviously anticipating a kind of philosophical inquiry.

We see in the writings, in the teachings of such eras, myths that often involve a voyage or journey of some kind. To get from A to B, there are obstacles that must be overcome. To overcome these obstacles, a kind of wisdom or knowledge is necessary. This might be borne in by birds or by other kinds of animals, by omens and prophesies, visions and voices, some of the guides being revelatory. There might be oracles to explain the right choice or direction. Very often, it is the wise man's counsel that is sought. One sits in the presence of the wise; one sits next to the wise man and addresses questions to him.

The etymology of the word *Upanishad* carries the action of "sitting next to," to "sit next to the master," and I say between 800 B.C. and 300 B.C., the Hindus would develop the Upanishads, which address questions regarding knowledge, conduct, the right sort of life, the nature of authority. This is part of the quasi-mythical and, at the same time, pre-philosophical thought of a highly developed culture, a highly developed civilization.

Well, what sorts of questions does one address to the wise man, to the prophet thought to be divinely inspired, to the sage whose years of reverential prayer and self-denial seem to have carved wisdom into his very bones?

The questions are the abiding ones: Where do we come from? How do you explain that some things live and other things don't? How did this great Earth come about, and what are we to make of the objects in the sea and sky, and do they portend certain things? How do we differ from other living things, and what is it about dead things such that they never seem to come to life, although we hear that sometimes they do? What kind of life should I be living? Why is there so much evil in the world? Why is it that we have wars?

Central to the Upanishads is the notion that the Universe itself, and everything in it, exists in virtue of some fundamental power or force or fire, a kind of cosmic soul, *Atman*, which in virtue of its presence, gives reality to things. It gives reality to us, too. We share something fundamentally in common with the Universe itself. We have the breath of fire within us. We have soul within us. It is an imperishable feature of our very nature. Everything that there is participates in the cosmic *Atman*, and there is this sense, then, in the Hindu Upanishads, that there is something fundamentally identical between the life of the person and the life of the cosmos, that indeed, one is the microscopic expression of the macrocosm itself.

Consider the *Khandogya-Upanishad* where, in the *Eighth Khanda*, three men are discussing the origin of everything, the Master expected to answer:

"Where," it is asked, "does 'tone' come from?"

To which the reply is, "Breath."

"And breath itself?"

"From food."

"And food?"

"From water."

"And water?"

"From heaven."

"And what is the source of the heavenly world?"

"This world."

Again, you see the essential unity between the fundamental explanatory device of the cosmos, including everything, and everything in its sharing.

Now, these are teachings that come to equate *Atman* not only with fire and life and creativity, but also through *Brahma*, a form of knowledge, knowledge as the manifestation of spirit, and, indeed, the quest for knowledge then becomes quite a natural undertaking for those invested with *Atman*, and *Brahma* then becomes the search that renders life meaningful.

Well, all comes from the soul, *Atman*—even space itself. Creation is attributed to an imperishable and heavenly person, Purusha, who, though breathless, gives breath: "Fire is his head; his eyes the Moon and the Sun."

Again, what is *Brahma*? It is breath, it is thought; it is enlightenment. Thus, it is the macrocosm within the microcosm, which is oneself—

both the self and the cosmos now endowed with *Atman*: "He who knows *Brahma* as the real, as knowledge, he obtains all he desires."

Again, though, who or what is *Brahma*? Initially, in the Hindu mythology, Brahma is one of the three supreme deities, along with Vishnu and Shiva, but is found in later developments to be the one deity that animates the entire cosmos. "Out of Brahma's mind were born the seers, but out of Brahma's body came sons named for greed, anger and the vices in general." You see the body as the grounding of what is vice.

Brahma is also a kind of introspective activity, however. It is a communion with the cosmic mind, with a deep, meaningful, initiatory quality. Here we have the beliefs of an ancient culture, a distinctly Eastern culture, with a set of religious values and over-arching precepts that must remain unchallenged, if these subtle teachings are to make sense and, indeed, to be incorporated into nothing less than a given form of life.

The Buddha lived some 25 centuries ago, and his teachings were placed, it is said, in three baskets, one of them containing the so-called *Bodhisattva Precepts*. What are these, other than rules against killing and theft, against any form of moral degradation, against any form of cruelty or deception? These are neither "Eastern" nor "Western;" they are the sort of counsel that can be ignored only at peril. Nonetheless, the teachings do not stand as philosophy, as such, nor does the mode of instruction fit the philosophical template.

Let me move now from East to West, and offer certain comparisons between the Upanishads and those famous epics composed by the blind poet, Homer. I'll not even attempt to answer the "Homer" questions: "Who was Homer?" "How many were there?" "What was 'her' real name?"

The "Homer" of history is operating out of an epic tradition that is already enduring. The early dating of Homer is in the early 800s B.C. The late dating, the more recent dating, would have him composing *Iliad*, and later *Odyssey*, circa 750 B.C.

Now, I want to go the epics themselves, and draw certain comparisons between *Atman* and what moves the heroes in Homer's epics. What moves the heroes of *Iliad* and *Odyssey* is generally found not in the cosmos, but in their chests, in *thumos*, places in the viscera.

The reason the Homeric hero steels himself for battle is because, on the basis of *thumos*, he is impelled to do certain things. When Diomedes turns around and does something as rash and unimaginable—namely, he takes his sword out and strikes out against Aphrodite herself—what is it Homer tells us? He tells us, "Well, Diomedes was overcome by something called *lyssa*, the 'wolf's rage.'" Diomedes, now in the pitch of battle, is simply overcome by something inside himself. What he is overcome by is something that is at least quasi-natural. It's something occupying him at the corporeal level, at the level of his very body and being. There is something utterly and uncompromisingly earthly about the Homeric epics.

The gods themselves have a very earthly—I'm inclined to say, a very "earthy" character. They have this penchant for mating with human beings. You never know when one of them is going to show up on someone's doorstep, finding your daughter or son particularly attractive. Myth has it that the great Minos of Crete was the direct offspring of Zeus, as was Helen of Troy, Achilles; scores of those celebrated in Greek mythology have this divine ancestry. In the pedigree of the great figures of the ancient world, then, one will often find the pairing of mortals with the gods of Olympus.

There is something terribly immediate, terribly proximate, awesomely human and portentous and real in the Homeric epics. We find ourselves on every page, so to speak. We find the same perplexity, no final answers. When Homer sets out to tell us the causes of the Trojan War, well, what are they? Is it the curse on the house of Atreus? Is that the cause, or is it because at a wedding of Thetis and Peleus, to which the goddess Eris, in the Latin "Discordia," had not been invited? Well, arriving and angered, Discordia throws a golden apple into the setting, on which is written—as Zeus reads it aloud—"*Kallisti*," "To the fairest."

Paris now must make a choice among the three contestants: Hera, Athena and Aphrodite. Each attempts to bribe him; you know, "Pick me as the fairest." Hera bribes him with wealth, Athena with wisdom and what is Aphrodite's bribe? Promising him a woman as beautiful as Athena herself, and the woman turns out to be, yes, Helen of Troy.

There are no lasting, finally settled answers to the question, "What caused the war?" The problem of knowledge is understood in the Homeric epics in the form of delusional dreams, gods imitating mortals, hallucinatory experiences. The actors can be rendered as mere playthings by deceiving them. The origin of conduct is illustrated repeatedly by our vulnerability to our own passions, our loss of rational control, and the problem of governance in this war of princes and kings is written in blood and gore, where the destinies are more powerful than the rule of law.

Iliad and *Odyssey* are entirely open-textured at the level we are pleased to call "epistemology, ethics and political science." What we learn is that it is very easy to get oneself into the labyrinth, and far more difficult to escape. The best course, then, is to pay homage to the jealous gods, and to avoid hubristic pretensions to divine powers.

The Upanishads would merge us with the eternal cosmic soul, and *Iliad* and *Odyssey* say instead, "Not a bit of it, that's not our fate; that's not our place of being. Our place of being is Earth." It's a place of war, love, failed aspirations, a place of heroic gestures that sometimes succeed, but often fail:

> The best laid schemes o' mice an' men
> Gang aft agley
> An' lea'e us nought but grief an' pain
> For promis'd joy!"

—said Robbie Burns, and in this, he might as well have been Homer.

The first word in *Iliad* is *menin*, anger. This is an epic about anger. It's about the prideful anger of Achilles, Achilles sulking in his tent, Achilles, who has to give up the booty of victory to Agamemnon, because Agamemnon, in order to propitiate Apollo, must return the young woman that he had chosen for himself and taken to be his prize for valor in battle, and if Agamemnon has to give up Briseis, then, of course, Achilles is going to have to give up his human prize. Well, you see, the entire epic begins with two heroes ready to kill each other over injured pride.

Now, as often in disguise, as in herself, Athena tells Achilles, "No, no; this is no time for the two of you engage in swordplay," but Achilles is angry beyond consolation. He retires to his tent. Not only will he not participate in the battle; he pleads with the gods that his own people, the Achaeans, the Greek-speakers—that they be defeated, so prideful is he, so angry is he, so possessed is he, in his chest, by an anger that will not subside.

Later in *Iliad*, the two are reconciled. Achilles now is going to join the fray and behave heroically. He knows that the one who kills Hector will die himself, and he sets out to do just that. The deed accomplished, Achilles drags the body of Hector around the walls of Troy. The body is being torn asunder. Its royal garments are shredded.

How does Homer end his song? It ends with Hector's once beautiful body being dragged by horses. Here, then, says Homer, is the end of Hector, "Breaker of horses."

Often the feature that identifies one is also present as he is undone. There's a kind of matching here between the achievement and the downfall, not a causal connection, but an ironic one, and one that suggests that the origin of the story may be found elsewhere.

Well, throughout, the focus is on Earth and on the problems of Earth, on the beginning and the middle and end of human life, the unpredictability of it, the need for a kind of conservative approach to it, the recognition that we are part rational and part passionate, and that there is an internal conflict taking place within us. Only under the most favoring circumstances, in times of peace and tranquility, and through the sufferance of the gods, through a kind of cosmic process that is only hinted at in our mythologies, but cannot be fully penetrated, we might, in fact, come to have a stable and wholesome form of life.

One character given to us in Homer, described as the most pathetic of all, the person in the worst imaginable situation, is a character described by Homer as "the hearthless, lawless, stateless man." What Homer is claiming here is quite different from the Upanishads. It is a kind of introspective and, indeed, isolating form of contemplative life that we get in the Upanishads, but what Homer is telling us is that there's nothing worse than to be outside the civic order of things, to be separated from people of one's own kind, to be separated from the laws and customs and habitats of the people who are your people. There's something wonderfully civic and, in the fullest sense, civilizing, about this depiction of the worst possible fate that can befall us: to be hearthless, and lawless, and stateless.

I return to Theseus. How ungrateful for him to abandon the brave woman who saved his freedom by giving him the means by which to escape the labyrinth created by Daedalus. Sailing away from Ariadne at Naxos, Theseus return to Athens to face still other trials. On one mythological account, his ultimate destiny turns out to be eternal life in the Underworld seated on—what? On the Chair of Oblivion.

Perhaps here is a symbol for what awaits one oblivious to true love and the gratitude that is due it, but I conclude with another chapter in the varied life of Theseus. We learn that when he returns to Athens he does the "Dance of the Cranes," and that dance allows him to pace out the steps involved in solving the labyrinth.

Now, in the 20th century, we find hive mates are informed by bees where flowers are by bees doing a particular dance; the "dance of the bees" shows everyone where the pollen is. Well, everywhere in Homer, nature is the guide, and in philosophy, we will see, at least in its earliest stages, nature as a guide.

How apt, in this connection, that one of the great philosophers of the 20th century, Ludwig Wittgenstein, would say of his own mission as a philosopher, that he attempted no more than "to show the fly the way out of the bottle." The "Dance of the Cranes, the "dance of the bees," the fly getting out of the bottle—philosophy has this perpetual characteristic, and we shall explore it, chapter and verse, as best we can.

Lecture Two

Philosophy—Did the Greeks Invent It?

Scope:

Philosophy is created when the mind turns from practical matters of avoiding danger and uncertainty to a form of critical inquiry in which its own resources are objectified and subjected to critical scrutiny. The ancient Greek world transformed inquiry from an essentially practical or ritualistic/religious enterprise into a form of abstract and theoretical thought. Was there something about the Greeks or their culture that brought about this transformation? The Greeks' relation to their gods, who had large but limited powers and business of their own to mind, was one influence. The fact that the religious establishment had little authority to pronounce on ultimate questions of reality was another. Further, the Greeks' commercial and military encounters with other cultures led them to questions of social organization. These things induced the Greeks to weigh themselves in relation to others, to examine the powerful influence of custom on thought, and to recognize no viable alternative to the use of their own limited intellectual resources.

Outline

I. Why is it that whether the subject is philosophy, or mathematics, or biology, or political science, even economics, our thoughts constantly recur to the ancient Greek world as we search for origins?

    A. There are theories that it had to do with sunshine, clean air, a slave economy, and abundant seafood, which provided leisure hours for the affluent.

    B. But other kingdoms had greater physical resources, yet never produced a semblance of philosophical thought and practice.

    C. The breadth and depth of ancient Greek accomplishment are too vast for single theories to embrace.

II. Before we can address the question of whether the Greeks invented philosophy, we must be clear as to just what the invention is. What is *philosophy*, and is it of such a nature that any people can be said to have *invented* it? Above all, why should our thoughts always go back to the Greeks to find the origins of our own modern thought?

A. There is no known society so limited in its thought and practices as to be totally unphilosophical, for the very existence of a society requires the recognition and solution of problems that are philosophical in the nature of things.

    1. Why not begin the history of philosophy with Buddha, Confucius? What about the scientific, medical, and engineering achievements of ancient Egypt and the mathematical discoveries of India?

    2. So, too, with great literary works.

B. But there is a difference between folk wisdom and philosophy.

C. Philosophy tests the most fundamental beliefs, convictions, and values that we have.

    1. Central to this process is *criticism*—of society, of received wisdom, of oneself.

    2. Philosophy's purpose is not to solve practical problems or to solidify civic bonds.

    3. Philosophy is the love of wisdom—not for its consolation or its finality but for the possibility of *getting it right*, even if that means bad news.

D. Yet, in most settings—including the most developed and modern ones—the philosophy employed in addressing such matters is a most *practical* affair, arising out of the need for an intelligible world in the face of danger and uncertainty.

    1. This took place from the first time *Homo sapiens* dropped from trees.

    2. Children raise pre-philosophical questions.

    3. Only rarely are there periods in which the very terms of debate are closely examined, periods in which even the most abidingly successful practical measures are held up to critical scrutiny.

E. Philosophy does not begin with the need for an intelligible world. The need for an intelligible world begins with the fearfulness of pre-philosophical, pre-literate societies, facing an unpredictable world of change and trying to make sense of it.

F. The ancient Greeks felt themselves to be outside the divine order, strangers in the world, self-determining.

    1. They found themselves among peoples whose behavior they didn't understand.

    2. Despite their oracles, priests, folk wisdom, and Olympian deities, there was no ultimate authority on matters of truth in their culture.

    3. The way to understand was to ask questions.

III. The first age in which this rare form of inquiry became common enough to emerge as whole schools of critical inquiry was that of ancient Greece in the 6th century B.C. If it is fair to say that the Greeks "invented" philosophy, then it is important to consider the conditions that may have favored or at least encouraged this rarest of human achievements.

    A. Was it the Greek "civilization"?

        1. Earlier and perhaps greater civilizations failed to reach an academic level of inquiry.

        2. It is a common mistake to think that civilization somehow matches up with philosophical and abstract modes of understanding.

        3. Great civilizations come about by solving practical problems. Occasionally, wealth, power, and inspired patronage add a lasting and influential record of artistic and literary merit.

    B. What explains, then, ancient Greek philosophy, and the fact that it would guide much of what would become Western civilization in its finest hours?

    C. Was it the climate? The Greek climate was not milder or easier than others, nor was their land more fertile.

D. Was it the gift of a slave-based economy? This theory of a leisure class now free to exercise philosophical genius is implausible: Slavery was coextensive with civilization.

E. Did it arise from the unique nature of Olympianism?

    1. The Olympian gods were largely unconcerned with human life and largely separate from the sphere of humans, who were left to solve their own problems.

    2. The Greek religion, unusually for the period, was not a state religion, but neither was Greek society secular: The reverential and the political were highly integrated; there was a religious attitude but not a state religion.

    3. Priests were the managers of ritual and oracles but had no authority to pronounce on ultimate questions.

    4. A philosophical approach arises when religious authority is not regarded as all-powerful.

    5. In one of Plato's dialogues, humans are described as puppets of the gods. But they have one string to pull back on—the golden cord of reason.

F. Is the reason for Greek philosophy more or less immanent in Greek culture and language itself?

    1. It has been observed that the Greek language does lend itself to a kind of analyticity.

    2. The speeches of Isocrates are masterpieces of rhetoric.

    3. In his *Panegyricus*, Isocrates defines the term *Hellenes*, not as a race, but as all those who share an overall philosophical and aesthetic outlook—a commitment to self-perfection.

    4. Isocrates credits philosophy with being the source of institutions that shaped Athens and, philosophy, in his words, "was given to the world by our city."

Recommended Reading:

Garland, R. *The Greek Way of Life*. Cornell, 1990.

Isocrates, *Panegyricus*, George Norlen, trans. Harvard University Press, Loeb Classical Library, 2000, Vol. 1, sections 45–51.

Robinson, D. N. *An Intellectual History of Psychology*, 3rd ed., University of Wisconsin Press, 1995, chapter 2.

Questions to Consider:

1. Explain how the conception of the Olympian gods liberates Greek thought.

2. Describe factors usually offered to account for the Greek philosophical achievement that were *not* present in earlier and highly developed civilizations.

3. How does Isocrates intend *Hellene* to be understood, and does this sense of the term retain its meaning today?

Lecture Two—Transcript

Philosophy—Did the Greeks Invent It?

Ah, philosophy—what is it, and did the Greeks invent it?

More than a few qualifications are required when the question is posed this way. Ours is an uncommonly sensitive time, when it comes to attributing all sorts of things to one people and leaving out the rest.

Sensitivities aside, however, one really should be expected to explain why it is, when one approaches "the house of intellect," or at least many of the rooms within it, that most of the foundations were laid— and nearly all of the early rooms were occupied—by the Greek-speaking people of the ancient world.

Why is it that whether the subject is philosophy, or mathematics, or biology, or political science, even economics, our thoughts constantly recur to the ancient Greek world as we search for origins? Additionally, in some cases, the early development of these subjects compares quite favorably with all that came later.

What was it about these ancient Greeks that would have them achieving so much, and in a relatively brief span of time? Was it something ethnic? It certainly was not "genetic" in any scientific sense of the term, and to say it was "cultural" is to confuse the effect with the cause.

Perhaps it was something about the climate. There are theories to that effect: ample sunshine, clean air, a slave economy, and abundant food from the sea—all this provided leisure hours for the affluent to—to what? Lay the foundations for the succeeding two millennia of systematic thought in the full range of scientific and humanistic study? No, this gives far too much credit to vitamins A and D.

It is not churlish, but to the point, that out of the kingdoms of Mesopotamia, Egypt, and Persia—all of these had far greater physical resources, more slaves than decency is eager to recall, and that none of these empires produced even a semblance of philosophical thought and practice. Such achievements in science and technology, as history claims for them, never generated or grounded that rule of law, that mode of civic life, that perfectionist ideal that mark out the ancient Greek way of life. Clearly, the breadth and depth of accomplishment are too vast for single theories to embrace.

Before we can address the question of whether the Greeks *invented* philosophy, we must be clear as to just what the invention is. What is the difference between a philosophical perspective and let's say the perspective that Homer had in composing *Iliad* and *Odyssey*, or the perspective the singers and writers of the Upanishads had, or that of the Hebrew prophets? In what sense did Pythagoras have the right to call himself, for the first time, a philosopher, over and against, say, Moses or Isaiah? Why not begin the history of philosophy equally with, say, Buddha, Confucius, and Socrates, instead of distinguishing the last of these from all earlier non-Greek thinkers? What of the scientific and medical and engineering achievements of Egypt, and the mathematical discoveries of India?

Sharp lines can be drawn here only at peril. Indeed, the more developed thinking becomes, the more philosophical and scientific thinking tends to merge—so, too, with great literary works, with the poetic imagination, with the realized dreams of great architects and good kings, with the noble and improving teachings of saints and prophets. Just where personal genius and virtue in such figures rise to the level of impersonal and trans-historical significance will always be a topic of joyful dispute among scholars.

There is, nonetheless, a special feature of philosophy that really does mark it off from all the rest, not in the sense of being "better," or more advanced, or reserved to a privileged few. The philosophical perspective is one of *criticism* and, yes, *skepticism*. I hope this won't be taken as indelicate or, worse, heretical, but if God were to declare a truth to the community of philosophers, at least the best of them would say—and one would hope worshipfully: "But how can we be sure of that?"

The point, of course, is that philosophy carries its truths, earns its truths, the hard way: by working for them. What the scientist actually sees through aided or unaided sight, what the poet dreams and the prophet has revealed to him, the philosopher must find through argument, analysis, doubt, and, yes, disinterest. The operative word here is "dis-interest," not "un-interest." The blindfold that decorates the face of Justice is intended to signify just that "judicious disinterest" that would have the chips fall where they may. The verdict will depend on evidence, not on the rhetorical skill of the advocate, or the wealth of the defendant.

This, needless to say, is the judicial ideal, and we know it is rarely achieved, but it is the recognized ideal—so, too, in philosophy. Let the successful arguments fall where they may. We are prepared to abandon one that was long a favorite, and accept one that we find personally odious.

Philosophy takes a systematically and critical perspective on all of the assumptions and claims that we in the other compartments of human endeavor accept. It isn't that the others have no epistemological or quasi-epistemological aims. The playwright, indeed, is attempting to get at a kind of truth, even a "fundamental" truth. Indeed, the great playwright reaches the deeper levels of human sensibility and thought, and presents the discovery in a memorable way. Are not the greatest "depth psychologies" served up by Euripides, Sophocles, and Aeschylus? We reach levels of self-understanding by way of such dramatists, and in a manner that would be almost impossible to approximate in any other way.

Still, philosophy is different. The bottom line in philosophy is not to solve practical problems; it's not to solidify the civic bonds among people. It's not to make us feel better—or worse. Rather, it is to test the most fundamental beliefs, the most fundamental values and convictions we have, and to test them for the purpose of getting them right, while at the same time realizing that basic questions as to what it could mean to *get it right* are finally unanswerable.

The central aspect of the philosophical perspective is a critical aspect, then. Criticality, criticism, self-criticism: This is what is at the very center of the philosophical project, the philosophical way of thought. It's at the very center of the philosophical enterprise. What is believed by way of the philosophical worldview is wisdom itself. Not wisdom "so that," not wisdom "in order that," not to get more of this or more of that. Not to be reassured, not for the good night's sleep. Not for its consolations, with all due respect to Boethius. No, it's to get it right, and where *getting it right* might, indeed, be bad news as well.

It is not inevitably good news. Sometimes, it is not news at all. It's a question that is answered with yet another question, and answered with yet another question. I sometimes say that profound philosophical insights should always be followed not with exclamation points, but with semicolons, because the long debate goes on. If it wasn't concluded by Plato or Aristotle, we can be sure that it will not be ended in the editorial pages of *The New York Times*.

Well, did the Greeks invent this sort of thing? They certainly didn't invent thought. I should think the first *Homo sapiens* started dropping from the trees, or landing from a different planet, and then had to civilize his litter, find the evening meal, fill the larder; some persistent questions emerged from the very nature of things. "Should we stay here? Should we leave? Is this a safe place? Are these our children, anyway? Are these children little adults? How come they don't know how to do this or that? Why do they make these meaningless sounds? Then, at a certain point, they seem to be making some sense. How is it that these dogs keep following us around? They are awfully nice creatures, after all. Yet, these other furry things aren't following us around, except to eat us. How do we tell the difference between one and the other? Can you know at a distance whether something is prey or predator? Who is that chap over there with feathers on his head who says if we don't do what he tells us to do, he is going to kill us? Maybe we should do what he says. Anyway, he is the oldest one among us; he survived longest."

I say, these queries are insistent. Listen to children. Children are raising what might be called pre-philosophical questions. We do a parody on this when we have the child saying: "Why is the sky blue, and why can't I have more ice cream?" However, these are questions that begin to take a philosophical orientation. I mean the answer: "Because I said so," is never convincing to the child who has asked: "Why can't I have more ice cream?" After all: "Shut up, I explained" is not a philosophical reply, but the question itself is a kind of philosophical question in a child-like idiom.

"Why can't I have more of something?" is getting at "What is the rule or principle that governs what I can have? Make this decision intelligible to me," and if you say: "Because you won't eat your supper," suppose the child says: "Let me have the ice cream, and I promise I will eat my supper." You then must move to points of greater refinement and explanatory power: "Ice cream in that quantity isn't good for you, and it won't mix well with what..." Before you know it, there is a kind of debate going on, one that parents very often find quite frustrating, but one that reveals the philosophical disposition of a rational being.

"Why is the sky blue?" is a very interesting question, and, indeed, most textbook answers to that question, which fail to take into consideration the unique properties of the visual system and the chemistry and physiology of color vision, do not do justice to the question itself.

Alternatively, consider the child looking at a cat. A child sees many cats; she sees alley cats, cats in the street, and then, watching a nature film, she sees a tiger for the first time, and she is told it's a cat. "That's a cat? My goodness, it's 20 times the size of a cat! The colors are different. The teeth are longer. The sound isn't a meow; it's a roar. How can Tabby and that both be cats?" There is, here, a searching for some scheme of classification by which to reduce the otherwise unmanageable chaos of experience to order.

Philosophy doesn't begin with the need for an intelligible world. The need for an intelligible world begins with the fearfulness of pre-philosophical, pre-literate societies, facing an unpredictable world of change and trying to make sense of it. The ancient Greeks, from the earliest record we have of them, tend to see themselves, as it were, estranged in the world. They are not part of the divine scheme. The Olympians are something very different from themselves, and they are aloof to their struggles. They are here alone, in an intimidating place. They are engaged in trade with people who speak a different language, who have different beliefs, who bow down in the presence of leaders bedecked in gold and taken to be gods. The Greeks in Asia Minor, in the settlements Miletus and Samos, and nearby places where philosophy is actually founded, are the near neighbors of people whose cultural practices strike them as bizarre. They are trying to make their estrangement from the world less dangerous by coming to understand the world. There are oracles, of course, and priests, folk traditions and folk wisdom—but there is no final, ultimate authority on matters of truth in this culture. Whatever may be said of the Olympian deities, they are not scholars, and they have bequeathed no book of truths.

Well, this isn't yet philosophy, but it's on the track, and we can ask the question again: "Well, why the Greeks? Why those people? Why at that time? Why there, in that place?" The era of earliest productivity in the matter of philosophy is in the 6th century B.C. Pythagoras died at about 500 B.C. Parmenides, the pre-Socratic philosopher, comes later in the 6th century B.C. This is less than two centuries since the Homeric epics, and yet, a philosophically rich body of thought is already being developed.

I return to the question: "What is it about this time and place and people that would foster such an intellectual achievement?" Earlier, and in some sense "greater," civilizations have been noted, as have their failure to reach what might be called an "academic" level of inquiry. There can be—and have been—vast and enduring civilizations utterly destitute of philosophical energy and originality, and I think it is a common mistake to think that civilization somehow matches up with philosophical and, indeed, scientific and abstract modes of understanding.

Great civilizations come about by solving practical problems and by developing the wealth and might with which to preserve themselves. Occasionally, wealth and power and inspired patronage add to these civilizations a lasting record of artistic and literary merit capable of influencing posterity long after the wealth and power have disappeared.

Only once, however, has an age set the very standard of excellence, the very means by which to assess it, the very perspective by which persons and nations come to grips with their potentialities and their limitations. That age is the age of Hellenism, and of all its achievements, it would be ancient Greek philosophy that would guide much of what would come to be Western civilization in its finest hours.

It should be clear that the climate is not going to explain this. The Greeks had no more sunshine and far fewer slaves than Pharaoh. Something about the Greek mainland, however, is informative here, for two-thirds of it is utterly unaerable. You can't grow anything on it. It is a rocky place, a place of "hard dealing." Olives do well, as do lemon trees, and fish surround the country. However, surely you would not say that the Greek-speaking people were blessed by having a place where if you scatter seeds, your food requirements are thereupon met.

As early as the 7th century B.C., mainland Greek speakers are found colonizing Sicily and the east coast of Italy, as well as islands off the coast of Asia Minor, largely for the purpose of producing food that can be sent back to the mainland. In other words, by about 700 B.C., they are already having trouble feeding themselves.

Nor is the availability of slave labor a credible explanation of the Hellenic achievement. Through military conquest, the Greeks did acquire large numbers of slaves, and there was, indeed, an aristocratic class whose members are found in the company of the great philosophers. This, too, will not do much explanatory work for us; though slavery was not unique to the ancient Greek world, it is, lamentably, coextensive with human history. In the context of ancient Greece, one could be enslaved through indebtedness; indeed, only after the reforms of Solon was it no longer permissible for Greek to enslave Greek.

Far more common was slavery resulting from defeat in battle and forming part of the reparations. However, such slaves were not barred from having slaves themselves, earning money. There are instances enough of slaves earning enough in the ancient Greek world for them to buy their own slaves and, indeed, enter into banking arrangements.

The majority of slaves were actually domestic servants. There is no evidence of a conception of slavery based on ethnic or racial grounds. The bulk of servants in the ancient Greek world are engaged in domestic service. Few of the major architectural achievements made use of slave labor. There was slave labor working on the silver mines at Laurium, but even this harsh and productive institution was ended when the mines dried up.

Moreover, there was a low ceiling on just how many slaves could be imported without causing significant disruptions in the domestic economy, which was a fragile one. The more slave labor, the fewer jobs for the locals.

Thus, again, this theory of a leisure class now free to exercise philosophical genius is just implausible on its face. We have long periods of economies grounded firmly, and much more lavishly, in slave labor without so much as a ray of philosophical light emanating from them. The Hellenic world depended far less on slave labor.

There is greater agreement among scholars regarding the influence of Olympianism as a religion on the invention of philosophy. Now, this is a subject unto itself, and I must touch on it all too briefly; but, recall from the previous lecture, the particular epistemological vulnerabilities of the gods. They don't know everything. They don't think they know everything. They don't claim to know everything. Except for certain lapses, they don't care too much about us.

Zeus is found admonishing the lesser gods and goddesses not to spend so much time concerned with human affairs. Consider his admonition to Aphrodite after Diomedes has turned on her and cut her with his sword. He says: "You know this sort of thing; it inevitably happens when you get yourself mixed up with these characters, you see, spending all your time worrying about what they are going to do," so that there's this relative indifference.

There is a wonderful little vignette that comes out of the blood and gore of *Iliad*. When we don't have hecatombs of ox being sacrificed, we've got great crashing helmets with eyes falling out and blood and bones littering the plains of Troy. We find a fallen hero being attended to by his chums. They stuff the open wound with herbs and work to close the wound. He gets up, returns to the field of battle, presumably with a limp he will never lose. He surely is not the man he used to be, but at least he is still serviceable to the cause.

Now, Aphrodite goes back to Olympus, and—after Diomedes had turned on her—she says to Zeus: "Look at what he did," and as Zeus puts his hand on Aphrodite's wrist, on her wound, it removes all evidence of a wound. There's no sign that anything ever happened!

This underscores further the total separation between—to use contemporary parlance—heaven and earth. We have to solve our problems. We propitiate the gods. We engage in rituals. We strive not to anger them. We surely do not adopt them as patrons of the *polis*, only then to shame them with our conduct within that *polis*—so there is a reverential attitude. However, the ancient Greek world never hosted a state religion.

It is an interesting fact; it's a rarity in the human experience. It never has a state religion, but, of course, it is never an entirely secular place either. Rather, there is a remarkable integration of the secular and the reverential, the secular and the religious—an integration of belief and myth with action and thought, an integration that I think has probably not been matched since. It is difficult, I should think, for a citizen of the contemporary world to enter empathically into that frame of mind in which one has a deeply religious attitude, but not a religion as such.

Now, what are the priests doing in this ancient world? Well, they are presiding over rituals, but they have no epistemological authority. It is not to the priest or priestess that you go with a bona fide philosophical question. You might consult the oracle, but this was mostly on practical matters. The oracles were not as much "for hire" as is sometimes suggested. However, it is not for no reason that what the oracle at Delphi says is described as "Delphic." In any case, no one consults the oracle to determine whether ultimate reality is atomic, or the cause of the lunar eclipse. There are no oracular answers to such questions. The religious aspect of the ancient Greek world calls by default for a philosophical approach to the problems of life and mind.

There is something about philosophy that is at once humanizing and utterly human. It's the court of last recourse, when the oracles have failed us, when the saints have grown silent, and when God has chosen not to reveal Himself. Then we stand back, in the dark shadows of confusion and fear, and ask: "What sort of being am I? What kind of life is right for me? How should I govern or be governed?"

This much granted, there is also an elusive relationship between the religious and the philosophical outlooks, both promising to reveal what falls beyond the ambit of passive experience. The spiritual dimension of life is coextensive with human experience and seems to be a vital ingredient. I believe that a life devoid of the spiritual dimension has been emptied of one of the chief sources of action, contemplation, and sublimity, but the inquiring mind is restless and demands a justification for its favored beliefs. It requires "warrants" and is fearful of self-deception. If the life devoid of a spiritual dimension is too thin a life, then one devoid of philosophical vigor is too complacent.

The philosopher doesn't enter the arena of philosophy as one devoid of belief, values, hope, or aspirations. No, all of that is in place, for it goes with the territory. There are those rare moments when we say this: "No matter how much this means to me, no matter how centered my being is on this pattern of beliefs, no matter how close I am personally and emotionally, and even romantically, to those who hold such convictions, I must reserve the right to question and to doubt. I will retain this skeptical bias as an obligation owed to my own rationality, my own integrity. I am prepared to follow the golden cord leading me out of the labyrinth, no matter how many twists and turns there are, because once I let go of that, my intellectual life is not my own."

In one of Plato's dialogues, we are told that we are all like puppets, and the gods can move us any which way they will by pulling on these strings, but we have one string that we can pull back on. Socrates tells us it's the "golden cord of reason." There's that string again! With it, we can resist the gods themselves, even if ultimately our fate is not in our hands. Win or lose in such contests, we are not simply foils—merely material objects to be moved around by the whim and caprice of hidden forces. Lose that reason, suspend that criticality, become gullible, accept anything that custom serves up, and you enter the life of a puppet on a string, the life of a slave.

It should be clear that what we resist when entering into philosophical modes of thought are not merely external influences, but our own habits of thought and cherished certainties. We are now willing, even if fearful, to raise the most basic and searching questions about reality, about right and wrong, about justice, about the grounds of our relations with others, about war and peace.

Well, if in the fullest academic and scholarly respects, the Greeks *invented* all this, we might ask again if there's something uniquely "Greek" about it. Is it something in the very language? It has been observed that the Greek language does, in fact, lend itself to a kind of analyticity, but it is better here to turn the question over to one of the ancient Greeks who considered it.

In the 4th century B.C., one of Aristotle's famous contemporaries, Isocrates, headed the leading school of "Rhetorick." It was in such schools that students learned how to prepare legal cases, this in a highly litigious world. Isocrates's own speeches are masterpieces of rhetoric, understood here as the art and science of persuasion. In one of these, in the *Panegyricus*, we find him urging Athenians to stop making war on fellow Hellenes and to see clearly just who the real enemy is.

It is at this time that Athens is a shambles, under the so-called "protection" of the Persian Empire sapping its wealth and effectively stripping it of its democratic character, but it is in this speech of praise for all that Athens has achieved that Isocrates pauses to remind his audience what it means to be a Hellene.

He speaks of the far ranging influence of Athenian culture, such that the pupils of Athens have become teachers of the world. He says that the term *Hellenes* now is no longer a race but a form of intellectual comprehension; in the Greek, it is no longer a *genos* but a *dianoias*, and he follows this with the statement that what Hellene now encompasses are all "who share our culture, rather than those who share our blood": "*Mallon Hellenas kaleisthai tous tes paideuseos tes emeteras e tous tes koines phuseos metechontas.*"

It is those who share *paideia*. Yes, the word translates as "culture," but in the wider and deeper sense of an overall philosophical and aesthetic outlook. "Those who come together with us, in what we take to be the most significant aspects of life—those aspects that find a limited creature committed to the doomed but defining task of self-perfection, are Hellenes." Here, then, is a statement on the birth of philosophy.

In this same work, Isocrates will credit philosophy itself with being the source of the very institutions that have made Athens what it is and, as he says, "made us gentle toward each other." "Philosophy," he says, "was given to the world by our city."

'Twas ever thus.

Lecture Three

Pythagoras and the Divinity of Number

Scope:

Pythagoras was born on the island of Samos in or about 570 B.C. and was perhaps the first to call himself a "philosopher." He traveled in Egypt and possibly in India, where he may have adopted his ascetic practices and the belief in transmigration of souls. In the course of his long and productive life he would find a sect that formed around his teaching, would assume the political leadership of the city of Crotona, and would lay claim to an astonishing number of original discoveries, including the theorem that bears his name as well as the musical scale.

For Pythagoras the ultimate reality was abstract and relational, depending on number: the four integers 1, 2, 3, 4 were quasi-divine generating entities. Pythagoras's teachings were to exert a strong influence for centuries, but markedly on Socrates, at least as Socrates is presented in the dialogues of Plato. This influence is seen in the Socratic theories that investigation of natural phenomena will always lead to the abstract, that abstractions such as number and form are capable of generating physical reality.

Outline

I. Though the Greeks of the 6th century are developing descriptions of the world that are naturalistic, one among them is not naturalistic but transcendent, and it is the view of Pythagoras. Who was Pythagoras?

    A. Pythagoras is a figure shrouded in mystery but one of the towering figures in the history of ideas. Before his birth, the oracle of Delphi predicted that he would "surpass all men in wisdom."

    B. Pythagoras spent many of his early years traveling, especially in Egypt; he was acquainted with the technical achievements of Egyptian civilization, including applied mathematics.

C. Did he also travel in India? One account asserts that Pythagoras was sent to Babylon as a prisoner, where he studied with the magi. Other sources claim that Pythagoras became famous as a teacher in India. We do know that in the 6th century, the ascetic Hindu sect of the Jainists arose, with beliefs in the transmigration of souls and the sacredness of all life, beliefs the Pythagoreans also held.

D. Pythagoras may have spent 40 years traveling in distant lands before returning to Greece, at which point, a cult had formed around him. He became the governor of Crotona for a short period of time, where the people were contemplative, committed to sustained inquiry into the ultimate nature of things.

II. We begin with the contrast between Pythagorean abstract, transcendent thought and naturalistic thought, which was so dominant in Aristotle and in ancient Greek medicine and science.

A. This contrast is important because Pythagoras was a significant source for what would become Platonic thought.

B. Pythagoreanism saw that reality was created out of something that is itself not material but is architectonic for all that can be material. That "something" is the abstract plan or idea on which reality is constructed. For Pythagoras, that abstract idea is number, through which material reality becomes accessible to the senses.

C. The sacred integers, 1, 2, 3, 4—the *tetraktys*—were the grounding, respectively, of the *point*, the *line*, the *plane*, and the *solid*, and it was with these integers that the soul of the cosmos then generates the sensible world of material things.

D. Pythagoras is known for the theorem $a^2 + b^2 = c^2$ and for the discovery of the musical scale and musical harmonies. Indeed, the harmonies of music are but the sensible manifestation of relations between and among numbers; relationships that determine which combinations will be concordant and discordant.

    1. For Pythagoras it was not coincidental that what is heard as "harmonious" is what obeys the divinity of number, for the soul itself can naturally perceive the same harmonic relationships that keep the planets in their orbits.

2. Creation is itself harmonic, expressive of a divinely rational plan: We resonate to the harmony of the universe, which is not material but *relational*.

3. Predictably, Pythagorean medicine included music as therapy. The body, which may manifest disorders, is the material manifestation of something that is, fundamentally, not material but relational.

4. Looking at geometry, we are told that a right-angle triangle has angles totaling 180° and that one of its angles is 90°. No material rectilinear triangle, however, is perfect, but the relationship $a^2 + b^2 = c^2$ is perfect and eternal.

5. There is a wonderful correspondence between the realm of matter and that of abstraction. Often mathematical abstractions predate physical discoveries which, however, they describe exactly. Our wonder at this, and our sense that it is no coincidence, are Pythagorean.

E. If we take the creative force behind all existing things to be a divine force, then we can only conclude that number is a kind of divinity, that number, in its abstract, transcendental nature, is divine.

F. Consider, however, numbers that do not match up with anything material, such as π or $\sqrt{-1}$. Nonetheless, π is needed to calculate the circumference of a circle.

1. For the Pythagoreans, coincidence cannot explain this. Further, the odds are long that a mathematician would come up with a complex equation that, 200 or 300 years later, would perfectly explain some brute physical fact.

2. Such occurrences, then, must express some plan. The ultimate plan must be abstract but capable of generating the physical reality. The abstract plan must also be a plan of relationships.

III. What kind of governor was Pythagoras? The answer is: "not successful."

A. The people of Crotona ultimately staged riots in reaction to Pythagoras's "old-time religion."

B. How could Pythagoras be a man of affairs at all? Is politics the sort of activity in which a philosopher engages?

    1. As Aristotle teaches, we seek precision only insofar as the subject allows it. There could be no Pythagorean theorem for political life.

    2. A philosophically guided state is unlikely to survive the reality in which it finds itself.

C. What can we say about Pythagoras as "first philosopher," a title that he arrogated to himself?

    1. The word *philosophy* means "love of wisdom."

    2. The Greeks had several words for *intelligence* or *knowledge*, some denoting scientific knowledge and some, practical knowledge.

    3. *Sophia*, however, was what the wise person possessed, the person who delves into core questions about the meaning of life.

    4. Pythagoras appropriately called himself a philosopher because he devoted himself to an inquiry serving the purposes of knowledge. He sought to discover what it is that makes anything possible and real and, as in chemistry and particle physics today, found the answer in number.

Recommended Reading:

Fideler, D. ed. *The Pythagorean Sourcebook and Library*. Phanes Press, 1987.

Questions to Consider:

1. Summarize in what ways Pythagorean "numerology" is like and unlike modern mathematical models of reality.

2. Explain the striking agreement found between abstract mathematics and actually occurring natural items.

Lecture Three—Transcript

Pythagoras and the Divinity of Number

I've titled this lecture "Pythagoras and the Divinity of Number," and I do so to put into quite vivid contrast a transcendentalist or abstract philosophy, and the naturalistic philosophy that is going to become rather more common in Hellenic philosophy at large and, of course, central in the philosophy of Aristotle.

Pythagoras is a figure shrouded in mystery, but the subject of relentless lore, both ancient and modern. He is one of the towering figures in the history of ideas; this, we are told, having been predicted by none other than the oracle at Delphi. It is said that when the oracle was consulted by Pythagoras's parents-to-be—by his wealthy merchant father, Mnesarchus, and mother Pythais—they were told their son would surpass all men in wisdom. On their way back to Samos, their son was born, in Sidon, we are told, and would amaze many from the first.

Pythagoras spent many of his early years traveling. His Egyptian travels lasted for a period of years, as he became well acquainted with the technical achievements of the Egyptian civilization. These included advances in what today we would call "applied mathematics." The Egyptians had worked out techniques for calculating acreage, for example, a kind of planometric mathematics, in which you could tell how large fields were even though very uneven in shape and distribution. The so-called "Reisner" and "Moscow" papyri, dating from about 1700 B.C., contain some 112 mathematical problems, mostly practical but a few being of an abstract nature. In one, the Egyptian student must determine how to divide various numbers of loaves of bread to give equal shares to various numbers of persons, all this requiring the use of fractions. As early as 2800 B.C., the Egyptians had a calendar with a 365-day year, and the means by which to predict the flooding of the Nile. Thus, Pythagoras had much to learn from this ancient people.

There is less evidence about his time in India. On one account, the invasion of Egypt by Cambyses resulted in Pythagoras being sent to Babylon as a prisoner, there studying with the magi and learning their secret crafts and rituals. There are sources that claim he not only studied in India, but became famous as a teacher there—where he was, it is said, known as "the Ionian teacher."

We do know that in that same period, in the 6th century, the great religious figure Jina surfaces in India. Jina had come from a very well-to-do family. However, his mother and father, it is said, starved themselves to death in old age—that is, they adopted an extreme asceticism in life, and carried it to its spiritual conclusion at the end, now finally and fully abandoning the materiality of earthly life. Pythagoras was surely taken by this. He was, I suppose, in his early 30s at the time. He would come to devote his own life to ascetic teaching, and thereby absorb himself into the great cosmic order of things.

Perhaps through the teachings of the ascetics, Pythagoras accepted that every living thing has the same class membership, the same familial membership. With so many of his contemporaries, and as part of Hindu belief, he believed in the transmigration of souls, the fact that at death something in us is liberated. I mentioned *Atman* in the earlier lecture. Something in us is liberated and is able to reclaim its transcendent life, as it were, and as his teachings consistently oppose all forms of destruction, all forms of intentionally caused death to any living animal, we see this surfacing in his philosophy. This is vegetarianism with a passion. His followers would take to walking down the streets—the Jains of India do this to this day, with brooms to sweep out of the way insects they otherwise might step on. Today's Jains consume liquids through a filter, lest some small organism enter into their bodies and be destroyed. Jainism is a great ethical school, exemplary for the celebration of life as such.

Of Pythagoras, writing some eight centuries later, Iamblichus would say that, "He unfolded the friendship of all things toward all, so that even now, those who are benevolent in the extreme are called Pythagoreans."

On some accounts, Pythagoras spent nearly 40 of his first 56 years in distant lands, finally returning to the Greek-speaking colonies. At this point, he has a cult or sect forming around him, committed to his teaching. Nonetheless, he's a politically active person. He becomes, for a short period of time, the governor of Crotona, then a Greek settlement in Italy. It's a settlement that is almost constantly at odds—and sometimes in open war—with Sybaris, which hosts those peoples whose form of life and conduct comes down to us in the form of the word *sybarite*.

In Sybaris, we find youth all decked out in finery. They are all powdered, in purple tunics, their sandals of the best sort. They make themselves up, and they are bejeweled; believe it or not, some of them actually wear earrings, whereas in Crotona under the tutelage and the directorship of the ascetic Pythagoras, we find a sect of contemplative people paying little attention to the needs of the body, to the day-to-day and mundane affairs of their own materiality and material life, and committed instead to the deepest and most sustained inquiry into the ultimate nature of things.

Of course, an old school of philosophy before Socrates is, among the pre-Socratic schools, the school of philosophy known as the Cynics. One of the leading Cynics was Diogenes. I just offer you this as perhaps an apocryphal story, but it's perfect for Diogenes.

It is said that when Diogenes would attend theatre in Athens, when the Sybarites, the young men of Sybaris, came in all decked out and perfumed, walking past Diogenes to take their seats in the theatre, Diogenes would lean back and say as they walked by, in the Greek, "Affectation," and then some minutes later, the Crotonian youngsters would come in their tattered sandals and shabby tunics, their hair unkempt, and as they would walk by, Diogenes would say, "More affectation," in this, recording that almost constant theme in Hellenic thought, "Nothing to excess."

I wish at this point to juxtapose the Pythagorean attention to transcendental and abstract considerations against the naturalistic perspective that is so dominant in Aristotle, and in ancient Greek medicine and science. This is important for two reasons. First, Pythagoras is an important source or forerunner for what we will come to understand to be Platonic thought, or at least one phase of Platonic thought. The most economical way to pick up on this is within the context of Pythagoreanism, that reality as we know it is created out of something that is itself not material but is architectonic for all that can be material. That "something" is the abstract plan, the abstract "idea," on which reality is constructed, and that abstract idea ultimately is, alas, number. Hence, the divinity of number, the creative power of number itself, the creative power of the cosmic soul, the ultimate creative force in the universe. It is through number that the material and physical reality all around us becomes accessible to the senses.

The Pythagoreans placed great stress on the first four positive integers in the Greek, the sum of them yielding—referred to as the *tetraktys* in the Greek—the sum of the first four integers yielding 10: 1, 2, 3, 4—just four positive integers. Now, what are they going to do with this "1, 2, 3, 4"?

Ah, well, what is "1"? "1" is a point; that is, the abstract character of the number "1" is the basis on which there can be a *point*. "2"? "2" constitutes the basis on which there can be a *line*, the bridge between two points. "3" constitutes the abstract primordium of the *plane*; and "4", the abstract grounding of the *solid* of the tetrahedron, which always had a special place in Pythagorean teaching.

The cosmic soul makes use of number to fabricate a material reality, then, and needs very little with which to do this. Of course, as you arrange the "1, 2, 3, 4," the sum is 10. The number "10" takes on a very special value in Pythagorean thought and teaching, as well.

Now, when I say the "divinity of number," I am referring to something that is not quantitative, as such. 1, 2, 3, and 4 are not mere integers. Pythagoras is probably best known to students today for the theorem *a* squared plus *b* squared equals *c* squared ($a^2 + b^2 = c^2$)," and many also understand Pythagoras, who was the first to call himself a "philosopher," as the discoverer of the musical scale and musical harmonies, the arithmetic or, shall we say, the mathematical principles of harmony. Now, there is some controversy as to whether Pythagoras actually discovered this, but certainly the Pythagorean School was known for this, and Pythagoras himself was credited with it.

Now just as for Pythagoras, 1, 2, 3, and 4 are not mere numbers, neither can it be a coincidence that the harmonic structure of music should have its reliable effect on our auditory system—that is, that we should hear as "harmonious" what, in fact, is governed by the mathematical laws of harmony. Why is it that the perfect fifth sounds the way it does? Why is it that, right up to and throughout much of the medieval period, moving from C to F sharp was actually considered a sinful maneuver? It wasn't something simply discordant; it was something that violated what is profoundly important, something violative of a harmonic precept thought to be part of the intended design and order of the cosmos.

This proved to be an understanding that spanned centuries. Now, what's underneath all this? It is the view that creation is itself an expression of an essentially harmonic and mathematical structure expressive of a divinely rational plan. It is in the rational relationships between and among abstract entities that the lawfulness of the cosmos itself comes about, and the lawfulness of our own bodily processes will come about, and the lawfulness with which we might enter into social and civic life. Number is at the bottom of it all. The reason why chords are harmonious is because we are constituted in such a way as to resonate with certain combinations of numbers, and to find discordant other combinations. The Pythagoreans thought that there was an ultimate truth here, grounding all other truths.

Predictably, Pythagorean medical therapy included music centrally. Disorders, at a certain superficial level, are corporeal disorder. Smith has indigestion, or facial tics, or drags his left leg behind him. Well, that's at the level of the body, but, of course, the body is just the material manifestation of something that is itself, and ultimately and fundamentally, not material. If it isn't material, what is it? It is *relational.*

Now, how should this be understood? Let's be guided by geometry as we learned it in school. What is a rectilinear triangle anyway? When we are told that a right-angle triangle, like all triangles, contains 180 degrees, one of these angles being 90 degrees, how does one know that? You might say you take out some sort of measuring instrument and draw a right-angle triangle with it, making sure that you've got two acute angles and that one angle is 90 degrees. The problem is you'll never do it! Try as you may, you'll never do it. You might humor yourself into thinking that you've done it. In fact, if your measuring instruments are crude enough, you'll be absolutely satisfied that you've done it. However, the better and better the measuring instrument, the more obvious it is that you did not hit 90 degrees, plus or minus nothing.

In addition, certainly, anything you draw is an utterly impermanent thing. Put it on a blackboard and ultimately, as planet earth suffers the heat death, there will be no blackboards. There'll be none of us. There'll be no classrooms, or textbooks, or anything, but there will be rectilinear triangles.

Oh, they won't be drawn rectilinear triangles. They won't be chalk on slate. What will they be? They will be the eternal, immutable relationship: $a^2 + b^2 = c^2$. What a rectilinear triangle is, is that which answers to the Pythagorean theorem. It is not something material or physical, but a formal relationship abstractly conceived.

Now, just as the harmonic musical scale matches up with something in the soul with which it resonates, so the rectilinear triangle, as given by the Pythagorean theorem, certainly matches up with—what? Well, it matches up with three-sided figures that have one angle of 90 degrees. There is this wonderful correspondence, not perfect mind you, but a most useful and remarkable correspondence between the realm of mathematical abstraction and that realm of material reality so accurately described and fashioned by way of these mathematical abstractions.

This is a feature of reality that continues to excite and perplex. Ask yourself this question: There have been mathematical discoveries, at the level of pure abstraction, that pre-date by decades, and sometimes by centuries, what science with technical advances comes to discover to be the case in the actual universe. That is, the mathematics pre-dates—by decades, or even centuries—an actual physical reality. It actually describes, it lays out, the central characteristics, with great precision, of something actually found in the universe, or in the shell of the conch, or in the snowflake.

How is it that abstract mathematics, initially utterly uninterested in the things of this world, nonetheless ends up providing the best, most accurate, most precise, and most revealing characterization of the things of this world?

You can actually generate things of this world starting off with a mathematical equation, whose discoverer was simply thinking: "Now, what we are inclined to say is, 'My goodness, what a happy coincidence this is.'" Isn't it just remarkable that, every now and then, some sort of furrow-browed mathematician comes out of a room, takes the green shades off, coughs a bit, and says: "I've got this multi-term equation here. It doesn't match up with anything. It is entirely meaningless at the level of daily experience. It came to me in a dream, and, by the way, I am going to die now," and he keels over? Then, 175 years later, someone is studying arachnids, or platyhelminthes, or some distant galaxy or quarks, or something else, and says: "Goodness gracious, we actually have an equation that describes this."

How is it that basic mathematical equations describe everything physics knows about the physical world? How is it that the cosmos is "regulated"—I'm using "regulated" within quotation marks—that the cosmos is, as it were, dictated to, it is authorized, as it were, by differential equations, which had nothing to do with this at the outset?

Well, let me not get too excited by this, but I do think it is one of the exciting moments in the history of thought when we discover that something at the level of pure and abstract mathematical thought corresponds almost perfectly, hip and thigh, chapter and verse, to the nth place after the decimal with some brute material of fact of creation.

Pythagoras was not a man who thought that such connections were accidental or coincidental. He was prepared in a philosophically reflective way to test the implications of that kind of agreement, and he was satisfied that the result of the test led inevitably to an essentially transcendentalist and abstract view as regards the foundation of all there is. If we take the creative force behind all existing things to be a divine force, then we can only conclude that number is a kind of divinity, that number—in its abstract, transcendental nature—is divine.

Then, too, there are numbers that will not and cannot match up with anything material or perceptible. Consider the transcendental number p, or the square root of −1, or e. Mathematicians have a whole host of such constructs for which there are no physical analogs. Nonetheless, to calculate the circumference of a circle, you must use p, and still other practical problems require the incorporation of still other irrational, transcendental numbers.

For the Pythagoreans, coincidence cannot account for this. Pythagoras died long before probability theory, which is largely a 17th- and 18th-century invention, but he, as we, certainly could claim an intuitive sense of what might be called "long shots" or "long odds." Now, what do you think the probability would be that someone speculating abstractly in the domain of mathematics would come up with a complex equation, which—200 or 300 years later—perfectly described some brute physical fact available, accessible to the senses?

The question answers itself, and as such occurrences exceed chance expectations or the work of accidents, they must express some sort of plan. The ultimate plan must itself be abstract but capable of generating the physical reality experienced at the perceptible level. The abstract plan is also a plan of relationship, because the salient facts of the physical world are the relational features that make things what they are.

What is the harmonic scale, except relationships among sounds? You can recognize a familiar melody played in any key. Yet, as you move from key to key, the actual frequency of the notes change, so what creates the melody is not the frequency of the separate notes. It's not the physics of the sound; it's the relationship among the participating elements. Some of them work perfectly. Some of them are highly discordant. The ones that work perfectly match up with something in us that is comparably "tuned," something that is itself expressive of a relational principle, finally, a "rational" principle. That's the thesis on which any philosophy worth having must be erected, and that is the Pythagorean bequest. That's the debt Plato owes to Pythagoras.

Well, what sort of a governor was he? I told you something about how his followers and disciples showed up for the theatre. I've always thought, when I read these accounts—and they tend to be rather late accounts—but I've always thought it was quite remarkable they went to the theatre at all. Well, what kind of governor was he?

The people finally staged riots and rebellions and drove the Pythagoreans from Crotona. That "old-time religion" wasn't wearing very well as the 6th century B.C. moved inexorably toward the 5th century B.C.

But how was it that Pythagoras could be found to be a man of affairs at all? I mean, is this the sort of thing philosophers do? Do you know that a little later on, Socrates is going to be arguing that there will be nothing but strife and misery within the *polis* until philosophers become kings and kings, philosophers? Well, I wonder what Socrates would have had to say if someone had said: "Well, what sort of a job did Pythagoras do in that regard?"

Here, I think it is important to point out that you can't judge the philosophical dimensions of a body of knowledge in terms of how it works practically in the political arena. This will become clearer as Plato and, especially, Aristotle start making distinctions between custom, man-made law, and the laws that we regard as the laws of the physical universe, the difference between nature, as in *phusis*, *nomos* as in custom—*nomos* as in legislated custom. As Aristotle will teach, we seek precision only insofar as the subject allows it, and there is not to be a Pythagorean theorem for political life.

The answer to the question, then, of: "How did Crotona fair under the guidance of Pythagoras and his followers?"—I think the right answer to the question is: "Not too well at all," and it's not quite clear that a philosophically guided state is likely to survive the reality in which it finds itself.

Now, what about the sense in which Pythagoras, as it were, arrogated to himself the title "first philosopher"? He may well have been. The ancients declare that he was the first one to call himself a philosopher. I say "arrogate to himself." Did he make the claim arrogantly, as in: "I am a philosopher, and you're not?"

Well, what is a philosopher? Well, it is someone who loves something. It's someone who has befriended something. Do you see? *Philos*, *philia*. Aristotle will tell us, later on, that the property the law has that attracts us to it is a kind of friendliness toward us, the Greek word here being *philicon*, Philadelphia, *philos, sophos, sophia. Sophia* is wisdom.

Now, the Greeks had several words for what we try to get at with notions of intelligence or knowledge. A scientific knowledge—which is the knowledge of, shall we say, the causal principles that govern things—was covered by the word *episteme*. The practical knowledge by which one deals with day-to-day affairs and makes prudential and correct choices consistent with the right kind of life is covered by the word *phronesis*, but *sophia* is something else. *Sophia* is what the wise person possesses. The one in possession of *sophia* is the one you consult when you finally are taking yourself seriously enough to ask core questions about the meaning of life, the ultimate point and purpose of things.

Pythagoras—non-arrogantly, and I think quite aptly—called himself a philosopher because he had devoted himself to an inquiry serving the purposes of wisdom itself. He wanted to know the truth of things. Not "so that," but because he had befriended wisdom itself. He saw the realization of his own humanity as inextricably bound up with a form of life that was a critical and inquiring form of life. He understood that he could only come to know the kind of being he was by coming to know what it is that makes anything possible and real.

Now, of course, we can dispute into the late hours whether what makes anything possible is ultimately and fundamentally number, but consider the periodic table, on which modern chemistry depends. Surely the relationships that obtain—among the chemical constituents of the world—are expressed in terms of numerical relationships, numerical powers that come about as a result of numbers of electrons, and bonding forces, and the like, so one might say that to the extent that things really exist in our chemical things—well, we might not want to say that they are made possible by number, but we would surely say that the most accurate description of what they are is going to be fundamentally numerical.

Then there are those in particle physics who will say that it is ultimately quarks held together by gluons that constitute "reality"; that is to say, there are quarks, and there are gluons holding quarks together. Now, what is it that allows a gluon to hold together a quark, and what combination of gluons would be necessary to hold quarks together in order for there to be a cosmos, or a sailboat, or a cuttlefish?

When we ask a question like this, we're likely to be regaled with a series of—ready? Equations! If we press on to ask why one theoretical account is judged to be superior to alternatives, we are likely to be told that it is because the theory matches up with, of all things, a set of equations, a set of numerical relations.

In fact, one of the characteristic features of scientific theories that enjoy a great reception and popularity within the advanced reach of theoretical physics are the properties of elegance and simplicity, where elegance and simplicity are themselves expressed in terms of mathematical precision—mathematical, formulaic simplicity.

Here, again, then, we see that on this very difficult question of what the necessary conditions are for anything to come into being, even the greatest advances in contemporary physics do take a very strong position behind number as such: numerousness, a kind of "informed numerology."

Well, "Ah, yes, the divinity of number," but now, with the divinity removed, at least for a time.

Lecture Four

What Is There?

Scope:

How many different kinds of "stuff" make up the cosmos? Might everything be reducible to one kind of thing? Can we know what it is?

The subject of *metaphysics*, as it would be developed in the 4th century B.C. by Aristotle, had already been founded by Greek philosophers. *Metaphysics* refers to two distinguishable but interconnected sets of questions: first, the question of just what there is—what *really* exists, and second, the question of how we know such things and whether the way we go about knowing is defensible or hopelessly defective. The first of these questions is the subject of *ontology*; the second, *epistemology*. Both sets of questions preoccupied the philosophers known as the *pre-Socratics*.

The thought of the pre-Socratics was chiefly cosmological, an attempt to discern what really is. But the problem of how we can know the truth of such things (Is knowledge relative? Does it come from the gods? Why does it differ from people to people?) raises issues that the moral questioning of Socrates in the dialogues of Plato will have to address.

Outline

I. The word *metaphysics* derives from the writings of Aristotle and means, "after the physics," or "after the study of natural science." It asks, essentially, two questions: "What is there?" and "How do I know?"

    A. The first question is ontological, that is, concerned with questions regarding the constituents of reality. For example, do minds exist, or thoughts?

        1. How do we go about answering such questions? Observation alone is insufficient. There is far more to reality than what is accessible to our senses.

2. Pythagoras had an abstract, rationalistic method for answering ontological questions that was largely intuitive and in which observation played no part.

B. We have at least two methods with which to approach the problem of knowing what exists, but we are left with the task of choosing between them. The rationalistic method may offer an account of reality that is not supported at the level of perception. Which account is to be preferred and on what basis?

C. Thus, we arrive at the second question, which springs from epistemology—the study of our claims to know. How do we know that reality is one thing or many things? To ask *what* there is is always to ask *how we know* what is.

1. Further, to declare that our senses deceive us or are incapable of reaching certain levels of reality is to make an epistemological claim.

2. If we know that our senses deceive us, we must have some non-deceptive—and non-perceptual—mode of discovery against which we can weigh the evidence of the senses.

3. What is this method of discovery for registering the truth of the world? Logic? Mathematics? Science? Religion?

4. These are questions of *epistemology*, meaning the study, criticism, and refinement of our very modes of knowing, the study of our knowledge as such.

5. Many of our most significant claims are actually *beliefs* rather than knowledge. We believe, for example, that the laws of science will still be operating tomorrow, but we cannot actually "know" what tomorrow will bring. Clearly, however, our belief in the laws of nature is different from a guess. How do we justify such a belief and distinguish it from guessing? This question pertains to what is referred to as *epistemic justification*.

D. Obviously, the two branches of metaphysics—ontology and epistemology—are inextricably bound together. To answer the question "What is there?" is already to have adopted a method. To adopt a method is already to have taken a position on the sorts of things that method might uncover.

    1. It is not solely in the philosophy seminar that these matters tax the intellectual resources. In daily life, we are continuously confronted by ontological and epistemological questions. Should I believe what I read in the newspapers? What medical advice is really sound? Do I die with my body or might there be a life after this one? Is there such a thing as goodness?

    2. As we begin to supply answers to these questions, we have adopted a method and may discover that the answers we've reached were more or less guaranteed given the method.

II. What does have *real* existence? Democritus of Abdera gave the materialist answer.

    A. Democritus argued for an essentially *atomic* theory of reality, according to which the ultimate constituents of the universe are invisibly small particles.

    B. This answer seems counterintuitive. We all have dreams and desires and thoughts and sensations. Are *these* "atomic"? The ancient atomists took a firm position: what exists does so because of its atomic composition. In the end, nothing transcends the level of physical materiality. Everything is ultimately reducible to that level.

    C. This reducibility is not at the expense of complexity, because the configurations of atoms may result in any number of things—buildings, turtles, people. But such collections are ephemeral. When the forces that hold things together become weakened through injury or disease, the atomic structure breaks down.

    D. What, then, is the atomists' position on the soul? For them, the soul is a finer kind of atomic structure.

    E. How many kinds of particulate, atomic "stuff" must be assumed to account for everything that exists? The materialist's answer is: "Only one kind—matter."

F. Returning to atomism, if what there is goes beyond the senses, how do we discover existence? Obviously, the atoms must come together in large enough ensembles to be accessible to the senses. Things take on defining properties in virtue of their atomic organization.

III. Does this search for what is real extend to the realm of morals? Are there such things as *beauty* and *ugliness, right* and *wrong*? To raise these questions is to trigger further questions about the means by which answers are found, that is, the method used to identify *right* and *wrong*.

A. Some have argued that the ultimate grounding of morality, law, and aesthetics is nothing more than conventional wisdom, one's social conditioning. We know, however, that different cultures or historical eras disagree widely on questions of right and wrong, good and evil.

B. The ancient Greek philosophers were not unaware of this dilemma. The pre-Socratics had grave doubts about our ability to answer fundamental questions without introducing our own prejudices into the equation.

C. Protagoras, who figures in the dialogues of Plato, insisted that "Man is the measure of all things." In this view, each person's experiences and perceptions constitute reality for that person—a reality that can claim as much ontological validity as any other.

    1. What Protagoras claims is that judgments of any sort—right or wrong, beauty or ugliness—must have some grounding, and that grounding can only be the experiences of a lifetime.

    2. We cannot occupy an epistemic position external to our own human ways of thought and feeling. If there is a standard independent of human nature, we could not even comprehend it.

    3. In this light, epistemology is a fit subject for cultural anthropology or sociology, examining the extent to which social and cultural values shape our metaphysical speculations. Indeed, if the answer to the philosophical question "What is there?" is known only from the vantage point of the person making the judgments and if philosophical inquiry is a search for truth, it seems that asking the question is misguided. Truth turns out to be the perceptions and perspective of the individual, rather than some objective or transcendent and eternal state.

D. Protagoras's position on religious matters, reminiscent of Homeric epic, appears in the only surviving fragment of his treatise *On Gods*:

> About the gods, I cannot say either that they are or that they are not, nor how they are constituted in shape. There is so much that prevents knowledge of this kind: the unclarity of the subject and the shortness of human life.

1. The fact that our lives are measured in hours sets a limit on what we can know. Truth comes from no transcendental realm beyond the human ken; all we can know is that opinions vary and that what one man will die for, another will scoff at as absurd.

2. In this way, each man becomes the measure of all things, and the possibility of a coherent transpersonal body of knowledge is beyond reach.

E. The contribution of pre-Socratic philosophers takes the form of robust skeptical challenges to customary beliefs. Socrates, too, examines these beliefs but also the challenges. In the process, he shifts philosophical attention from the cosmos to the human condition itself. He will argue that each of us not only fails to be the measure of all things, but we are generally very poor in our understanding of our very selves.

Recommended Reading:

Barnes, J., ed. *Early Greek Philosophy.* Penguin Books, 1987.

Hussey, E *The Presocratic Philosophers.* Cambridge University Press, 1983.

Questions to Consider:

1. Conclude whether there are similarities between the effects of skeptical philosophy on attitudes in ancient Greece and the effects of modern science on contemporary attitudes.

2. Given that nearly universal human customs (*nomoi*) are taken, therefore, to be "natural," explain how exceptions can be dealt with.

3. Give examples of nearly universal customs that are brought about by essentially local conditions.

Lecture Four—Transcript

What Is There?

In titling this lecture, "What Is There?" I realize I am playing into the well-established prejudices of the many against philosophy, prejudices according to which philosophers spend most of their time raising questions that everybody has ready answers to and that no sane person would have thought about asking anyway.

"What is there?" is answered by as many things as we can point to. There are carpets and doors and puppies and people, and all the rest of what fills our cluttered world, so the answer to the question, "What is there?" is: "Look around."

Well, of course, philosophers, too, look around, and otherwise live their lives as others do. They do look around, but they then press on to determine whether they can trust what it is they are seeing, or whether behind what they are seeing there might be something more fundamental, something more ultimate. In the process, the philosophically inclined, seeing what is "there," may also wonder, in a disciplined way, whether it is really there, or whether the very process of perception has transformed the real object into something of a distortion.

Now, ancient man engaged in spear fishing, and he must have learned pretty early that the actual location of the fish in the water is not quite where the fish is perceived to be. We all, from time to time, have to learn how to adjust to the fact that our senses might deceive, but then the question is whether they *always* deceive and how it comes about that we would be able to discover this. Might all the things we take for granted as having real being actually be just apparitions or manifestations of a peculiar sort, and behind such apparitions might we be able to find something worthy of the title "reality"?

Again, then, "What is there?" This is an example of a metaphysical question. Now, in the course of these lectures, such questions will be persistent, so this would seem to be the right time to define *metaphysics*. In matters of this sort, the brief dictionary definitions are not particularly helpful.

Let's begin at the beginning. When does the word begin to be used? In a monumentally important treatise composed by Aristotle, the great philosopher notes, for the benefit of his students, that they have just completed a systematic consideration of "nature," or what we would call the physical world. The words for this subject are *phusis* and *phusikos*, "nature" and what is "natural."

Centuries later, commentators giving titles to Aristotle's major works noted this reference and adopted a phrase to refer to the treatise that came next, *"Ta meta ta phusika,"* which translates simply as, "after the natural science work," "after the 'physics." Thus, this most subtle and original of philosophical works receives as its formal name one that simply places it after another work—but what's in a name?

The actual subject matter of the work known as Aristotle's *Metaphysics* is the subject of "real existence." More needs to be said here by way of definition.

A fairly settled understanding is that metaphysics embraces two primary sets of questions. One set, as Willard Van Orman Quine, the Harvard logician, put it, is exhausted by three monosyllabic English words: "What is there?" This part of metaphysics is called *ontology*, from the Greek *on*, which just is "being." *Ontology* is the branch or division of metaphysics concerned with questions regarding the constituents of reality as such. Do ghosts and witches *really* exist? Any number of complex issues are then generated. Something may exist merely accidentally, or by being the effect of a cause, or even in some sense, necessarily, and as an object undergoes change, there arises the ontological question as to whether the original still exists or could exist, etc.

Now, most will agree that there are neither ghosts nor witches as such, but what about "minds" and "thoughts"? Are there minds and thoughts, or are they just peculiar states of the brain that we describe in a mentalistic language? Do thoughts really exist? Which is to say, are thoughts bona fide ontological entities, or are they merely terms, terms of art hearkening to a period of superstition and ignorance?

How does one go about answering such questions? Presumably through some mode of inquiry, but what is the right mode of inquiry? Should we answer the question, "What is there?" by making observations? That is, what there is, is just what we can see, touch, hear, taste, or smell? Well, if we adopt that method, then surely there can't be quarks, neutrons, protons, or anything at the subatomic level.

Now, as it happens, the maximum visual sensitivity of the honeybee is actually in the ultraviolet region of the spectrum where we can't see anything at all, so the ontology of the honeybee is radically different in content from our ontology.

This surely is an unsatisfactory state of affairs. It would make no sense to say that what *really* exists varies from person to person—from sighted to blind persons, from persons with normal hearing to persons with defective hearing, from persons to honeybees, etc. We surely resist the conclusion that things come into being and go out of being depending upon what sensory apparatus might be at work at a given time.

The deeper implication of all this is that there is far more to reality than meets the eye, or that is accessible to any of our senses, so: "What is there?" is a philosophical question. Like all worthy philosophical questions, it's anything but idle, and when we consider the ontological questions implicit in the famous maxim recorded at the temple of Apollo in Delphi, the maxim, '*Gnothi seauton*," "Know thyself," we are driven to ask: "What am I? What sort of being am I? What am I made of? What am I made for?"

 Now, I say, if the method of observation is insufficient, are there other methods? Pythagoras was fairly confident he had a method. The method was an essentially abstract mathematical method by which to discover and create coherent relationships constitutive of all possible realities. Observation, as such, takes no part in this. The "method," if we may call it that, is largely intuitive and rational. We might call it an "abstract rationalistic" method.

With at least these two methods of approach to the problem, to the problem of knowledge, we are left with the task of choosing, but then this would seem to require some other method or device with which to make choices between various methods. There is here a worrisome "infinite regress" that seems to be lurking. The rationalistic method may offer a conception or an account of reality that is not supported at the level of perception. Which account is to be preferred, and on what basis?

These are questions not about "real being," but about the basis on which we claim and defend our knowledge of reality. We say that these are—what? These are "epistemological" questions. To declare that the senses deceive or are incapable of reaching certain levels or aspects of reality is to make an "epistemological claim."

Now, presumably, if we are sure that the senses deceive us, we must possess some non-deceptive—and, one would think, non-perceptual—mode of discovery against which we can weigh the claims of the senses and say, "Alas, the senses got it wrong."

Now, the only way we can say this with confidence is if we have some non-deceptive, or as we say, "veridical" mode of registering the truth or the facts of the world. What would that be? Is it logic? Is it mathematics? Science? Religion? Revelation? Intuition? General agreement? By vote? By custom?

These are epistemological questions, the root of this adjective being the Greek *episteme*, which refers to systematic knowledge—not the mere assembly of facts, but the organization of facts and principles in such a way as to provide a systematic understanding of things, a systematic understanding of events. Taking off from this etymological root, we employ the term *epistemology* to stand for the study, criticism, and refinement of our very modes of knowing, the study of our knowledge as such.

Many of our most significant claims are actually *beliefs* rather than knowledge. We believe, for example, that the laws of science that worked up to this very moment will still be operating tomorrow, and will permit us to move ourselves and other objects with the aid of, for example, the internal combustion engine. To be precise, we must admit that we cannot actually "know" what tomorrow will bring. Clearly, however, our belief in the continuing operation of the laws of nature is different from a mere guess. Now, how do we justify such a belief and distinguish it from guessing? This question pertains to what, in philosophy, is referred to as *epistemic justification*, an important area within epistemology.

It must be obvious that the two branches of metaphysics—ontology and epistemology—are inextricably bound together. To answer the question "What is there? What is really there?" is already to have adopted a method. To adopt a method is already to have taken a position on the sorts of things that method might uncover, so there is a continuing dialectic between the ontological and epistemological aspects of metaphysics.

It is not solely in the philosophy seminar that these matters tax the intellectual resources. In daily life, ordinary citizens are plagued, and they recognize themselves as tested, by ontological and epistemological questions. "Can I trust rumors? Should I believe what I read in the newspapers? What do we really mean by 'poverty'? Is there such a thing as 'victimless crime'? What medical advice is really sound? How do we know that the counsel of the wise is wisdom itself? What standard do we use against which to weigh those things that prevail on us for our allegiance, and our belief, and our convictions? Do I die with my body, or might there be a life after this one? Is there some transcendental realm above the realm of materiality, in which one meets the saints of the world? Is there such a thing as goodness, really, or is this simply a habit and a certain form of speech that a particular tribe uses to describe what it likes? Is there a moral reality such that moral questions can be settled once and for all? Is there moral objectivity? When we use moral language, are we referring to something that has bona fide ontological standing?"

Now, as we begin to supply answers to questions such as this, we have adopted a method—consciously or by blind habit—and we may discover too late that the answers we've reached were more or less guaranteed given the method we chose.

Metaphysical analysis is clearly not a game that just anyone can expect to play well, but it is a game that everyone must play seven days a week, and it often stands as the game of life itself. We have good reasons to be thankful for those metaphysicians who have devoted themselves in a quite systematic way to helping us find the way out of one or another labyrinth.

Well, again, what is there? One famous answer to this most basic of metaphysical questions was supplied by Democritus in the ancient Greek world. He is the father of one of the major ontological traditions in philosophy, that of "materialism." Democritus defended the thesis that the ultimate reality is but an unimaginably large number of atoms—the Greek "*atomos*" referring to that which is so small that it cannot be "cut" further. Democritus answers the ontological question by declaring that all that is really there are atoms and a void, atoms and the spaces between them.

This answer seems utterly counterintuitive. We all have dreams and desires and thoughts and sensations. Are *these* "atomic"? Nonetheless, the ancient atomists took a firm position here: What exists—what has *real* existence—has *real* existence in virtue of its atomic composition. When we see a rose or smell it, it is the result of atomic emanations, or what in the Greek were called *eidola*. What the object impinges on is also atomic in structure. In the end, nothing transcends the level of physical materiality. What there is finally is material, atomic. Everything is ultimately reducible to that level.

None of this is at the expense of the seeming complexity of the world, for the configurations of atoms may result in large buildings, turtles, and, indeed, metaphysicians. But such collections are ephemeral. Sooner or later, the fate of everything is dictated by the atomic structure of everything. When the forces that hold things together become weakened through injury or disease, the atomic structure now breaks down—then, "Dust thou art, to dust returneth."

Now, the poets tell us that, "Dust thou art, to dust returneth" was not spoken of the soul. You know:

> Tell me not in mournful numbers
> Life is but an empty dream.

Et cetera.

Well, what's the atomist's position on the soul? The soul, we learn, is a finer kind of atomic structure. That is, what we refer to as the "spiritual domain" is itself particulate, atomic, but now the ontologically real entities are just of finer stuff. Note: stuff—still stuff!

If the fundamental ontological question is "What is there?" it may be rephrased this way: "How many kinds of 'stuff' must be assumed to account for everything that there really is?"

"You need only refer to one kind—and that is matter." What it means to be a materialist, then, is to defend an ontological position—namely, that there is no real existent that is not material. Facing such a claim, we might then insist that it be defended with argument and evidence, and through a mode of inquiry that is proper for the task at hand.

Let me stay with materialism for the moment. It is useful to point out that defenses of it often rely on evidence gathered by methods that presuppose the validity of the claim—namely, methods suited to identify and quantify matter, or material things. There tends to be a certain circularity, even a vicious circularity, between the ontological position we take and the methods that we employ to vindicate or confirm or, as we like to say, "objectively" test it. This will be apparent in more than one major theory considered in subsequent lectures.

Returning once more to the ancient atomism, if it is the case that what there is goes beyond the senses and involves particles so small that no one can see them, how do we go about the task of discovery? Obviously, the atoms have to come together in large enough ensembles to be accessible to the senses. The atomist is not skeptical about chairs and apples, or people and birthday cakes. What atomism asserts has to do with the ultimate constituent of things, and not their gross, perceptible features.

Obviously, things take on defining properties in virtue of their atomic organization, so that the next-door neighbor is different from a birthday cake, not in that a next-door neighbor is made up of something other than atomic entities, but is comprised of radically different atomic configurations.

Nevertheless, it reassures this same ordinary citizen that what is perceived is really there, insofar as it has an atomic configuration agreeable to our essentially empirical or sensory modes of knowing. Here is that *naturalistic* orientation that plays off very nicely against, for example, a Pythagorean worldview.

Suppose we now raise the question: "What is there?" in the domain of morals, or politics, or art. Is there, in reality, *right* and *wrong*? Is there, in fact, real *beauty*? Is there, in fact, truth and falsity in statements about good and evil? To say "yes" or "no" is to trigger basic questions about the means by which answers are reached, the method used to identify *right* and *wrong*, etc.

Some have argued today, as well as thousands of years ago, that the ultimate grounding of morality, law, aesthetics, and principles of governance is nothing more than conventional wisdom. At work is nothing more than one's social conditioning. One's values are reflections of nothing more than the way one was raised and acculturated. Jack knows that there is right and wrong, and all Jack's friends and neighbors know that there is right and wrong. Why, all red-blooded Americans know there is right and wrong, but so, too, do all red-blooded ancient Babylonians, Aztec tribesmen, European witch-hunters, and Oriental believers in the divinity of their emperor.

The anthropological record makes clear that there has not been a stable and universally accepted scheme of moral rectitude or aesthetic value. As we examine one tribe or culture, or one historical era or another, there seems to be wide disagreement as to questions of right and wrong, truth and falsity, good and evil. Certainly, what the Greeks revered as sublimely beautiful in their commitment to harmony and proportion, balance and measure, is not what the Kwakiutl might regard as beautiful, with feathers sticking out, and wild plumage, and distortions of the body. Certainly, the medieval depiction of human forms struck Renaissance painters and sculptors as hopelessly defective.

The ancient Greek philosophers were not unaware of this as they attempted to find truths not otherwise discovered through the shifting perspectives of the non-philosophical world. Thales, who might be regarded as the first philosopher of note in ancient Greece, flourishing around 580 B.C., reasoned that everything is composed of some sort of spirituous or watery material. His student, Anaximander, reasoned that the ultimate composition of things was neither watery nor solid, but some sort of ineffable substance. Others defended what came to be something of the conventional view, that all reality was a composite reality, the composition being of earth, air, fire, and water.

However, among the pre-Socratics were also those who had grave doubts about our ability to answer fundamental questions without introducing our own prejudices into the equation. Heraclitus, flourishing about 500 B.C., and famous for the maxim, "No one descends twice into the same river"—seeing nothing but flux and change everywhere—had yet another maxim: "The donkey prefers garbage to gold."

When we turn to more systematic forms of skepticism, however, the thinker who comes to mind immediately is Protagoras, an older contemporary of Socrates, who will figure in two of the main Platonic dialogues, the one named after him, *Protagoras*, and another in which his teaching is critically assessed: *Theaetetus*.

Protagoras is famous for the maxim, "Man is the measure of all things." If philosophers ever come to grips with the fact that they're probably going to be remembered for one sentence or merely vagrant utterance, no matter how many qualifications they added, they might choose a life of silence.

Well, from Protagoras we have two gems, and we wish we had much more. First, though, is, "Man is the measure of all things." How is this to be understood?

Protagoras is a founding father of *Sophist* thought. And we can tell from the dialogue, *Protagoras*, which he is having with a still less-than-ripe Socrates, that he is a formidable philosopher. We will meet him again, but here it is sufficient to note that there is certainly more to Protagoras than the single and arguable idea that "Man is the measure of all things."

What Protagoras is claiming is that judgments of any sort—right or wrong, truth or falsity, beauty or ugliness—must have some grounding, and that grounding can only be the experiences of a lifetime. We cannot occupy an epistemic position external to our own human ways of thought and feeling. If there is a standard liberated from—or independent of—human nature, we couldn't even comprehend it. To that extent then, each man does turn out to be the measure of all things. It's you who will decide whether this is a sweet or sour substance, and what's sweet to one person might be sour to others, or even to the same person on separate occasions. "One man's fish is another man's *poisson*," as the pun would have it.

Now, this relativizes epistemology. Understood under this light, epistemology is a fit subject for cultural anthropology or sociology. In fact, we do have a flourishing field of inquiry called "the sociology of knowledge," and it's applied even to the most developed branches of science, the extent to which social values and cultural values shape—and even dominate—our metaphysical speculations.

Thus, Protagoras's answers to the question "What is there?" is going to be guided by knowledge of the vantage point of the person making the observations and the judgments. Accordingly, if philosophical inquiry is a search after the truth, it seems that this is a misguided undertaking from the first. Truth turns out to be one of those elusive entities that finally records more the perceptions and perspective of the individual; little more than some transpersonal, or objective, or transcendent eternally true state of affairs is certainly not going to be within reach—not that there aren't truths of such a nature, but we're scarcely equipped to comprehend or unearth them.

We have but one more *bon mot* from Protagoras. So much of his philosophy is lost as is that entire system of thought developed by the pre-Socratic philosophers. All we have now can be fit into a single volume, but one suggestive enough to stimulate whole libraries of commentary.

Let me go back to the second snippet from Protagoras, though; this is from a treatise he composed about the nature of the gods. In that treatise, he says something that always reminds me of what it is the Homeric epics are depicting as we wrestle with the problem of knowledge. Protagoras says:

"About the gods, I cannot say either that they are or that they are not, nor how they are constituted in shape. There is so much that prevents knowledge of this kind: the unclarity of the subject and the shortness of human life."

"The unclarity of the subject and the shortness of human life." We are mortal. We do not live on Olympus. Our life is measured in hours, and this sets a limit on what we can know, and with respect to the gods, the ultimate source of all there is and all there could be—these are questions beyond the human ken. These are matters we cannot reach. "I cannot write to you about the gods. I can write to you about what I can see and hear and taste and touch. I can write to you about where I've lived and where I've visited. And what I've discovered," Protagoras seems to be saying, "and what I've discovered in these travels, in these journeys, in journeys of thought and journeys of body, is that opinions vary widely." And what one person is prepared to die for in virtue of what he takes to be its truth, another regards as just another example of the absurdity of the human condition. Thus, each one, in his way, becomes the measure of all things, and the possibility of a coherent transpersonal body of knowledge is ever beyond reach, if not realistic hope.

Well, this really is surely a melancholy prospect for a philosophy. "Put the books away, put away the pens and pencils, find another day job! If each person is the measure of all things, there can't even be an argument!" However, as Socrates will show throughout his productive life, there is much to argue about, including the proposition that each person is an ultimate measure of all things.

The significant contribution of philosophers before Socrates, or among his older contemporaries, takes the form of robust skeptical challenges to customary beliefs. Socrates, too, examines these beliefs but also the challenges. In the process, he shifts philosophical attention from the cosmos that so arrested the attention of the pre-Socratics, turning it into the human condition itself. He will argue that each of us not only fails to be the measure of all things, but we are generally very poor in our understanding of our very selves. With him, philosophy now becomes an utterly humanizing and humanistic enterprise, a significant place on the map of thought, from which there will be no retreating.

Lecture Five

The Greek Tragedians on Man's Fate

Scope:

In the drama of the ancient Greek world—in the works of Aeschylus, Euripides, and Sophocles—the tension between fate and striving can never be relaxed. Medea is illustrative. Here is a woman whose magic is used to rescue Jason, only to have their subsequent marriage set aside by him as he pursues another woman. In blind vengeance, she kills their two sons. Was Medea's crime mitigated by Jason's treason against their love? Was she a murderer or the victim of uncontrollable impulses? *Nomos* or *physis*—better still, perhaps, *nomos* as *physis*.

Consider, on the other hand, Antigone, as presented by Sophocles. Against the express orders of King Creon, she buries her brother, then appears before the king to defend herself. But her defense is not that of Medea, not that she was overcome by grief or that passion got the better of her. No, Antigone's defense is that her allegiance to her brother is a veritable law of nature—something as causal as the laws of nature themselves. Indeed, if there would be kings at all, there must be a capacity for unrepentant faithfulness.

Is human nature within or beyond the natural realm? What is it in our nature that inclines us toward good and evil? Is everything but the result of whim and chance and fate, or is there something in the person that might rise above both custom and brute nature itself? It is in the major dramatic works of Aeschylus, Sophocles, and Euripides that the problem of self-knowledge is underscored—a problem made ever more difficult by the variety of factors, both seen and unseen, that operate on us in the course of a lifetime. How can we limit the destructive force of those "slings and arrows of outrageous fortune"? What form of life, what mode of conduct, might yield sanctuary?

Outline

I. Pre-literate societies had limited resources for recording what was of value to them, but one method used was dance, such as the dance of the cranes that Theseus performed to communicate the secret of the labyrinth to his people.

- **A.** Chorus and singing add vividness to dance, and narratives of consequence can be acted out before the whole people to remind them of who they are and what their responsibilities are.

- **B.** As individual speakers arise who are able to carry on colloquies and embody characters, the chorus addresses the audience, evaluating, commenting, and analyzing.

- **C.** Thus, out of gesture, dance, ritual, bardic story comes a world of stories and philosophical disquisitions cast in the form of dialogue: the world of the Greek dramatists that will issue eventually in the dialogues of Plato.

II. The psychological depth and philosophical complexity of Greek classical drama can be seen in the dilemmas of Euripides's Medea and Sophocles's Antigone. We first look at Medea.

- **A.** Was Medea guilty of murder? The killing of children by a parent is the most "unnatural" of acts, but her act might be seen as a natural revenge proportionate to the crime committed against her and, thus, fitting or "meet."

- **B.** Revenge of this sort harks back to an earlier, pre-juridical world—the world of the *law of revenge*, when the chthonic gods of the earth held sway and the Olympian gods of light were still in the future, a world in which the pleadings of the heart trump the demands of rationality.

  - **1.** This older religion was associated with birth and renewal, with crops and nurturing, and identified the female with all that was sustaining; the bond of mother and child was the fundamental social bond. At this most primitive level is where Medea's creative and destructive energies reside.

  - **2.** In the classical period, this pattern is reversed. The Olympian religion installed Zeus as chief among the gods, and the superiority of the male was uncontested. In Aeschylus's drama of Clytemnestra and Agamemnon, Clytemnestra's crime (killing her husband) is judged to be worse than Orestes's crime (killing his mother) by the Olympian Athena, because Clytemnestra's crime is that she killed a man.

3. Medea harkens to an older perspective, so different from our own that she seems to us, and to Euripedes's audience, as simply mad. Indeed, Medea seems to be more driven than driving. Something of the mystery of earth itself impels her movements, has her sacrifice her sons to return them to the earth, to revive the cycle and have it conclude more satisfactorily.

4. In a key moment, as she kisses and caresses the children she is about to murder, Medea describes her own dilemma without being able to alter it:

> Go, leave me; I cannot bear to see you any longer.
> Overcome by grief, now I understand what I am
>   about to do;
> Passion—that cause of our most dire woes—
> Has vanquished my rational power.

5. Euripides develops characters more accessible than the Olympians: the mysterious and powerful but jilted woman, cheated by her opportunistic and aggressive husband, who finds "honor" chiefly in externals. Medea's impulses spring from beneath the earth; his, from what is above it.

6. Perhaps because this is a rather modern saga, many of Euripedes's contemporary critics thought it was uninstructive. It didn't accomplish what they regarded as the mission of theatre—not to depict the entities we are but to show us how good character leads to good ends. Euripides understood the tension between the earthly, chthonic life as it is lived and the ideal realm of moral imperatives.

C. We also find in Euripides, and in nearly all the Greek dramatists, the central canon that *character is destiny*.

1. The word *nomos* is pivotal here. As understood in the vocabulary of the ancient philosopher, *nomos* is not what is merely customary, but what is lawful, as in the very

laws of nature. And in this same age, in the context of law and society, *nomos*, again, is not merely the customary practices but what is utterly binding as a legal precept.

   2. How are we to understand the law? Is the law something naturally right? Is it something imposed? Does it arise from our very nature? Is it counter to our nature?

   3. Medea's crime is "unnatural," but being driven by passion *is* natural. It is possible to recognize that you have passed beyond reason and be unable to stop yourself.

D. Medea is one of the commanding women of the ancient Greek world, a group that includes Aphrodite, Athena, Antigone, Andromache, the Theban women, Clytemnestra, Penelope, and others.

   1. Despite their actual position of reclusive subservience in the ancient world, women are portrayed with greatness by the ancient Greek dramatists.

   2. This prominence in literature seems to be a recognition of the power of Eros, the ancient understanding that what brings men and women together is not just a creative force, not just something that brings about life and repopulates the world, but also a powerfully destructive force. Because what we will do at the bidding of Eros is what Medea does.

III. *Nomos* as custom, *nomos* as law, and nature (*physis*) begin to merge and diverge as the classical world faces increasing complexity of thought and practice. The story of Antigone illustrates.

A. Where Medea surrenders to her passion, Antigone's passion reaches a universal principle.

   1. Antigone violates Creon's order not to bury her dead brother out of her conviction that *nomos*—the law of the land—is more ancient than the orders of kings and that her duty to bury her brother is a *universal* one; a later age will call it *natural law*.

2. Beneath all our allegiances to king and custom is a deeper allegiance to nature that we must have in order for there to be kings and customs. To this allegiance, Antigone subscribes.

B. Medea's passion is a form of madness in which reason is surrendered: a form of ignorance. Antigone's passion is akin to knowledge. Antigone *knows herself*: She knows what she should do, the wishes of kings notwithstanding. She doesn't want to have to do it, hates the idea of dying for it, but she does it.

IV. Both Greek drama and Greek philosophy would propose "Know thyself." The resulting knowledge was scarcely reassuring. Even if we are careful, wise, and moderate and avoid *hubris*, dreadful things often befall us. Philosophy will have to address this tragic dilemma at the core of existence.

Recommended Reading:

Boardman, J., et al., eds. *The Oxford History of Greece and the Hellenistic World*. Oxford University Press, 1991, chapter 7, "Greek Drama."

Dane, N., and J. Ambrose, eds. *Greek Attitudes*. Scribners, 1974.

Vernant, Jean Pierre, ed. *The Greeks*. University of Chicago Press, 1995.

Questions to Consider:

1. In casting Jason and Medea as less than heroic figures, Euripides may be said to have humanized the psychological forces at work in tragedy. Euripides was criticized in his own time for presenting characters who defied the settled values of the *polis*. Summarize, in this context, what is the artist's responsibility in relation to morality.

2. Antigone is the quintessential exemplar of "civil disobedience." Conclude whether she was right to oppose the authority of the king or whether her sister was right in recommending the prudent course of compliance.

Lecture Five—Transcript

The Greek Tragedians on Man's Fate

In the first lecture, I noted that when Theseus found his way out of the labyrinth, he set sail, and, after abandoning good Ariadne on the island of Naxos, he returned to the Greek mainland and decoded the labyrinthine maze through the "crane's dance."

Now, in those dance steps, he performed a series of movements that would guide others out of the labyrinth. There is something of a parallel between Theseus's Dance of the Cranes and, as I noted, the "dance of the bees" that locates the flowers with the greatest amount of nectar.

Dance figures importantly in the classical literature—in Homer, and Ovid, and other classical writers.

It has been noted by more than one cultural historian—Yale's Eric Havelock is the one that comes to mind in this connection—that pre-literate societies, having limited resources with which to set down, as it were, what is worth knowing, routinely employ the dance for such purposes. Through certain dance steps, which can be rehearsed and repeated and learned by others, one can symbolize events of great moments, not only symbolize them, but lay them out in a definite and choreographed order, reflecting time and space.

To some extent, then, the earliest cultural memories of a community are recorded, coded as it were, choreographically as it were, "inscribed" in movement. This can be greatly enriched by having the dance accompanied by a chorus. Consider the expressive power of modern ballet and opera, and imagine the content repeated regularly and connected to matters of profound importance to oneself and one's community. Add the metric and melodic character of the music lyrics of heroism, pathos, and tragedy. Here are the ingredients of preliterate history, preliterate moral thought, performed to teach and to remind, and to allow those witnessing the event to go home at the end of all this and recognize what kind of people they are, what they stand for, what their obligations are.

Now, out of this background, something quite precious and productive develops. The chorus breaks up, and there are actual participants whose activities now are commented on by, or otherwise illuminated by, a group providing a gloss on the activity. The chorus sings a commentary, but the participants themselves are engaged in one or another kind of drama, designed to teach a lesson or present possibilities otherwise unforeseen, or remind people of events that must always be kept in mind if the *polis* is to be preserved, if the tribe is to be kept intact.

What we have here is the foundation of drama itself, whether it is ever to be recorded in written form. In the classical world, the dramas are composed and performed not only in a society that is literate, but in a society that has an exquisitely precise and supple language.

Out of the developed drama comes—what? The dialogue. That is, out of this dramatic enactment we now can find a much smaller ensemble of participants who address, frontally, questions that the drama is otherwise about, but that the drama itself cannot resolve. The drama presents possibilities, and it's in a later development, in a later and more philosophical or intellectual development, that out of the possibilities of the dramatic is carved a dialogue for the purpose of dispute, analysis, and evaluation.

It might be said then that philosophy arises from cultural resources that begin in a pre-literate world possessed of choreography, and painting, and certain natural movements, and natural language, by way of which one can communicate thoughts and feelings. Then, to this world of the dance and the painting, this world of murals and body postures and signs and symbols, is added a chorus, a lyric, a story to be told, an epic poem, the benefit of minstrels singing away memorably, with tunes that one remembers all the way back to one's tents.

Out of this, through the imagination, the fertile genius of the literary mind, whole stories are spun in rich, dramatic form, and out of this same set of dramatic possibilities, but only rarely, arises nothing less than philosophical disquisitions on the path toward authentic and critical philosophy in the form of dialogue. From the dance of Theseus to the dialogues of Plato, we are witnesses to thought refining itself.

I wish to dilate on the dramatic form first, because the dramatists not only appear on the eve of Socratic philosophy, but even pre-date Socratic philosophy. More than this, the drama envisages possibilities in ways that are vivid and deeply suggestive, often connecting to actual life with an immediacy missing in formal philosophical discourse.

Problems are not clarified or resolved the way they are in philosophy, but a kind of philosophical challenge is set down, once we learn how the lives of the characters are being lived within the drama. It is surely not accidental that the dialogues composed by Plato have a dramatic form. Indeed, were Plato not acknowledged to be among the greatest philosophers, he might well be included among the leading dramatists of the ancient world.

The great "depth" psychologists—principally Sigmund Freud and Carl Gustav Jung—were no strangers to the ancient Greek tragedians, and saw them as penetrating to levels of psychological understanding deeper than that reached by psychiatry itself.

A few words then on how the human condition was understood by the dramatists. Let's begin with this question: Is Medea a murderess? Is she a murderess in just the sense that would be meant today by a prosecutor in possession of the same facts? Now, Medea, dramatically resented in theaters all over the world and in scores of languages—audiences have no doubt but that she kills her sons. She's forlorn. She's enraged. She's been abandoned by Jason, whose faithlessness was to improve his own situation in the world. He has taken up with another woman, the daughter of King Creon. We're going to meet Creon again, as he admonishes a very different sort of woman, Antigone.

Here's Medea, though, who has been the victim of an act of treason against her own love. She seeks a form of revenge proportioned to the offense. What will cause in Jason the unrelieved pain and grief he has caused her? Even in this rage, even in what might be regarded as a kind of madness, we see an attempt to find a proportionality, to find something fitting and "meet." Even in the act of what we would take to be a violent and "unnatural" crime, there is something that tries to match up with the depth of feeling—the depth of resentment—that is experienced by this jilted lover.

Now, when Euripides gives us Medea and Jason, he is knowingly controversial in his own time, because he does not offer heroic figures. His are all-too-human, possessing but few redeeming qualities. Oh yes, Jason and the Argonauts engaged in all sorts of daunting tasks to get the Golden Fleece, but Medea's help was there at many turns. When they escaped together to Corinth, Jason would sire two sons with her, only then to turn around, marry the daughter of the King of Corinth, and shamelessly assure Medea that he did this with her interests in mind.

One does get the sense that in all this, including the demanded search for the Golden Fleece, Jason has been prompted by what I'm tempted to call "middle-class values." I mean, they are off to get the Golden Fleece. Here is an opportunistic fellow, moved around by his own passions rather too easily; it could make the evening news.

Meanwhile, we have Medea, and what we know about Medea is that service to Jason was in the form of sorcery. She is the daughter of a nymph-witch, and she is practiced in the arts of magic, a figure surrounded in mystery. There is something about her that is at the subterranean level. She is redolent of a religion in a Greek world that pre-dates Olympianism. It is the *chthonic* earth religions, the religions devoted to deities judged as controlling birth and renewal, agriculture, husbandry, crops, fertility.

The Olympians came to replace the chthonic gods, but in this earlier form of devotion, pride of place was held by women because of their procreative power, their life-giving power. Life then was identified centrally with womankind, not at the practical level of political or economic life, but at the most primitive level, which is the level at which Medea's creative and destructive energies reside.

I might digress here to mention another interesting event in Greek literary and legendary history. Avenging the sacrificing of their daughter, Clytemnestra kills Agamemnon when he returns from the Trojan War. Their son, Orestes, now avenges his father's death by killing his mother, a faithless wife, and this sets the stage for a trial that leads to a hung jury. They can't decide between the crime of

Orestes (killing his mother), and the crime of Clytemnestra (killing Agamemnon)—and who is to cast the deciding vote?

It is to be cast by a woman, and not just any woman, of course, but Athena. Her vote favors Orestes, because the crime of killing the man ranks higher in negativity than the crime of killing the woman, and you begin to see the patriarchal perspective replacing that older chthonic matriarchal outlook.

Well, enough of that. Now, Medea harkens to an older perspective, so different from our own that she seems to us, and to Euripides's audiences, as simply mad. Indeed, when Medea is played right, she herself is less aware of precisely what she's doing than too many actresses are inclined to make her seem. She should be more driven than driving. There should be something of the mystery of earth itself that impels her movements, that will have her sacrifice her sons to return them to the earth, to revive the cycle and have it worked out in a better way next time round.

I did scratch out just a couple of lines where she is explaining herself, as she kisses the children she's about to kill. It is one of the poignant moments in the history of theatre. "Go," she says. "Leave me." She wants them to disappear back into the fundament of things. "Leave me. I cannot bear to see you any longer." That is, your presence in my senses is defiling, but not because of anything you've done; it's because of something I've done. I gave birth to you as a result of love for a traitor.

"Overcome by grief, now I understand what I am about to do," she says. "Passion—that cause of our most dire woes—has vanquished my rational power." Plato might just as well have been sitting in the audience taking notes. Here we go again, from that rage that launches Homer's *Iliad* to Medea's passion. Passion does it all. The movements are to be understood in that chthonic sense of something driving us—we know not what. We call it passion, but what Medea is about to do has the character of the involuntary, the *akousios* in the ancient Greek, not unlike a gripping addiction or seizure. Is she a murderess, then, or are these motives irresistible?

Euripides develops characters now more accessible than the Olympians: the mysterious and powerful but jilted woman, cheated by her opportunistic and aggressive husband, who finds "honor" chiefly in externals. Medea's impulses spring from beneath the earth; his, from what is above it. Perhaps because this is a rather modern saga, many of Euripides's contemporary critics—because of that—thought it was uninstructive. It wasn't accomplishing what they regarded as the very mission of theatre: not to depict the sorts of entities we are, but to show us how our good character leads to good ends.

However, Euripides knew what he was doing, and Euripides knew, in his day, that this tension now was a real one—this tension between the Chthonic and the Olympian, this tension between our origins and our ideals, our humanity, and that perfectionist scheme believed to obtain among the Olympians. Alas, "Know thyself."

What we do find in Euripides, and in nearly all the Greek dramatists, the central canon that at the end of the day, *character is destiny*. This is clear in Homer, of course. Once you can peg the type of character on display, all the rest seems to fall into place. No one is surprised when finally Agamemnon stands up during that brief period of rapprochement with Achilles and says of their previous and angry encounter: "Oh, look, you know that day, I didn't really do it. It was the *Erinyes* that takes you over, and the gods make you do things," etc., etc.

There is something so true to character in Agamemnon taking that particular way out. There is something so characteristic of Helen of Troy in *Iliad* and *Odyssey*, when, on the few occasions when we meet her, she never utters a sentence in which she does not refer to herself, or the faithfulness of Penelope, the valor of Patroclus, etc., etc.

The dramatists are attempting to work out something else. There is a dangerous conflict brewing between the ageless customary practices of the Greek-speaking people and this new philosophical thought that is producing new insights and discoveries.

The word *nomos* is pivotal here. As understood in the developed vocabulary of the ancient philosopher, *nomos* is not what is merely customary, but what is lawful, as in the very laws of nature. And in this same developed age, within the context of law and society, *nomos*, again, is not merely the customary practices but what is utterly binding as a legal precept. How are we to understand the law? Is the law something naturally right? Is it something imposed? Does it arise from our very nature? Is it counter to our nature?

Now, the dramatists play this out at the level of fiction, but fiction that is often more real than reality itself. What we find in Medea is someone behaving "unnaturally." Mothers do not kill their sons, even when they are married to faithless husbands. She's doing the most "unnatural" of things, a mother killing her own offspring. Nonetheless, she is doing something that is intelligible, because she's driven by passion. Well, if driven by passion, then, is the act the "natural" sort of thing? When she says herself that "direst consequences ensue when reason is trumped by passion," is this a rational reflection on her part? Isn't that precisely the point where she could stop herself?

No. Precisely not. To be driven by passion is to have passion rule reason, if even as a kind of parallel development, you know better, as when a chorus reflects on the actions of a play's principal characters. You recognize that what you are doing is beyond reason. Nonetheless, you are beyond reason. And no private narrative to that effect stops the action from taking place.

Here, then, we find in Medea one of the famous women of the ancient Greek world—and note how many of the really commanding figures in that ancient Greek world are women: Aphrodite, Athena, Medea, Antigone, Andromeche as brave Hector's wife, the Theban women, Clytemnestra, Penelope—the list is long and revealing. It's very similar to what we will find in Shakespeare later on. That is to say, it's difficult to find a bona fide male hero in Shakespeare, certainly any hero of Homeric proportions. One might want to think about that a bit. The heroic figures tend to be women in Shakespeare—the self-sacrificing, committed, stolid characters. Not with Hamletian indecision does Lady Macbeth proceed with the business at hand.

There is also a greatness in Homeric women, and a greatness in the women of the ancient Greek dramatists. It's worth noting this because of the position women actually occupied in the ancient world, and particularly the ancient Athenian world, which was a position of reclusive subservience, but this, I think, should be understood more in cultural terms than what might be finally and validly psychological terms. It is more a recognition of the power of Eros, the ancient understanding that what it is that brings man and woman together is not just a creative force; it's not just something that brings life about and re-populates the world. It is a also a powerfully destructive force, because what we will do in the name of Eros, what we will do at the bidding of Eros, is what Medea does.

This recognition of the power of Eros has more to do with the relative standing, the actual relative standing, of women in the ancient Greek world, than some theory like Aristotle's, according to which women are incomplete men, closer to children than to male adulthood. That's philosophers' talk, but I don't think in that talk, Aristotle is recovering the thought of his age, and he is certainly not recovering the thought of Sophocles, Euripides, and Aeschylus.

Well, there is another woman that warrants attention, and that is Antigone, as presented to us by Sophocles. Antigone finds that her brother, Polyneices, has been killed. His body is left out in the open for the dogs and wolves to devour. King Creon of Corinth has ordered that no one shall touch this body, let alone bury it—Creon taking him to be a mere traitor. Creon, you know, is the chap whose daughter Jason takes up with, a fact that is not irrelevant.

Thus, there's Creon: "Don't touch the body." Antigone sits with her sister and says: "We've got to do something about this. That's Polyneices out there. He must be given a proper burial." Her fearful sister will have none of it. "Don't do it, Antigone!"

Utterly undissuaded, though, Antigone proceeds to do what she is compelled by conscience to do. Now brought before the king, she is queried harshly by Creon, sort of a "Don't you know who I am?" and "By what right do you disobey?"—that sort of interrogation. What his questions express is the ageless maxim according to which the will of the prince is the law of the land, in one sense of *nomos*. How, in this context, is the law, *nomos*, to be understood?

What Antigone replies, in so many words, is that that the law that requires that a sister bury the body of a dead brother is more ancient than kings. It's a universal precept. It's not just customary. Some might insist that Antigone's defense includes the recognition that such has always been the case, but that is not what the Greek says. What the Greek says is that what she is doing is *universal*, that she is impelled by something universal. Antigone is serving up, by way of Sophocles's play, a version of what today might be called *natural law* theory—that is, that there is something in us, something at an intuitive but a reachable level, that tells us the course of action that is right for beings like ourselves.

When, many centuries later, Thomas Aquinas will say: "If our nature were different, our duties would be different," he's recording the same insight that we find in Sophocles's Antigone. "It is in my very nature, do you see, that I must do this." She might just as well have said to him—and every ancient Greek watching this play would know she is saying as much—"If there would be kings, we must have the unreflecting capacity for the kind of allegiance that I am now showing toward my dead brother. That is, what impels me to do in his behalf what I am doing is exactly what you would have to rely on for there to be kings at all."

Now, I find the contrast, or the comparison, between Medea and Antigone quite interesting. Antigone is, of course, a woman of passion. There is no question about it. She loves deeply and reverentially. She is a woman of fear. She doesn't want to be locked up behind stone by this ruthless king. In the 11th hour, however, what she responds to is the summons of her nature, just as Medea, in the most forlorn of terms, is lamenting the fact that passion prevents her from matching up with the summons of her nature.

In the one case, we have Euripides giving us a form of madness, which is the madness that overtakes us when we surrender reason to passion, and in Antigone, Sophocles is giving us a woman who recognizes who she is. She has answered the command "Know thyself," and she understands herself to be constituted in such a way that what she does must be done. It must be done whatever kings might say.

Ideally, kings encourage us to do, and command us to do, what the best of our natures would have us do in any case, but when they don't, ultimate authority is retained by the light of conscience and not by holder of the scepter.

When Aristotle comes to define tragedy, he will say that tragedy is when bad things happen to good people. In his characteristically Aristotelian way, he would reject the notion that there is anything tragic about bad things befalling those who deserve it. It is entirely just when bad things happen to bad people, but there's something awful about bad things happening to good people.

Nonetheless, terrible things do happen to the good, the brave, the innocent. The question that has to arise in the ancient mind, as it arises in the contemporary mind, is this: If there is a providential and all-seeing God who loves us, how do we account for the presence of evil in the world? The ancient Greek dramatists wrestled with just this question, but with no acceptance of an all-good and all-loving God. For them, it was clear enough that one may honor the gods, perform sacrifices, be reverential, shun *hubris*—you can do all this and more, and nonetheless come to endure what is dreadful.

It falls to the philosophers, then, to pick up the baton and carry the race for insight and understanding a bit further down the track, toward the finish line still not visible. However, the promise is that, with sure steps and a disciplined mode of approach, progress will exceed anything gained by mere literature. Surely it was one of the presumptions of the philosophical mind that it was capable of going beyond what mere literature might produce.

Audiences of both great ancient theatre and great ancient philosophy will make that choice for themselves. Does philosophy get us further down the track than did Euripides? Perhaps.

Lecture Six

Herodotus and the Lamp of History

Scope:

Does history teach? Herodotus thought so, and this because of what he took to be certain universal human aspirations and deficiencies.

Herodotus, born in 484 B.C., is said to be the first historian in the accepted sense of the term. His treatise, *The Persian Wars*, is filled with details on character, armaments, battle strategies, and perhaps most significantly, attempted explanations of why events took the form they did.

As something of the "father" of historical scholarship, Herodotus would inevitably be found limited by succeeding generations of historians. There are patent impossibilities to be found in his major work; consider only the famous meeting between Solon and Croesus in chapters 30–32 of Book I. Given their respective chronologies, these two men could not have met; however, the point of their inclusion by Herodotus is not to relate a historical encounter but to tell something of a "moral tale." Such defects are not uncommon in Herodotus and have been subjected to deserved and predictable criticism by those who are now ranked as "professional" historians. Herodotus invented the subject, not the profession!

Outline

I. Herodotus is usually accepted as the first historian in the modern sense of the term. This is not because he was the first to chronicle major events or to establish dates for occurrences of interest to his contemporaries. The writing of history is not the occupation of the mere chronicler.

    A. Herodotus writes *The Persian Wars* to record the causes of the events and to ensure that brave deeds not be forgotten.

        1. In this way, he recorded the ancient Greek sense of the past as prologue but, as we shall see, in a form less indebted to myth and religious notions of retribution.

2. But he is also wrestling with the *problem of knowledge*. What could be a more burning question, at least at the level of daily life, than to determine the causes of war?

B. Men make war not out of hate and aggression but out of devotion to irreconcilable values, expressed in cultural symbols—themselves a form of discourse. Herodotus thus devotes many pages to customs, religious beliefs, the form of dress, weapons, and so on. He understands that an informing account of a world war calls for more by way of explanation than can be found in mythology.

    1. Herodotus teaches that, to account for events of historic proportions, one must go well beyond the mere chronicling of the events. One must undertake a veritable "sociology" of those events and a "psychology" of the participants.

    2. We see Homer's influence here, which suffuses nearly every aspect of the ancient Greek world and its achievements.

C. Herodotus also recognized that history teaches and inclines people toward actions, but how does history teach?

    1. The answer must be found at a level Herodotus takes to be more fundamental than ethnicity and culture: the level of our common humanity.

    2. The lamp of history illuminates the very commonalities that constitute human nature itself. History teaches that wherever you find human beings, certain lessons are worth learning.

    3. There is a root humanity that is reached by certain events and that allows us to predict how we are likely to behave under certain conditions and how those conditions, therefore, should either be promoted or shunned.

D. Does the account teach us of the gods? In Herodotus, the religious and mythic elements are relegated to secondary importance. Rather, events are to be understood in terms of actual patterns of motivation, in terms of local conditions and contextual factors.

1. The Persian wars were caused by *us*. Religious *beliefs*, not divine will, were a factor. As he says in chapter 64 of Book II, when speaking of Egyptian religion, Herodotus will not attempt an explanation for, to do so, "I should be led to speak of religious matters, which I particularly shrink from mentioning."

2. This perspective *humanizes* human history. It helps us address the command "Know thyself." To know thyself is, among other things, to know what we've done. The problems of knowledge and of conduct and of governance may not be solved by historical study, but they can be thus illuminated.

II. If Herodotus's history of the Persian war succeeds as a descriptive psychology of human nature under conditions of stress and strain, it is less successful as an accurate historical account of events.

A. Herodotus has been accused by later ages of having written bad history, telling of encounters between people who could not have met. Yet throughout the work, Herodotus pauses to alert readers to interpretations that are based chiefly on the opinions of the author or to records of events that he did not witness.

B. His account includes parables, morality tales that communicate the lessons of history: What happens if we are cowardly? What do we stand to gain if we are brave and decent? In this way, Herodotus addresses the *problem of conduct*.

1. The dialogue of Croesus and Solon—the man famous for wealth and the man famous for knowledge—is not intended to be historical; it is a disquisition on the nature of happiness.

2. Croesus asks Solon who the happiest man in the world is, obviously expecting the reply to be that it is Croesus himself. Instead, Solon tells the story of Cleobis and Biton, asserting that they are the happiest men in the world because they died in a state of being that all would honor and aspire to emulate.

3. Happiness is not fame or riches or heroic virtue, but a state that will inspire posterity to think, in reflecting upon another's life, that it was the life one would wish to live. We can say of no man that he is *eudaimonios*, that his was a truly flourishing life, until his days are over.

III. These two elements that Herodotus addresses—the problem of knowledge and the problem of conduct—raise the issue of the problem of governance.

A. We know that the ancient Athenian democracy had to save itself from what would have been the tyrannical rule of the Persians. It turns out, however, that the Athenian democracy was not saved by the Athenians but the Spartans.

B. In illuminating this fact, Herodotus passes to Plato and Aristotle a historical perspective on a paradoxical question of governance: In the attempt to cultivate virtue, must one be battle-hardened?

C. Plato, like Herodotus, would recognize that in the spectacle of war, the truths of our mortality can be learned as in no other way, but this conclusion is worrisome. Are strife and conflict necessary if character is to be formed? Perhaps as an answer, Herodotus gives us the story of Cleobis and Biton, suggesting that there are alternatives to warfare in the cultivation of virtue.

Recommended Reading:

Collingwood, R. G. *The Idea of History*. Oxford University Press, 1994.

Herodotus. *The Persian Wars*. G. Rawlinson, trans. Random House, 1942.

Questions to Consider:

1. Explain whether the past is prologue.

2. Summarize whether the writing of history presupposes what is now widely doubted—namely, that events taking place at one

time under unique conditions can help explain yet other events, widely separated in time and context.

Lecture Six—Transcript

Herodotus and the Lamp of History

Herodotus is usually accepted as the first historian in the modern sense, or the nearly modern sense, of the term. This is not because he was the first one to chronicle major events or to establish dates for occurrences of interest to his contemporaries. Herodotus's treatise, *The Persian Wars*, is a genuinely historical treatise. It is the first item, the first entry, in this genre, and, in many respects, it is paradigmatic for the historical scholarship that would follow over the course of centuries.

Now, one might ask oneself why someone would undertake a project of that kind, particularly since precedents for it were not ample. And you might say that "Well, don't chroniclers do these things?" After all, fans of the New York Yankees want to pick up the newspaper every day to see whether and how they won or lost. It's quite understood that few other than Yankee fans will care much about this kind of thing, nor will anyone two or three weeks later, but this is what the news is all about.

However, Herodotus's history of the Persian wars is not a species of news reporting, newsgathering. This is a genuinely historical work, and I again want to refer to the metaphor of Ariadne's golden cord. This is an historical work in much the sense that Theseus getting out of the labyrinth is retracing steps in order to extricate himself from a bind. Herodotus tells us in the first sentence of this work the account is given "so that the deeds of these brave men not be forgotten." He wants people to know what we can rise to do, how we can rise to truly heroic levels of behavior, and he also wants us to recognize the multiplicity of factors that participate in any genuinely historical event, the number of vantage points one would have to occupy in order to understand any complex social phenomenon.

In today's lecture, I will touch upon just those features in Herodotus that turn out to be very important and, in their own way, deeply philosophical—not extra-philosophical, but philosophical in their own right. The connections are subtle but pervasive.

In his *Persian Wars*, Herodotus is wrestling with what I have referred to as the *problem of knowledge*, and what could be a more burning question, at least at the level of daily life, than the causes of war? Think of it. War and mayhem, the death and destruction that it produces, the deep suffering, the rift between and among peoples, the collapse of trade, the creation of suspicions that might take generations to subside, the redrawing of boundaries, political boundaries, alterations in the economy, the sudden increase in a class of slaves now won victoriously by the winning side. How to understand the causes of something like this?

The problem of knowledge presents itself most vividly when we ask the question "Why are we like this?" Now, Freud, of course, would tie this in with certain instinctual, aggressive tendencies that are outgrowths of our evolutionary animalistic heritage, that sort of thing—that we are the way we are because at the instinctual level we are driven by blind, self-protective, self-gratifying impulses.

Herodotus—I think I can say, if I may say—knows better than this. When you actually look at men at war, they don't hate each other. The sources of action—the drives, impulses, and motives—are not at the level of uncontrollable hatreds. It is not aggression that moves armies—it is devotion. Moreover, what brings about such conflicts— at the most fundamental level—are irreconcilable values, perceptions of a radically different nature. What brings these things about actually is a form of discourse. Sometimes we call it propaganda—but whatever it is, legions are moved by words and symbols, and in a way that I think Freud, with all due respect, missed.

Herodotus recognizes this, and this is why he spends so much time on who the participants are in this world, in this world war, for it is a kind of world war in a smaller world than our own. The Persian wars feature not just Greek-speaking people and people from Persia— rather, every clan and sect and petty province will be dragged into the conflict, each moved by its own particular understanding, its own enlarged set of grievances.

These are the reasons for Herodotus telling us so much about their dress, about the particular weapons that they use, how they decorate them, what they say as a battle cry, what they eat and how they dine, what their economies are, their trade relations. He understands that an informing account of nothing less than a world war calls for much more by way of explanatory resources than one will find in mythology or the contrivances of fate.

More than "The devil made me do it," or, "Instinctually I'm like that," people do not go to war because of their evolutionary history. They go to war for stateable, discoverable reasons bound up with politics and culture, civilization, and religious and moral values. Herodotus teaches that to account for events of historic proportions, one must go well beyond the mere chronicling of the events. One must undertake a veritable "sociology" of these events and a "psychology" and "social psychology" of the participants.

If the echo of Homer is audible here, it is no accident, for Homer's influence suffuses nearly every aspect of the ancient Greek world and its achievements.

There is something else involved in historical scholarship, and I think we can say that Herodotus certainly recognized it. Why is it you would want posterity not to forget brave deeds, the brave deeds of these men? Why, unless such a history teaches and inclines?

How can history teach, though? Consider the implications contained in the question. We will choose Herodotus as historian, and proceed to the vexing question as to how or what or whom history teaches: We've already got the historian, a writer by the name of Herodotus, who if nothing else, recognizes the great variety of factors that incline whole peoples toward warfare. He establishes that these factors are deeply imbedded in culture, and that cultural differences create yet other differences. Then, too, there are these problematic language differences.

Thus, totally aware of all of this, how can he believe that his treatise can teach? Teach whom? Can it teach Persians the way it teaches Hellenes? Can it teach Assyrians the way it teaches Egyptians? Can it teach Phoenicians the way it might teach Spartans, or those from Megara or Argos? Now, the answer must be found at a level Herodotus takes to be more fundamental than ethnicity and culture. Indeed, it is at the level of our common humanity.

The lamp of history is what illuminates beyond the reader's desk, the reader's village, the oceans that surround the reader's nation. When properly constructed, the lamp of history—the study of history—illuminates the very commonalities that constitute human nature itself. What is taught is this: Wherever you find human beings, these lessons are lessons worth learning, and no matter how different the language, or the culture, or the customs, or the diet, there is a root humanity that is reached by such events and that will allow us to predict how we are likely to behave under certain conditions and how those conditions, therefore, should either be promoted or shunned, depending upon whether our behavior is to be laudable or reprehensible.

Well, again, the Homeric voice is audible, but it speaks to us of Zeus, and Apollo, and Artemis, and Hephaestus. Homer tells us that they are behind momentous historical events. Now, contrast this with chapter 64 of Book II, where Herodotus, writing about Egyptian religious prohibitions and rituals, declares that he simply will not even attempt an explanation when it comes to this sort of thing. On matters of this sort, Herodotus is like Protagoras: "The subject is too complex, and life is too short."

What do we hear Herodotus say? He says: "I'm not going to do this at all. To do so, I should be led to speak of religious matters, which I particularly shrink from mentioning." Now, of course, this is the sort of sentence that could be subjected to a variety of interpretations. I think this is not just a version of Protagoras recording the evanescent nature of life and the inscrutability of things divine. Rather, I think this is Herodotus saying: "The Persian wars were caused by *us*, and I can offer an account of this without dilating on questions of religious belief in Egypt, etc. Oh, these beliefs are going to count for something as regards the causes of the war and the outcome of the war, but they are not going to account for it because the actual gods referred to in that religion are doing it; it's because the *beliefs* are doing it."

There is something utterly *humanizing* and humanistic about this, for it is a philosophical perspective on human nature. It's a philosophical perspective presented in the form of a history, and history, of course, is not only one of the humanities and a form of humanistic study, it is a humanizing study, because, in fact, it is an account of what we do, and, therefore, it helps answer the question "Who am I?" It helps us address the command "Know thyself." To know thyself is, among other things, to know what we've done. Now I say, what "we've" done. We as Persians? We as Egyptians, or as Assyrians, or as Athenians? No. We as human beings; what we have done. What we believe. What moves us. How we move each other.

If Herodotus's history of the Persian War succeeds as a descriptive psychology of human nature under conditions of stress and strain—a misguided, self-deceiving, ambitious human nature—it is less successful as an accurate historical account of events. Scholars the world over still publish papers establishing their own celebrity by showing how Herodotus, obviously, got one thing or another wrong; he was wrong about numbers of ships and casualties, wrong in his staging of certain encounters between people who couldn't possibly have met, etc.

Much of the criticism is well earned by the text itself, though I don't think all of it is. Recall that Herodotus never tires of pointing out where in his treatise he is expressing what are merely his own opinions. Furthermore, at many places in the text, he points out that what he is about to relate are the opinions he has heard from others. As he was not an eyewitness and cannot actually corroborate this or that bit, he notes instead that it has been reported and is worth passing on anyway.

This is not defective historical scholarship; rather, it is an example of the scholar's burdens and how they are permissibly borne. In so many words, Herodotus is saying: "Look, you're never wrong providing all the data. There will always be the problem of sifting, and judging, and analyzing, and establishing the validity of claims, but let's not start out with the assumption that we should deny readers access to information that is clearly affecting the historian's own thinking. No, here's the record. Let me give it to you straight out, entirely."

Well, of course, once you do that you are going to fill pages with gossip and innuendo, guesses and hunches, out-and-out propaganda. There is plenty of that in Herodotus's *Persian Wars*. Perhaps in considering one such instance, we might comprehend more fully what is at the bottom of some of the "tricks" that Herodotus includes in his otherwise worthy history.

An encounter that always amuses scholars of the period finds Solon having a colloquy with Croesus of the "rich as Croesus" fame. Croesus is all puffed up with his own wealth and power, and he is looking forward to meeting Solon. He knows Solon is the wisest of men. Of course, given the dates, the two could not possibly have met.

In any case, we learn that Croesus is looking forward to meeting Solon, so that Solon, among other things, can put the wise man's seal of approval on Croesus's own greatness.

The encounter finds Croesus welcoming Solon. It might have been something like this: "Very, very happy to meet you. You're a wise man, etc., etc.," and the conversation doesn't go very far before Croesus asks—he's asking Solon this question: "By the way, who would you say is the happiest of men?"

Now, you know the answer he's expecting. "Who would you describe as the most fortunate of all human beings of your acquaintance? Nothing personal here, mind you; just sort of tell me here in this royal setting, in which you will find me with a smile on my face, this temple of opulence,"—perhaps a temple of vulgarity—"filled with healthy children, and loyal and obedient subjects. Well, who would you say is the most fortunate of people? Who would you say is the happiest of men?"

Solon mentions first somebody that no one has ever heard of, and Croesus wants to know who that is. "Well, oh, he's just someone greatly admired by his people."

"Oh, well, all right. Well, who would you say is the second most fortunate man you've ever known?" You see where this is going, of course. You should say this is the "top 10" list now, and Croesus wants to be on it, so we've got Croesus waiting to finish high in the league tables.

Solon then says: "Happiest of men; well, Cleobis and Biton, perhaps, would be the happiest of men."

"Who?"

"Yes, Cleobis and Biton."

Who are they that they should show up on this very short list?

Well, Cleobis and Biton, we learn then, were the finest young men, loyal and faithful sons, paragons of virtue, decent in every respect, beautiful in all relevant ways, and their mother, a temple priestess and good woman, so fearful of being late in showing up at the Temple of Hera for devotional exercises, found her sons, Cleobis and Biton, yoking themselves to a chariot because the servants had not yoked the oxen. They thus carry their mother swiftly some three miles in the heat of day so that she is not late for her appointed rounds. Let's get the picture, here.

Now, as they come into town, people are in awe of these wonderful sons. Cleobis and Biton themselves are absolutely exhausted, as you might imagine. They offer their prayers in the temple, and then, in this total exhaustion, just lay down to sleep under a shade tree. Their thankful mother is inside the temple; she is supplicating Hera, thanking the gods for the sons that she was given, and she prays that they die the happiest of men—and Cleobis and Biton never awaken.

They did die the happiest of men because the happiest of men, the happiest of us all, are those who die in a state of being that we would honor and aspire to emulate. So, say of no man that he is *eudaimonios*, this happiest sort of person. Say of no man that he is truly flourishing in his life until his days are over.

The answer to the question: "What was your life like?" is to be rendered in that tense. "I can't tell you, Croesus, where you stand in the league tables right now, because right now is right now, and the future is mute. Let us see what you do with the balance of your life, and, more importantly, let us see how you are remembered. The Latin for memory is very good here, *monumentum*. Let's see what your monument is," you see.

Now, Herodotus is constructing a monument, a *monumentum*. He is constructing a memory of events participated in by the great and the small, by the hero and the villain, all operating under different and strained conditions, and in doing this, he sketches out the kind of life worth living. This is the record of history, in its own right a kind of ethics, addressing what I've called the *problem of conduct*. Not just an ethics, not just what people do, but positive teaching about the wages of cowardice, about what we can earn through heroism, what we can earn through commitment and devotion and decency.

Here is Herodotus pausing to give us this little vignette on Cleobis and Biton. Would we ever have heard of these chaps had it not been for these few sentences and an encounter between two people who historically could not possibly have met each other?

Why does Herodotus put this in? I would say with all due respect to contemporary scholars who say: "Ha, ha, Herodotus, historian? Well, how about that impossible Croesus-Solon meeting?" I offer just this: Herodotus was born in 484 B.C. As he is writing this for contemporaries who very well know that Croesus and Solon were not having conversations with each other, the vignette is not inserted by an historian who thinks he can gull his contemporaries or those coming later.

No, Herodotus is conveniently including a little morality tale within his elaborate history. He has already told us what is merely his opinion, and the opinions others have, to underscore the difference between an opinion and a fact. The vignette is inserted as a comment on our aspirations, because after all, the cause of war, the *causus belli*, is a complex of conflicting aspirations. Someone is trying to achieve something. Some group or people are trying to achieve something and are prepared to risk life and limb to do it, and to have others die for it.

Well, now let's rehearse the discussion, the conversation, between Solon and Croesus. What is worth dying for? What should the aspiration be?

Here is Croesus. Just about anything you can imagine an upper-middle-class or petty aristocrat seeking, Croesus has in abundance. Why, he is "rich as Croesus." Solon is nearly a Jungian archetype of the wise man, as in "the wisdom of Solon," so Solon is inserted emblematically to provide a précis on the nature of happiness, and Croesus is inserted for the same reason. Croesus's very life is, on some account, a précis on the nature of happiness. Who would not want to be "rich as Croesus"?

Perhaps in our own time, one might think of, perhaps, Princess Diana—a lovely woman, married to a future king, descendants from an ancestral family, raised on a great estate, loved by all. Do we say of this now-dead princess that she lived the happiest of lives? Not a bit of it. Imagine that young woman meeting Solon and, in a lapse of some kind—I don't think that this would have been at all characteristic of Princess Diana as a young woman—but saying, let's say after the second child was born, and the palace is set up, and so forth, saying to Solon: "Whom would you regard as the most fortunate of women?"

Of course, the answer would be—well, I don't know the person Solon might have picked out, but he certainly could not have picked Diana. Rather, he might have said something like: "Princess, you are 30 years old. I don't know. I can't even count you in the process until your days are over." All estimations of *eudaimonia* are, finally, retrospective. We look back on the life that was lived, and then come to some estimation of whether it was a flourishing life.

It's what others are going to finally come to regard as the life you've lived—what it has amounted to in the eyes of others who are in the position to make the judgment. You're living that life as best as you can, and it is posterity that will pass judgment on whether or not, all things considered, it was the life others of us wished we could live.

It's not something the actor himself is ever going to know, because the actor himself has not been told by Clotho just how much time he still has. In the encounter between Croesus and Solon, we are given an ethics, a kind of emblem book, as to what it is we should aspire to, and what it is that may cost us much of our very humanity.

What we should aspire to is what Cleobis and Biton have already attained, which is the admiration of good people, and an admiration based on virtuous conduct. Not celebrity *per se*, not really heroism per se. After all, what we want to say about Cleobis and Biton is not that in taking their mother to Hera's temple, they behaved heroically. There isn't anything Homeric about this; there is something fundamentally decent about it, and, more to the point, it tells us something about the kind of men they were, and what Herodotus's history presents are these very sharply defined characters.

We think we know Croesus when we hear him asking these questions. We're sure we are in the company of Solon when we hear the answers. We can almost picture those two boys pulling that wearying weight to get their mother to the temple on time. There is something very neighborly about this account, even as it is spread out on the canvas of a world war.

Now, I dilate on this approach to the problem of knowledge and the problem of conduct to raise a point or two about the problem of governance. We hear much about the ancient Athenian democracy, and we know that the ancient Athenian democracy had to save itself from what would have been the tyrannical rule of the Persians, but it turns out that the ancient Athenian democracy was not saved by the Athenians themselves. If it's saved by any part of the Greek-speaking world, more than by the rest, it is saved by Sparta—by Leonidas and the Battle of Thermopylae.

In Plato's *Republic*, we're going to see this again. We are going to see this reflection on whether, at the end of the day, it is an infantry trained for hand-to-hand combat that finally carries with it the core of precepts on which governments finally depend, or whether it is an Athenian navy striking an enemy at a distance, being remote not only from the scene of battle, but from the battle's most imminent threats. We are also going to discover that Plato, like Herodotus, and in an interesting way like Aristotle himself, sees in the conflagration, and the immediacy of one's own mortality, something so richly character-forming as, perhaps, to have no substitute.

Well, this is an awesome account and, indeed, something of a worrisome conclusion. After all, suppose it is the case that in the attempt to cultivate virtue, and to cultivate virtue in such a way as to have a flourishing life, one must be battle-hardened, that it takes nothing less than a world war of hand-to-hand combat in order to refine sensibilities, and focus attention, and draw us inward to those resources that we have—which, when they become habitual, are just the habits of virtue itself.

Is Herodotus now, before Aristotle, telling us what it takes to make life worth living? Is he providing an account not only of the many, and often frivolous, causes of war, but, in fact, something of the necessity of war, or at least, the necessity of strife and conflict, if character is to be formed at all?

I don't think this is the message of Herodotus, because of all of the characters that Herodotus might have pointed to when asked that question by Croesus, he pointed to two young men whose claim to fame was that they did the sorts of things good sons do, under the burden of their own consciences, with a love for their mother and a respect for what it was she was setting out to do.

They were good and great neighbors, members of a good family, understanding what their duty was, and prepared to expend such energy as was required to do their duty, and if all this is possible in the absence of war, and it can make them the happiest of men, then perhaps, indeed, there are alternatives to warfare and hand-to-hand combat in the cultivation of virtue.

I believe Herodotus thought so, and for what it's worth, I think so, too.

Lecture Seven

Socrates on the Examined Life

Scope:

Socrates (c. 469–399) is perhaps the most admired figure in the history of philosophy. Even when dismissing so many of the "pagan" thinkers, Saint Augustine would venerate Socrates, regarding him as a true philosopher because he was willing to die for what he believed.

What is known of his life comes by way of a good friend, Xenophon, and a loyal and loving student, Plato. The former provides a picture of Socrates as neighbor and fellow-citizen; the latter, a Socrates at sea on the endless voyages of mind and spirit.

Before Socrates, the major schools of philosophy emphasized cosmological and physical topics or, thanks chiefly to the Sophists, rhetorical techniques designed to highlight the ignorance of one's adversaries. In Socrates, however, at least as he is revealed in Plato's dialogues, there is a commitment to *objectify* the self and hold it up to scrutiny. As there is nature, so, too, there is a *human nature*, and it is a fit subject for discourse and dispute. But what vexations arise when the subject is the object is the subject! "The unexamined life is not worth living," but what form shall the examination take?

Outline

I. It was Socrates more than any predecessor, though there were ample pre-Socratic precedents, who worked to perfect the dialectical method of inquiry, the vaunted "Socratic" method that tests every assumption for its grounding and its implications.

    A. Socrates described himself as a gadfly—approaching those who were sure of what they knew and interrogating them until their certainty was shown to be groundless.

        1. In ancient Greek mythology, a gadfly knocked a chap off his horse, who had been trying to fly up to heaven and engage hubristically in arrogating to himself the powers of the divine.

2. Socrates is a gadfly, then, in the sense of unseating the confident rider who believes he is on the flight path to truth.

3. Socrates was well trained in the art of rhetoric and the great Sophist teachings of his time, but he goes beyond Sophism. His objective was not just to expose the ignorance of an interlocutor but to find the truth and, ultimately, defeat skepticism itself.

B. The first obligation of a philosopher, Augustine suggests, is the willingness to die for the principles of his philosophy. If this standard were generally applied, few philosophers would measure up—but Socrates did.

1. His friends urged him to flee after his trial rather than die—the trial had been a sham; no one would think less of him. Socrates preferred to die rather than abandon all that he had taught about the law as the corporate expression of rationality.

2. The charges against Socrates were that he had failed to respect the gods of Athens and had corrupted Athenian youth. The Socrates given to us by Xenophon, however, was a deeply religious and reverential man, not at all skeptical on the spiritual level, although perhaps less than obeisant to the customary devotional beliefs and practices of his contemporary Athenians.

3. That Socrates corrupted the youth of Athens also seems unlikely. In the *Symposium*, the one dialogue in which we might expect to find debauchery and corruption, Alcibiades complains that in attempting to be Socrates's lover, one gets nowhere. Socrates simply will not participate at that rich, lusty, corporeal level; indeed, given his wisdom and the depth of his thought, Socrates must have been among the loneliest people who ever lived.

4. Why did Socrates choose suicide? Because he recognized that the rule of law is the corporate or public expression of human rationality itself. Law is the means by which the rational power of corruptible man might

minimize corruption. Having devoted his life to rationality, Socrates would not abandon everything he had stood for and taught merely because his own situation was compromised.

II. "The unexamined life is not worth living": Why? And if this is true, how are we to examine our lives?

    A. What is the matter with a life of perfect satisfaction and gratification that is based on an illusion—provided by drugs or machines?

        1. Socrates did not live in our technical world of microsurgery and pharmacology; thus, in Plato's *Republic*, he considers prisoners in the depths of a cave who have objects and events projected on some parapet in front of them. They think they are experiencing reality, but this reality is no more than mere shadows and illusion.

        2. What Socrates makes clear is that behind every experience, there is room for an interpretation of the meaning of that experience. It's in the interpretation, the examination of what life amounts to, that in fact, life becomes worth living. For Socrates, it's not the sequence of passive experiences but the integration of those experiences into some intelligible whole that constitutes a form of life, and one subject to refinement through self-critical reflection.

    B. This returns us to the Delphic pronouncement: "Know thyself." But how we can do this?

        1. We must know what it means to be a certain kind of being, in this case, what it means to be a human being. The answer must reach toward something other than mere biology, which may be a way to understand a particular species but certainly can't answer the question: "What kind of person am I essentially?"

        2. Socrates's life as a teacher was devoted to the question: "What kinds of beings are we?" Only after reaching a defensible position on that question might we proceed to "How should we live our lives? What is the right form of government? What's the relationship between the individual and the *polis?*"

C. To know thyself presupposes the capacity to know anything. You may know many things and not "know thyself" in the Socratic sense. But to know thyself is, minimally, *to know.* Thus, Socrates begins with that core problem of knowledge: How do we know anything?

    1. If the skeptics are right in that we can't know anything for certain, then we certainly cannot know ourselves in any settled and certain way, and that means that one's life is uselessly examined. What would the examined life be? Simply a constellation of prejudices and self-deceptions.

    2. What must be defeated here is skepticism. We must come up with at least one kernel of truth that we can settle on as true and that will answer the root epistemological question: Is it possible to know anything? If we can settle on one thing that is true, then we can know that it is possible to know, and if we know the method by which we arrived at that truth, then perhaps we can use it to know other things.

D. We begin to see that the Socratic agenda is a fairly broad one. First, one must do philosophical battle with skepticism and cynicism. One must also contend with the problem of conduct. What kind of life is right for beings such as ourselves? Should we aim solely at happiness and pleasure? What of our values? Are they simply reflections of our own prejudices, giving us no right or reason to impose them on others or expect them to be shared?

E. Finally, what of the problem of governance and the vaunted "democracy" of the Athenian state?

    1. The Athenians treasured the democratic character of the *polis,* and a philosopher could well expect trouble when challenging its core precepts. Socrates raised grave questions about such precepts, while others, including Aristotle, defended them.

2. Nonetheless, Socrates reserves to himself the right at least to raise the question: How should we be governed? This question cannot be answered in the abstract. We can't answer the question of how we should be governed unless we have already established the right kind of life to live. And we can't answer that question until we've settled the question of what kind of beings we are and how we can come to know as much.

3. Until we have successfully defeated a skeptical position on knowledge as such, we can't have a defensible position on ethics. And until we've handled the ethical dimensions of life, we can't pinpoint what the political organization of the *polis* should be.

4. It is a credit to the lasting genius of Socrates that he understands the interconnectedness of these questions, that the problem of knowledge, the problem of conduct, and the problem of governance are various phases of the same problem: how we come to know ourselves and realize our humanity in the course of a lifetime. This, of course, will be the central agenda of the program of philosophy for centuries to come.

Recommended Reading:

Robinson, D. N. *An Intellectual History of Psychology*, 3rd ed. University of Wisconsin Press, 1995, chapter 2.

Xenophon. *Memorabilia*. Cornell University Press, 1994.

Questions to Consider:

1. Socrates assembles his friends in the years following the defeat of Athens at the hands of Sparta. Explain whether Socrates's philosophy is the thought of the "losing side."

2. If Socrates was undermining the values and received wisdom of his *polis*, conclude whether he was justly prosecuted.

Lecture Seven—Transcript
Socrates on the Examined Life

Who was Socrates? What is the famous "Socratic" method? What's so special about Socrates anyway, since we don't have so much as a sentence ever written by him, and there were a number of important philosophers who came before him? Everything we know about Socrates comes from two contemporary sources: his faithful student, Plato, and his friend and neighbor, Xenophon, who in the *Memorabilia* gives us the neighbor's and fellow soldier's view of Socrates, the man.

If we are to believe Plato—and in this I think we have no right to believe Plato—in one of Plato's *Epistles*, he says, that in the matter of the developed philosophical presented in the dialogues, all credit goes to Socrates, Plato doing little more than serving as a kind of recording secretary. Of course, this can't possibly be the case. Plato, obviously, was doing more than sitting as an amanuensis and recording what he heard.

Surely, though, what is the case is that Socrates profoundly influenced the people who were most closely associated with him, and more to the point, some he profoundly influenced turned out to be among the most estimable of figures in the ancient Greek world and, of course, chiefly, Plato himself. "Plato," by the way, is not the family name. Plato is a fellow with quite broad shoulders and so the nickname, Platon.

Now, Socrates's dates are 469–399 B.C., and perhaps the first social and historical fact warranting attention is that he begins his career, as it were, in an Athens that had lost a devastating and long war against Sparta. What one must understand as one goes through the dialogues of Plato is that these "Socratic dialogues" are conducted by the losing side. It is vitally important to keep that in mind. It certainly helps explain why so much in the political part of the Socratic program looks very much like the Spartan regimen for raising children and training armies, etc.

In one or another dialogue, we might be inclined to hear Socrates saying, in so many words—and this is not uncommon when we look at the postwar literature of a losing side: "Look, the winning side excelled in certain respects in which we Athenians found ourselves unable to measure up. Where is it we went wrong? Where is it we went wrong in our childrearing, in our military strategy, in our economics, in our social life?"

These are burning questions in a postwar period, of course, so there are utterly practical questions that animate the dialogues. We tend to think of the dialogues of Plato as the sort of ethereal, otherworldly kind of colloquy engaged in by people who don't quite have their feet on the ground. Quite the contrary.

Obviously, the man who comes to teach that the whole point of philosophy is to prepare us to die is not a person with an overweening interest in the merely practical affairs of daily life, but he's not indifferent to these, so I say, one point I want to make about Socrates is that he is a loyal and faithful soldier, a defender of Athens, who has seen his *polis* defeated by Sparta, and this clearly summons him to a deeper reflection on what Athenian life has been all about, where things went wrong, how it can be prevented in the future.

What shall we conclude from the fact that he didn't write things down, or establish a school, and that what we know about his philosophy comes through the words and recollections of others? He seems to be a figure shrouded in mystery, unless we are willing to take at face value things said about him by Xenophon, and the portrayal that's given to us in the dialogues.

Socrates described himself as a gadfly. He thought that his unique mission in life was to approach those most confident in their knowledge, and ask them probing questions. Not intended to be embarrassing, the questions, nonetheless, do require us to examine the grounds on which we adopt our beliefs and positions. Through such relentless questioning, we come to see that what we thought were legitimate grounds are either confused, or patently false, or contradictory—based on self-deception, or an entirely misapprehending vocabulary, a failure at the level of words, a failure at the level of definitions, a failure to appreciate even the importance of definition as we begin to defend one or another thesis. This is somebody who is going to irritate, then, the way gadflies can irritate.

Now—a word about gadflies. Recall that gadflies are very pesky creatures. In ancient Greek mythology, one of them actually knocked a chap off his horse, who had been trying to fly all the way up to heaven and engage hubristically in arrogating to himself the powers of the divine. It was a gadfly that Zeus sent to sting winged Pegasus, and thus unhorse Bellerophon. There lay Bellerophon, back on earth, even as Pegasus continued the ascent to Olympus.

Now, in casting himself as a gadfly, Socrates is claiming more than the rank of a busybody in the Agora. He is a gadfly in just that sense, of unseating the confident rider who believes he's on a flight path to truth. Do you see? "This horse takes me to heaven because I deserve to be there." Along comes a gadfly. The next thing you know, you're looking up at the stars.

In Socrates, we see the often whimsical and deft conversationalist, who really can catch you up short if you are not wary. Socrates was well trained in this art because he was well trained by the great Sophist teachings of his time, so he knows a sophistical argument when he hears one—and he can put one together himself, if the case requires it.

Was Socrates, then, just another Sophist, able in the art of rhetoric and the right sort of teacher for litigious Athenians? The Sophists, after all, were famous for developing arguments that would equip their students to score victories in debate, their adversaries caught up in logical contradictions and conceptual confusion.

We must be careful here. The philosophy of the Sophists is rich and variegated, not to be reduced to a sentence or two, so I don't want to libel or trivialize so-called "sophistical teaching." That teaching includes among its ranks Protagoras himself, but there is, I think, a defensible sense in which one of the central aims of, shall we say, "sophistical teaching," is a rhetorical aim. It has, as its goal, an argumentative form likely to be successful—not in quite the trite way that, later, schools of rhetoric might come to practice, but, to some extent, the aim of the Sophist is to expose the ignorance of his interlocutor. Socrates is going beyond that. It's not just to expose the ignorance of an interlocutor; it is to find the truth and, finally, defeat skepticism itself—so we would not want to say that Socrates, in his sophistical art and practice, is himself a Sophist.

Erasmus, who I think probably comes as close to being a thoroughly civilized human being as anyone would have the right to claim, used to refer to his "Saint Socrates." Augustine—who knew much about ancient Greek philosophy, and was quite wary about the teaching and philosophizing of those "pagans"—well, St. Augustine was fully prepared to reserve, almost exclusively to Socrates, the title "philosopher," and why was that? Because in Socrates, he found someone who was prepared to die for what he believed. Augustine here is establishing a very demanding standard, a mortal standard: The first obligation of a philosopher is a commitment to live according to the terms of his own philosophy.

Were we able or willing to impose that standard on all the major figures in the history of philosophy, I think we'd find any number of them leaving the field pretty quickly. I think most of the skeptics, for example, would be out of town before sundown. It is said that one of the great "fathers" of skeptical thought was Pyrrho of Elea, so-called "Pyrrhonism" being an early form of radical skepticism, and it is said that Pyrrho's friends used to accompany him everywhere, because, in his skepticism, he denied the reality of the heat of fire, or that one would actually drown in water, and so forth—so, it is said that in their solicitude, Pyrrho's chums would keep him out of self-destructive modes of behavior. Nonetheless, the story does come down to us that, on one occasion, he is found chasing his cook down the streets of Athens with a frying pan in his hand for having served his friends a bad meal—so, even the great Pyrrhonist skeptic, Pyrrho himself, drew a line under skepticism, below which he would not go, his line, apparently, having much to do with the ancient cuisine.

Now, Socrates was prepared to live, and I should say, more importantly, maybe—for him, surely more importantly—to die for what it was that his philosophical inquiries presented as true. I won't dilate on the well-known tale of Socrates's trial and self-execution— just to say these few things. The trial was, to some extent, trumped up. The charges were that Socrates had failed to respect the gods of Athens and had corrupted Athenian youth.

Socrates, the one given to us by Xenophon, turns out to be a deeply religious and reverential man. There's nothing in the record to suggest that he was at all skeptical at the level we would be inclined to call the "religious" or "spiritual." That he was less than obeisant to the customary devotional beliefs and practices of his contemporary Athenians, there is no doubt, but this is just to say that he regarded some of these customs as nothing but the habit of sloth, immunized against critical thought and its challenges.

Now, that he corrupted the youth of Athens, I think, is a rather different charge. The youth of Athens had any number of ways of corrupting themselves. In the one dialogue in which you might find debauchery and the corruption of the young taking place—I refer, of course, to the *Symposium*—it's Alcibiades who's complaining that in attempting to be Socrates's lover, one gets nowhere. The fellow simply will not participate at that rich, lusty, corporeal level. This is a plaintive Alcibiades explaining to everybody what one has to go through with this fellow, Socrates.

It's also quite interesting the way the *Symposium* ends. I've always found this to be one of the most poignant features in all of Plato's dialogues, the very end of the *Symposium*. This is an all-night drinking party, animated by discussions of the nature of love and kindred subjects. It is Socrates who leaves early in the morning and, as Plato tells us, "returns home alone." It's an extraordinarily vivid picture of how the man was perceived. This social gadfly, this skillful conversationalist, given his very wisdom and the depth of his thought, Socrates must have been among the most lonely people who ever lived, in any society, including that one.

As for the trial itself, the charges were trumped up; perjured testimony was given. He was found guilty, and then he was given a choice between death or exile. Exile was a customary sentence for offenses of this kind. It was called *ostracism*, and it usually carried with it a term of not less than 10 years. In fact, charges leading to the same punishment were made against Pericles himself when plague broke out in the city and the war with Sparta was going badly, so it would not have been totally dishonorable to be subjected to exile. I mean, it would have been a mark against one, obviously, but given the trumped up charges, the nature of the trial, Socrates certainly—with a smile on his face—could have accepted a period of exile.

Socrates was told truthfully by his friends that most of the Athenians knew the charges were trumped up; no one wanted Socrates to die, and that, were he to attempt an escape, the guards would simply look the other way. He could leave the city, could just go away for a time, and once things cooled off, return no worse the wear for it. Surely a good man shouldn't kill himself because a bunch of liars got together and made a mischief. You know, there's a kind of ethical proposition here. If, in fact, you've been done in by perjured testimony, why should you accept the punishment at all?

Socrates listens to all this patiently. He knows that his friends want him to live, and, of course, nobody knows more thoroughly than Socrates himself that the charges against him were indeed lies, perjured testimony, coming from envious and predictable sources, but he isn't going to hightail it out of Athens, for he is not going to break the law.

Why not? Because he recognizes that the rule of law is the corporate or public expression of human rationality itself. Law is the means by which the rational power of corruptible man might minimize the corruption. Decades later, in attempting to define the law, at the end of his treatise on politics, Aristotle will say: *dioper aneu orexeos nous o nomos estin*. "The law, therefore, is reason without passion." *Nous aneu orexeos*—reason without passion. It is disinterested reason. It's the application of reason, not in such a way as to benefit this person or that person. Rather, it is to be to the benefit of justice itself.

Unto the last, then, Socrates is a teacher, instructing his melancholy friends in what he takes to be this obvious fact. "Here," he says, "I've devoted my entire life to the cause of reason, and now, just because my own particular situation is compromised—you know, I'm facing a rather severe sentence—I'm supposed to abandon all that I stood for, everything I stood for, everything I taught, everything I believed to the very quick of my nature? I'm supposed to turn and run like a thief in the night, and then what would my life have meant?"

No. He drinks the poison, hemlock. It is in Plato's *Phaedo* that Socrates speaks his final words. Having reassured all and asking them to give him some peace, he grows cold, and then he says, "I owe a cock to Asclepius. Will you remember to pay the debt?"

His final words have to do with a sacrifice he owed to the god of healing. I have always found rich symbolism here, for Socrates himself was "sacrificed" for the healing power of philosophy, and, ironically, the dialogue ends with Socrates entirely faithful to custom, whereas the charge against him was that he had violated custom.

This ending, you see, is Homeric in all of its defining features. Do you think again of Hector, "Breaker of horses"?

Ah, "The unexamined life is not worth living." Here is a stock Socratic teaching; "The unexamined life is not worth living." Why is that? What's wrong, at the end of the day, with consuming narcotics that keep one in a state of pleasure and peace, or supplying them to others as a profession? What's wrong, if it is possible, with allowing surgeons to remove one's brain, and put it in a vat, and—through the proper application of electrical stimulation—play into that brain everything one could possibly desire, or think, or feel? Answer every need, or want, or whim?

One might have the experience of being Solon, or the Socrates of the dialogues, or Napoleon, but this time, let's say, victorious at Waterloo. What is wrong with that? After all, people do aspire to success and achievement. Remember the discussion that Croesus has with Solon. Would one not want to be the happiest of men, where every one of life's desires is realized?

Yet, it seems safe to say that no competent person would willingly enter into this sort of existence; I refer you to a brain in a vat. Now, I am reluctant to call it "this sort of life," for what is promised here is not life, but the illusion of life. What's wrong with this is that it is not a lived life. It is simply a screen on which events are played out.

Socrates did not live in our technical world of microsurgery and pharmacology; thus, in Plato's *Republic*, Socrates does not consider brains in vats, but prisoners in the depths of a cave who have objects and events projected on some parapet in front of them. They think it is reality, whereas it is no more than merely shadows and illusion.

What Socrates is at pains to make clear is that behind every experience, there is room for an interpretation of the meaning of that experience, and it's in the interpretation, the examination of what our life is amounting to, that in fact, life becomes worth living. It's not the sequences of passive experiences; it's the integration of those experiences into some intelligible whole that constitutes a veritable form of life, and one subject to refinement through self-criticism and reflection. For it to be a worthy life, the experiences themselves have to have validity. They have to have truthfulness about them. Otherwise, we are living the life of one in a drunken stupor, one chained in the bowels of a cave, one afloat as a brain in a vat.

Now, this takes me, again, to the temple dedicated to Apollo at Delphi, and that commanding inscription that figures in every introductory philosophy course, and even in fortune cookies in Chinese restaurants: "*Gnothi seauton*," "Know thyself."

How are we to understand that? Was Socrates urging some sort of 1960s West-Coast mode of "self-discovery"? Does the full weight of g*nothi seauton* finally yield questions of the sort: "Am I surfing too much and reading too little?"

No, it is not knowing oneself that way. It's knowing what it means in the fullest sense, what it means to be a certain kind of being—and in this particular case, what it means to be a human being. This must reach toward something other than our mere biology, because we have a common biology. There are human beings covering the face of the earth, as was known in Socrates's time, and, presumably, they have a common biology—so, to know the biological picture is not to know oneself. It might be to know the constituents that make up potentially self-knowing entities.

Nonetheless, take any large sample of such beings, each having the same biological constitution—more or less, anyway—and within that sample, you will find a riot of beliefs; convictions; superstitions; mystical, cultish orientations; forms of debauchery; forms of virtue; forms of genius; forms of self-degradation. Now, this is all taking place in beings who—at a biological level—are pretty much the same. They are all human beings. They all began as babies. They all bleed when cut, etc.

Thus, biology can't be the way one goes about knowing oneself in this Socratic sense. Biology may be the way you go about understanding a particular species or genus of things, what it means to be a human being, what it means to be a cat, etc., but that certainly can't answer the question: "What kind of person am I essentially?"

Socrates's life as a teacher was devoted to the question: "What kinds of beings are we?" Because only after reaching a defensible position on that question might we proceed to "How should we live our lives? What is the right form of government? What's the relationship between the individual and the *polis*?"—today we might say: "between the citizen and the state?"

To know thyself presupposes the capacity to know anything. I mean, if we are totally skeptical at the level of knowledge, then the question "Know thyself" is as unanswerable as the question "Know anything." Now, you may know many things and not "know thyself" in the Socratic sense. But to know thyself is, minimally, *to know*—and so, Socrates begins with that core question, that core problem, the problem of knowledge. How do we know anything? If the skeptics are right in being skeptical about any and every knowledge claimed, then they're going to be right in spades about a claim of not knowing oneself as well. If you can't really know anything for certain, then you certainly cannot "know thyself" in any settled and certain way, and that means that your life is uselessly examined. What could the examined life be? It simply would be a constellation of prejudices and self-deceptions. You might as well get into the vat, or at least allow your brain to be put there.

What has to be defeated here is skepticism, then. It has to be defeated at least insofar as one can establish a good philosophical basis on which to claim that there is something we actually can know. Descartes is going to do the same thing centuries later. We're going to have to come up with at least one kernel of truth that we can settle on as true and that will settle the root epistemological question: "Is it possible to know anything?" If we can answer: "Yes. Yes, it is possible to know something," and to know that you know it, and to know the method you used to come to know it, then maybe we've got a method for uncovering yet other things.

You, thus, begin to see that the Socratic agenda is a fairly broad one. First, one has to do legitimate battle, philosophical battle, gentle battle, with skepticism and cynicism. These schools of thought are in place at the time. Socrates must deal with them, and we will see how he does when we examine several of Plato's dialogues.

He must also contend with the problem of conduct. What kind of life is right for beings such as ourselves? Should we aim solely at happiness and pleasure? What of happiness? Are we all the same in this regard? Does it differ from place-to-place, time-to-time, culture-to-culture? What of our values? Are they simply reflections of our own prejudices, giving us no right or reason to impose them on others or expect anyone else to share them? As we say today, is it all "relative"?

What of the problem of governance and the vaunted "democracy" of the Athenian state? Of course, this was not the sort of democracy that today's citizens of the so-called "Western democracies" routinely describe as a democratic form of government, but by ancient standards, it is the first of its kind, and it is extraordinary. It was fully participatory, except for slaves and women.

The Athenians treasured the democratic character of the *polis*, and a philosopher could well expect trouble when challenging its core precepts. Socrates raised grave questions about such precepts. Suppose, for argument's sake, that the *polis* contains 11,000 people, of whom 10,994 are certifiable fools and 6 are wise men. Now, do you want to take binding votes on important matters, where democracy requires rule by 10,994-to-6 majorities?

As we shall see, Aristotle will defend democratic precepts on the grounds that, all other things being equal, you are likely to get more sheer cleverness, intelligence, and perspicuity out of 100 people than out of 1—that is, their strengths are likely to be additive, whereas their weaknesses might be self-canceling.

Nonetheless, Socrates reserves to himself the right at least to raise the question: How should we be governed? You cannot answer a question like that in the abstract. You can't answer the question of how we should be governed unless you've already established what kind of life is the right kind of life for us to live, and you can't answer that question until you've settled the question: "What kind of beings are we, and how is it that we can come to know as much?"

Until you've successfully defeated a skeptical position on knowledge, you can't have a defensible, let alone compelling, position on ethics. And until you've handled the ethical dimensions of life, you can't have much of a handle on what the political organization of the *polis* should be.

It is a credit to Socrates's lasting genius that he understands the interconnectedness of these questions, that the problem of knowledge, the problem of conduct, and the problem of governance are various phases of the same kind of problem, and that problem is: how we come to know ourselves and realize our humanity in the course of a lifetime.

Lecture Eight
Plato's Search for Truth

Scope:

There is much revealed by Plato in his dialogue *Meno*, including a successful counter to the Sophist challenge about the search for truth—the challenge according to which such a search is either impossible (for one doesn't even know what one is searching for) or unnecessary (for if one knows what it is, then no search is needed). If one knows what one is looking for, why is a search necessary? If one doesn't know, how is a search possible? In *Meno*, we get a particularly clear version of that famous Platonic solution to the problem of knowledge, knowledge as a form of reminiscence. The reminiscence theory of knowledge is opposed to the empirical, the latter grounding knowledge in perception.

Outline

I. The search for truth can only be undertaken once one has defeated, or at least neutralized, the most cogent of the Sophist and skeptical claims against the very possibility of truth. In any number of the dialogues composed by Plato, we see the skeptical position being taken head on and an attempt made to refute it.

   A. There is no final defeat of skepticism in every form, but there are fairly good counters to the more worrisome skeptical claims. Some of these are cogently developed in the dialogue Plato titled *Meno*, named after the young Athenian aristocrat who confronts Socrates.

   1. Meno has been traveling, perhaps to Thessaly, which has a great school of Sophist teaching. He begins a conversation with Socrates by asking whether virtue is acquired by teaching or practice, or perhaps, it resides within us by nature.

   2. What Meno is testing is the sense in which anything can be said to be known. Virtue is spoken of often and with confidence, but what is its source, and how is it to be

understood? If we don't know it by direct experience, we have no route to discovery.

3. When Socrates declares himself to be ignorant of an answer, Meno asks, "How will you inquire, Socrates, into that which you do not know? What will you put forth as the subject of inquiry? And if you find what you want, how will you ever know that this is the thing which you did not know?" This is the stock Sophist challenge to one who claims to search for truth.

4. In response, Socrates shows that Meno's young and uneducated servant, through probing questions and gentle guidance, "knows" that the area of a square is uniquely determined by the length of the diagonal drawn through it. The boy "knows," then, the Pythagorean theorem, though he never studied such subjects, nor did Socrates give him the answer.

5. How did he know it? The answer Socrates gives is that he always knew it and, under the proper guidance, remembered it. This is the original statement of the most famous solution to the problem of knowledge: knowledge as *reminiscence*.

B. There are two distinct kinds of knowledge: knowledge of the facts of daily life and truth, that which has always been and always will be true.

1. Observation of daily life can yield facts, but it cannot yield the second kind of truth; this kind of truth cannot be learned by experience, because experience is merely the encounter of matter with matter and is subject to constant flux.

2. How, then, is truth learned? The soul knows it. How is it that the soul can make contact with such truths? They exist in our souls as prior knowledge, a part of the gift of rationality itself.

3. One of Plato's debts to Pythagorean teaching is a belief in the proposition that there is some animating principle within us that is immaterial and abiding, that pre-dates birth and persists after death. Through its repeated

incarnations, it comes to possess a knowledge no single person could command.

4. With the death of the body, the soul is liberated and presented with the opportunity to gather its proper inheritance—pure knowledge.

5. Absent philosophical guidance, one remains a prisoner of the senses and the world of matter in motion—the world of fluxes and changes. Absent philosophical guidance, one cannot gain access to the truths possessed by the soul (mind) as a feature of its own rational endowment.

II. A philosopher is engaged in the search for truth—that which can be known certainly. That there is such truth is verified by the universal truths of mathematics.

A. The answer to the question "What is a right-angle triangle?" is: "Whatever figure satisfies the statement $a^2 + b^2 = c^2$." It is the latter that is the *true form*, whereas the drawn figure is but a transitory, defective, often misleading depiction. The true form suffers no change—ever.

B. Nothing drawn in the sand by Socrates is the Pythagorean theorem. The visible right triangle is, after all, soon to be swept away by the wind and the traffic of the road.

C. The difference between the *drawn* figure and the *true* right triangle is that the latter is, finally, not an object of sense but a formal relationship.

D. What is it about the soul, about rationality, that can make contact with a truth of that kind? We can't come up with mathematical truths experientially. Surely, Pythagoras did not arrive at that theorem by laying his measuring rod along various right-angle triangles, luckily finding the first one to be a 3–4–5 triangle.

E. Obviously, such ideas must exist, in a sense, in an *a priori* way, which doesn't necessarily mean temporally prior to experience, but logically prior to experience, because there is nothing in experience that will convey such truths. Given that rational beings are clearly in possession of these ideas, they must be in possession of them independently of experience.

F. This is an intuitionist's theory of knowledge, a theory of knowledge based on the proposition that what is firmly known, and known to be true, and could not possibly be known as a result of experience must be part of the very gift of rationality itself. It must be something co-extensive with the life and thought of a rational being.

G. We might note that Aristotle, commenting on Platonic teaching, insists that it was not Socrates but his disciples who conferred ontological standing on the "true forms." Our concern is with the larger issue: whether or not true forms in the Platonic sense can legitimately be regarded as having some kind of ontological standing, some immaterial but nonetheless real standing in the domain of actual things.

III. If the skeptic says, "How can you possibly stand behind the proposition that there is such a thing as unchanging truth?" one reply will present the truths of mathematics.

A. Plato was satisfied that the truths of mathematics were sufficient to put skepticism on notice. Mathematics has established that some things can be known with certainty. The problem of knowledge then becomes a search for the kind of truths that will match up with mathematical certainties.

B. But if such "true forms" cannot be reached through experience, what is left? The answer is: a rational enterprise that takes the form of a dialectical or argumentative approach, an *elenchis* in the Greek.

  1. This approach is not simply a rhetorical device; it's an investigative device. Through the philosophical mode of investigation, we come to consult whatever is contained in the rational resources of the soul itself.

  2. The truths we are looking for can't be held up and shown to anybody. We must discover them in the way Pythagoras must have discovered the Pythagorean theorem: by engaging in an internal contemplative discourse within the soul itself, a kind of introspective, spiritually guided form of inquiry into what Aristotle will call "first things."

    3. Only through the dialectical method and the guidance of the philosopher is one able to get past the ephemera of sense to truths possessed by the soul from the outset.

C. This approach gives us, if not a solution to the problem of knowledge, a recognition of just what it is that makes knowledge problematical. Knowledge is problematical owing to a slavish reliance on experience.

    1. As we have said, experience can't get at certain truths. Animals have experiences; wicked and foolish people have experiences. Further, if one person's experiences are insufficient, little is gained by adding those of another. Self-deception is not eliminated by increasing the number of those thus deceived!

    2. We begin to see that in the solution to the problem of knowledge, there is already skepticism about democratic approaches to questions of conduct and governance.

Recommended Reading:

Plato. *Meno*, in *The Dialogues of Plato*, 2 vols., B. Jowett, trans. Random House, 1937.

Questions to Consider:

1. Explain whether the "Socratic method" is able to do any more than disclose confusions—whether it has a *creative* as well as a critical contribution to make.

2. Summarize how the notion of "pure forms" and skepticism regarding perception stand up against modern scientific conceptions of knowledge.

Lecture Eight—Transcript

Plato's Search for Truth

Well, now for the search for truth. The search for truth is a search that can only be undertaken once one has defeated, or at least neutralized, the most cogent of Sophist and skeptical claims against the very possibility of truth, and in any number of the dialogues composed by Plato, we see the skeptical position being taken head on, and an attempt made to refute it. Of course, the history of skepticism is one of the most formidable in the history of philosophy. Victories over it are always tentative.

There is no final and telling defeat of skepticism in every form, but there are fairly good counters to the more worrisome skeptical claims. Some of these are cogently developed in the dialogue Plato titled *Meno*, named after the young Athenian aristocrat, Meno, who confronts Socrates and bids him "hello."

Now, Meno has been traveling, perhaps to Thessaly, which has a great school of Sophist teaching, as Socrates acknowledges at the very beginning of their conversation. Meno begins by asking whether virtue is acquired by teaching or by practice, or perhaps, it resides within us by nature. Socrates recognizes the Sophist source of questions like this, noting that one of their chief locales is the city of Larisa, which is Meno's hometown. You see, then, the knowing readers or audience for this dialogue understand what's going on here. We've got someone from a Sophist background raising one of these very interesting questions that are likely to undo one's interlocutor: "Where does virtue come from? Is it taught? Is it in us by nature?"—et cetera.

Now, unlike the Sophists who answer all such questions, Socrates declares himself to be just another ignorant Athenian: "You see, I'm not from Larisa. What do I know?" In thus confessing his ignorance of the subject, Socrates disappoints Meno, who asks: "Am I to carry that report back to Thessaly? You see, shall I go back to my home community and say: 'This man knows nothing about this important subject'?"

What Meno is testing is the sense in which anything can be said to be known. If it is not a subject to be taught, then it must be known in some other way, but if it isn't an object we can point to, or hear, or taste, then just what is it that is "known"? Virtue is spoken of so often and with such confidence, but what is its source, and how is it to be understood? If we don't know it by direct experience, we have no route to discovery, and if we can't define it, we really have no way of knowing just what it is we're looking for.

Meno puts it this way:

> How will you inquire, Socrates, into that which you do not know? What will you put forth as the subject of inquiry? And if you find what you want, how will you ever know that this is the thing which you did not know?

You thus begin to see the art of sophistical interrogation. Here we are, the stock Sophist challenge to one who claims to be searching for the truth. The search is shown to be an idle activity, and we can safely abandon such futile projects and get on with the serious business of life.

Now, Meno is attended by a servant boy, a young servant—in some translations, a slave, a *doulos*—a young servant, described by Meno himself as a "barbarian," and we want to recall the sense to be attached to the term "barbarian," when the ancient Greek writers use it. They are not referring inevitably to someone in a loincloth with straggly hair and grunting in no known form of language. Rather, they are referring to a non-Greek speaker, to someone who is not part of the Hellenic culture, to someone outside the bounds of Hellenic *Paideia*.

The Greeks did have a rather uppity attitude toward the non-Hellenic world. This was based on their own judgment that the non-Hellenic cultures had not achieved anything on the order of what the Hellenes had achieved, and, therefore, they should enjoy some pride of place when it comes to philosophy, the rule of law, the idea and realization of beauty—one might say, to some extent, an "earned" uppitiness.

Nonetheless, there was a full appreciation of the fact that these different cultures produced persons of great power and nobility. The Greeks had been defeated often enough by alien cultures not to underestimate the abilities of their adversaries or their friendly neighbors, whether those were in Egypt or Persia, or elsewhere in the known world. Thus, to refer to someone as a "barbarian" was not to refer to someone of an inferior stripe, except in the cultural sense.

Well, Socrates asks Meno if it's all right for him to ask this young servant boy some questions. "By the way, has he had any education?"

Of course, Meno says: "No, no formal education."

"Does he know mathematics?"

"Of course, he doesn't know mathematics." Barbarians don't spend a lot of time learning mathematics.

Well, this much established, Socrates calls the boy over, and as he engages him in a kind of colloquy, Socrates starts sketching some figures in the sand. Now, we have a good idea of the sorts of things he was sketching.

He asks the boy whether he realizes that if this is the case, then that's the case, and if this is so, then isn't that the case, and this goes on for a time. As this interrogation proceeds, it becomes quite apparent that the boy recognizes certain quite basic relationships of a mathematical nature, indeed, of a geometric nature, and in the culminating series of questions—this now depending on how one interprets just what it was that Socrates was drawing in the sand—we're led toward the conclusion—perhaps tentative, but we are led toward the conclusion that the boy appreciates the fact that the area of a square is uniquely determined by the length of a diagonal drawn through it. Which is to say, the boy comprehends the truth of—what? The Pythagorean theorem.

Well, this is a very interesting discovery that Socrates has made, although Socrates knew all along what the outcome was going to be, and he then says to Meno:

"Well, now, did I give him the answer to this problem? Did I solve it for him?"

"No, no, you didn't solve it for him."

"Well, is this something he learned in school? Was this in a course of studies completed or something he learned from tapes from The Teaching Company, etc.?"

"No, it wasn't anything like that at all."

Thus, the question that then naturally arises is: "Well, how did he know it? What is the source of this knowledge?" You can imagine the surprise here, now. You've asked a young servant, a slave, all sorts of questions, and you reach the defensible conclusion that the slave, without any benefit of instruction, seems to comprehend the Pythagorean theorem. How so?

Socrates sets out to answer his own question. The answer to the question: "How does Meno's servant know the Pythagorean theorem?" is that, in a certain sense, Meno's servant always knew it, that what was called for here was not for Meno's servant to learn something, but for him to recall something. Here in the dialogue, we get a particularly clear version of that famous Platonic solution to the problem of knowledge: knowledge as a form of *reminiscence*.

Plato's is indeed a *reminiscence* theory regarding what is true. At this point, however, it is important to distinguish between knowledge as an awareness of mere facts in the world, and the enduring "truths" that stand behind what are otherwise mere appearances.

To know the facts of the world, Socrates—and nearly every other philosopher—would suggest that you open your eyes, listen, walk around, and otherwise exercise the powers of perception, but truth is something different from fact.

Recall the Pythagorean position. Truth is that which does not change. It is that which is eternal. It's not part of the ephemera of daily experience. It's something that abides. What is true must always have been true. It always will be true. Therefore, it is removed from the domain of purely sensory experience. It's removed from the domain of mere materiality. This is now "Truth," then, with a capital "T," as opposed to "facts," with a lowercase "f."

Such knowledge—knowledge of this kind of truth—cannot possibly come about by way of perception, where everything we know that way comes about as a result of the world making contact with the sense organs—well, that can only be material things, because the sense organs themselves are material. The world is a collection of material objects, the sense organs themselves material objects—so, at the experiential level, what one has is an interaction between matter and matter, and, of course, everything that is material is constantly in a state of flux.

Heraclitus put it very well. If Heraclitus had written in Latin, he would have said: "*Nemo discensit bis in indem fluminem.*" "No one descends twice into the same river." We usually render this in Latin, by the way. "*Nemo*" is "no one." "Captain Nemo" is "nobody."

Now, the Heraclitian theory of the fluxes is a theory about the constant changing nature of what we would call the "real world." To accept this is to be skeptical in the matter of perceptually based knowledge. If everything is in a state of flux, any knowledge claim we make can only be good for the moment. This might be a valid knowledge claim about the facts of the world, but surely not about ultimate truths judged to be unchanging and eternal.

If such knowledge cannot be gained as a result of direct perception, how does one come to have it? Ah. Well, one has it, as it were, intuitively. That is, the soul possesses a certain power of comprehension, a certain reservoir of root understandings about ultimate reality, about ultimate truth.

One of Plato's debts to Pythagorean teaching is belief in the transmigration of souls—the proposition that there is some animating principle within us, some feature of *psyche*, that we translate as "soul," that is immaterial, abiding; it pre-dates the birth and persists after the death of the corporeal being.

Through its repeated incarnations, it comes to possess a knowledge no single person could command. With the death of the body, the soul is liberated. We find several times in the dialogues—in the Greek now—a play on words, *soma, sema. Soma* is the body, *sema* is a kind of prison cell, and the idea of the body now is as a *desmoterion*, a kind of penitentiary—the body as a place that has shackled the soul during earthly life, and death brings liberation of the soul and, therefore, the possibility of the soul recovering and gathering pure knowledge, which is its proper inheritance. If you are sensing some anticipation of Christian teaching in this, you're on the right track.

Well, much of this is at work in the dialogue *Meno*. What Meno's servant is doing is, by way of philosophical guidance, reaching into a level of intuitive knowledge that is otherwise clouded by sensory experience, distorted by the mere facts of the world. As long as Meno's servant is allowing his soul to be occupied by the flotsam of perception, he would never arrive at these understandings.

We have, then, this answer, as it were, to the skepticism that is inherent in much of Sophist teaching, and inherent in much of the teaching of the cynics, inherent in much of pre-Socratic philosophy. It's inherent in theories of fluxes, the constant change in the world, the changeable character of all things that exist—leaving us in the lurch with respect to knowing anything definite about it, anything you could really count on. I say this is an answer to all of that.

The other obvious debt to Pythagoras is in the very example that Socrates chooses, when he brings the servant boy over and starts drawing figures in the sand. What is it he wants this to lead to but a recognition on the part of Meno that what this boy understands is the Pythagorean theorem.

Now, recall that the true rectilinear triangle is not something drawn. We've been over that. It's not something physical or material. The true rectilinear triangle is what is instantiated by a mathematical relationship. Remember Pythagoras and the "divinity of number," a mathematical relationship that undergoes no change whatever because there isn't anything material about it. To the extent that a rectilinear triangle is a physical object, it's changing all the time. To the extent that it's a fundamental mathematical relationship—that doesn't change at all. a square plus b square equals c square ($a^2 + b^2 = c^2$) is the relational statement that just *is* the rectilinear triangle.

Now, drawn figures—drawn in sand, or drawn on papyrus, or drawn on paper—these are changeable sorts of things. They exist in a world of flux wherein the soul is distracted from its proper course. We must make a distinction between a *drawn* triangle and the *true form*. The drawn triangle is an empirical thing, accessible to the senses, inevitably undergoing change and degeneration, and ultimate destruction. The true form of the rectilinear triangle suffers no such fate.

"$a^2 + b^2 = c^2$" was a truth that pre-dated human history. You wouldn't ask the question: "On what date did the Pythagorean theorem become valid?" It is a truth that will remain when the last human being has disappeared from the face of the earth and the cosmos has suffered the heat death, depending on which of the cosmological theories you find most appealing—or, perhaps in this case, least appealing.

On the understanding that everything—everything that exists—is finally going to approach that maximally entropic state in which there is homogeneous distribution of an infinity of little particles spread out through a spaceless universe—even on that understanding, what? "$a^2 + b^2 = c^2$"—it remains true.

Now, what is it about the soul that can allow it to make contact with a truth of that kind? What is it about our rationality that can make contact with something like that? Well, you begin to see immediately that it can't be something about the psychology of the individual that is perceptual that is going to be able to do this. It can't be the retina that's doing this. Surely, Pythagoras did not arrive at that theorem by laying his measuring rod along various right-angle triangles, happily and luckily finding the first one to be a 3–4–5 triangle, which would make the arithmetic come out quite neatly.

Surely, except for the 3–4–5 rectilinear triangle, it would be unlikely that measurement would generate such a theorem. Three squared plus four squared does equal five squared, but matters become very, very difficult when different combinations of numbers are used. Consider cases where the altitude of the triangle happens to be 6.37 inches, and the base happens to be 2.4436 inches. Well, you begin to see, this turns out to be a rather difficult thing. You might even need a computer for this if you are trying to arrive at a theorem like that empirically.

Similarly, with p, you don't come up with 3.1416 forever and ever and ever as a result of some experiential undertaking, because that is an experience that would have to go on for all eternity, just as p is a series of numbers that would go on for all eternity—so, you can't come up with transcendental numbers, or imaginary numbers and the like, experientially. Nothing in the realm of fact is the square root of minus one.

Now, where do these notions come from, then, since they don't come from experience on this argument or analysis? Well, obviously, they must be there, in a sense, in some *a priori* way, which doesn't necessarily mean temporally prior to experience, but, as it were, logically or conceptually prior to experience—as there is nothing in experience that will convey something like this. Nothing in experience will convey the square root of minus one, and as rational beings are clearly in possession of ideas like this, they must be in possession of these ideas independently of experience.

Again, this is an intuitionist's, as it were, theory of knowledge, a theory of knowledge based on the proposition that what is firmly known, and known to be true, and that which could not possibly be known as a result of experience must be part of the very gift of rationality itself. It must be something coextensive with the life and thought of a rational being.

Now, on the Platonic account—and here let me pause for a moment and clarify what I mean by the Platonic account—the dialogues have been categorized by scholars into three periods: the so-called "early," "middle," and "late" dialogues. Ideas firmly espoused in the early dialogues sometimes are modified and even rejected later, so to refer to "the" Platonic position generally requires us to say whether this is early Plato, or middle Plato, or late Plato.

Note, for example, Aristotle commenting on Platonic teaching—and he had been exposed to it for 20 years. Aristotle insists that it was not Socrates, but Socrates's disciples who conferred ontological standing on the "true forms," that it was never Socrates's view that there is some really existing true form of the right-angle triangle over and against—do you see?—particular three-sided figures that have one angle that is 90 degrees. Aristotle is thus of the view that the original Socratic teaching was that something like the rectilinear triangle is the formal representation of what actually exists in the concrete, but that the formal mathematical representation doesn't have some independent, kind of floating, cosmic existence. This, at least, is

Aristotle making a distinction between Socrates's actual teaching and what the Socratics found to be affirming in Plato's dialogues.

Now, I don't want to broker the competing claims of Aristotle and writers in the Platonist tradition on the matter of just what Socrates's last word on this subject was, but, I say, as early as Aristotle's own writings, we see the controversial claim that teachings of Socrates were transformed by his students, and may not be reliable guides to Socrates's own thought. The dialogues themselves may not be reliable guides as to precisely what Socrates's own position was, and this is part of the general Socrates-Plato question: How much of the dialogues are Socratic, and how much is Platonic? There's a "Platonic Socrates," and a Socratic Plato." These are matters that we have fun with late at night, not so much right now.

I don't plan to make these fine distinctions here. Quite apart from the fact that much time would be consumed by attempts to make such distinctions, is the more fundamental consideration: When what is at issue is one of the great ideas in the history of philosophy, it's far less important to determine what Socrates really believed, than it is to determine whether the proposition is true and defensible. What Socrates's personal position might have been on whether or not true forms have bona fide ontological standing, or whether the "true form" simply refers to an abstract representation of that which can only exist in experience, is for Xenophon or some later biographer of Socrates to figure out.

Whether or not true forms in that Platonic sense can legitimately be regarded as having some kind of ontological standing—some sort of "real," immaterial existence in the domain of actual things—is a philosophical proposition worth our attention, again, whether Socrates finally subscribed to the view or not.

Now, if we take the position that mathematics is just the right model for getting at the "Truth," "capital T"—that is, that "Truth" inevitably refers to that which is an unchanging form—and that ready at hand is an abstract mathematics that vindicates that very belief—we may make progress in dealing with all of the problems of knowledge.

If a skeptic, therefore, says: "How can you possibly stand behind the proposition that there is such a thing as unchanging truth?"—well, one reply will present the truths of mathematics. You just say: "If you doubt there can be any Truth at all, get out Euclid, or get a trigonometry book, or a calculus text," you see.

Now, of course, there are rebuttals to that rebuttal, that riposte, and we will be confronting these in the course of later lectures. One can turn around and, in the spirit of David Hume, say: "Well, yes, these are truths, but these are truths about words, not truths about anything having real existence." We will get into revived forms of skepticism and firm defenses of empiricistic alternatives to the account discussed here.

Plato, though, was satisfied that the truths of mathematics were sufficient to put skepticism itself on notice. There really do seem to be things that can be known certainly, and mathematics has established that these things can be known with certainty—so, the problem of knowledge now becomes understood as a search for the kind of truths that will match up with mathematical certainties. We should be looking for relational truths of the sort instantiated, for example, by the Pythagorean theorem. The "true" right-angle triangle is expressed by this theorem, which is the triangle's "true form," as distinct from the sketched three-sided figure observable by perception. The former—the "true form"—is immutable, and the latter is what? It's a pure counterfeit.

Now, if the "true form" of something cannot be reached through experience, what's left? Well, what is left is an essentially rational enterprise. Not an experiential enterprise, but a rational enterprise, and what form must this rational enterprise take? It takes a form that in the Greek is referred to as the *elenchis*, a dialectical or argumentative approach, but not argumentative at the level of rhetoric. It's an approach that sets out simply to show your adversary as a dunce or a dullard. It's a bona fide search for truth—not a search for victory, where the rhetorician or the Sophist might want to show an adversary to be a dunce—one engaged in the *elenchis* is really trying to get at what really is the case without showing anybody up: "We're all in this together. Let's argue it through."

Now, I should say, as I said in a previous lecture, that it's quite easy to libel the Sophists in this regard. There were members of the

Sophist teaching fraternity, of course—one who comes to mind and who figures in Plato's *Republic* is Thrasymachus—who taught for pay, and who seemed to be engaged in a set of argumentative ploys that were rather showy and, I should think, intended chiefly to reduce one's interlocutor to utter confusion, and make him seem like an utter dunce. The original Sophist school, though, included men of great intellectual integrity, who were not indifferent or hostile to the idea of truth, but were wary of claims to the effect that "It's within our reach."

The argumentative or dialectal approach is not simply a rhetorical device—I want to emphasize that. It's an investigative device. Through the philosophical mode of investigation, we come to consult whatever is contained within the rational resources of the soul itself. As it were, we "talk" our way into this domain. It's the only thing we've got, because experience is not going to count for anything here. The truths we are looking for can't be held up and shown to anyone—so, we're going to have to discover them—how? Well, we are probably going to have to discover them the way Pythagoras must have discovered the Pythagorean theorem. Surely, not by running around and measuring three-sided figures, but by engaging in a kind of internal contemplative discourse within the soul itself, a kind of introspective, maybe spiritually guided form of inquiry into what Aristotle will call "first things."

The philosopher has committed himself to an inquiry of that kind, and what it means to be a disciple or student of a philosopher is just to be one who is prepared to cast oneself as an acute listener, the right sort of conversationalist, on a journey, the end of which is a form of knowledge attained by Meno's servant. The end is less a discovery of what has never been known, than the uncovering of what had always been possessed, but lost in the hurly-burly, in the flotsam and distraction of daily perceptual, sensory, sensual life.

We have at once, then, if not a solution to the problem of knowledge, a recognition of just what it is that makes knowledge problematical. Knowledge is problematical owing to this slavish reliance on experience, as if experience could teach us things like this.

Clearly, every man, woman, and child—as well as most of the creatures of the animal kingdom—have experiences minute-by-minute, seven days a week, 365 days a year, and yet the world is home to villains and fools, a few wise men, distracted people, the mad, the weird, and the mentally deficient. There's a panoply of human types and types of lives, and it is idle to attempt to discriminate between or within groups such as these on the basis of experience, for experience is ubiquitous.

The villains of history are rich in their experiential backgrounds, and few saints we've ever known are any richer in their experiential background, perhaps not very rich at all. Well, the point is this: You can't make distinctions between the wise and the foolish on the basis of who has had more experience, and if you can't make distinctions between the wise and the foolish on that basis, then on what basis will you make the distinction? That is to say, to add up that which itself never reaches the fundamental truths is to engage in an enterprise that is entirely nugatory.

Well, then, the experiences of 11 people would not amount to anything, versus the experiences of one, and if the experiences of 11,000 people amount to no more than the experiences of one person, the implications for democratic or majoritarian rule are clear.

We begin to see, then, that Socrates is going to get into trouble in the radically Athenian state in which he finds himself.

Lecture Nine

Can Virtue Be Taught?

Scope:

In the dialogue *Protagoras*, Socrates must learn from Protagoras how his young friend Hippocrates should be educated and where he should be schooled if were he to become a fine sculptor or an expert physician. Receiving predictable replies from Protagoras, Socrates then asks what it is that young Hippocrates should aspire to be for it to make sense for him to study with Protagoras! The answer given by Protagoras is "virtue," but then Socrates must ask whether this is the sort of thing that can be taught.

Outline

I. The skeptics ask: Why is the conduct of life problematical? Why is it that we cannot simply live in such a way as to maximize our own satisfactions and take others into account only insofar as they stand in our way and must be avoided or defeated?

    A. There may be truths in mathematics but not in the conduct of life, which is a matter of personal taste and desire. Nobody can tell others how to live.

    B. To counter the skeptics' position, Socrates must make a case that there is a problem of conduct and that it can be solved with the same argumentative and analytical resources that proved successful in the search for knowledge itself.

II. In the dialogue *Protagoras*, Socrates deferentially asks the famed Sophist Protagoras how his young friend Hippocrates should be educated: Where should he be schooled? What is it he might learn from Protagoras?

    A. Protagoras goes along with the inquiry: were Hippocrates to be a fine sculptor, he ought to study with Phidias; to be an expert physician, with the Aesculapian school. Socrates then asks what it is that young Hippocrates might become expert in studying with Protagoras.

B. The answer given by Protagoras is "virtue," moral excellence, *arête*. Socrates must then ask what is virtue and whether it is the sort of thing that can be taught. The dialogue explores these questions.

III. To teach anything one must know what it is. What *is* virtue? Is it one thing or many?

   A. Are justice, holiness, and temperance separate virtues or parts of virtue as a whole? It makes a difference, because if they are separate, it should be possible for a person to be, for example, just but intemperate or holy but unjust. Protagoras's answer, that these qualities are parts of virtue, introduces confusion. If justice is separate from and not in any way like temperance, then temperance must match up with what is not just, that is, with injustice!

   B. Socrates then pursues the question of whether virtue can be taught. Why would he raise this question? Socrates appreciates that there's something about moral excellence that defies merely academic exercises or pedagogical undertakings. There seems to be something in the human being that reflects, generates, expresses virtue. How can something of this nature be "taught"?

   C. We do not say of persons that they are virtuous in the morning but not so in the afternoon. We tend to think that a person is virtuous when there is a quality about the person that expresses itself in almost every context. For that to be the case, it must be because the actions of the person are guided by a principle or precept that is at once unified and universally applicable.

   D. Obedience to this principle is not blind, however. Expressions of virtue presuppose knowledge; courage, for example, arises not from ignorance of what is involved in one's actions but with full knowledge of the risks.

   E. Thus, virtue seems to be a quality regulative of conduct, but if it is a *universal*, then it cannot be accessed by the senses. The senses can pick up only particulars, not universals. If behind persons of virtue, there stands a universal principle, an impelling principle, applicable in all contexts and known in some non-sensory way, then virtue is like the Pythagorean theorem—a matter of relationships.

F. If virtue cannot be learned by experience—that is, by some sort of perceptual activity—then how can it be taught at all?

    1. In most contents, we teach by pointing to instances of what we are teaching, but we cannot point to virtue, which is a universal. A universal precept cannot be the subject of ostensible definition.

    2. For Socrates, if virtue cannot be taught, then there is no point in teaching at all. Teaching is reduced to a kind of training, as in training to be a welder.

G. We might argue that we cannot point to virtue, but we can point to instances of virtue, just as we can point to right triangles, which though not perfect, are instances of the relation $a^2 + b^2 = c^2$.

    1. This approach presents another problem: A one-year-old child shown the heroism of the Spartans at Thermopylae can learn nothing from it. The soul must be prepared and of the right disposition; there must be guidance, as Meno's servant required guidance to discover that he knew the Pythagorean theorem.

    2. Thus, Socrates argues that virtue cannot be taught as such. However, if knowledge attained by philosophical reflection is the necessary ingredient in virtue, this can be taught.

    3. Again, not all are ready to be "taught" virtue in this sense. The students for this instruction must have the background and propensity to resonate when a virtuous act presents itself. We cannot teach virtue by presenting instances of virtuous actions to a person whose soul has been so corrupted as not to be able to enter into a kind of sympathetic relationship with the exemplum.

    4. We have here the foundations for a kind of elitist position on who shall be virtuous, which we will confront again in Plato's *Republic*. The life of virtue is not available to anybody and everybody—it requires a certain kind of person.

5. We also see the foundations for an essentially developmental theory. If one is ever to be in a position where the lessons of virtue make some impact, it must be because from the earliest time in childhood, one's soul was conditioned in such a way as to be receptive to lessons of this kind.

IV. In a later dialogue, the *Theaetetus*, the authority of Protagoras is again challenged, this time as a result of the famous claim in his long-lost book, "Man is the measure of all things."

A. Socrates notes that if Protagoras claims that each man one at a time and for himself is the measure of truth, then why should we believe this or any other pronouncement?

> I am charmed with his doctrine...but I wonder that he does not begin his book with a declaration that a pig or dog-faced baboon or some yet stranger monster which has sensation is the measure of all things; then might he have shown a magnificent contempt for our opinion of him by informing us at the outset that while we were revering him like a god for his wisdom, he was no better than a tadpole.

B. In so many words, Socrates insists that we can't have it both ways. Protagoras can't stand as a paragon of philosophical wisdom and still contend that everybody, one at a time, is the measure of all things.

C. At the end of the day, the problem of conduct is a problem of principle. If the principle is right, it is universally right. It is not tarnished or reduced by the mere showing that large numbers of people don't embrace.

D. Each man is not the measure of all things. There is a measure of things, and it is the task of the individual to find a way to understand that measure and apply it properly.

Recommended Reading:

Julia Annas, *Platonic Ethics, Old and New*. Cornell University Press, 1999

T. H. Irwin, *Plato's Ethics*. Oxford University Press, 1995

Questions to Consider:

1. Explain whether the Socratic notion of *virtue* is taught in contemporary educational institutions.
2. Describe how Socrates would likely have been received by the politicians of this age.

Lecture Nine—Transcript

Can Virtue Be Taught?

Well, what is the problem of conduct? What makes conduct problematical? Why, after all, can't we just solve the problem of conduct by saying: "Well, let's act in such a way as to maximize pleasure and minimize the pains of the moment"? If that means suffering, or otherwise tolerating or putting up with others, well, we can do that, and we can do that for the sole instrumental purpose of personal gain, keeping out of trouble, and making sure that, at the end of the day, things went better for us than they did for anybody else, or at least we weren't caught crying.

Now, that's one solution to the problem of conduct. There are some philosophers who have recommended such a strategy, and still others that associate it with cads and highwaymen; so, there's a wide range of opinion on what the standards of conduct ought to be, and what principles should guide conduct.

Now, one might say instead that the problem of conduct is solved by just finding a community that is willing to tolerate one's eccentricities, a community of kindred spirits—and that's really the end of it. If one wants to be a member of the mafia, it would be counterproductive to join a community of saints, and vice versa, but surely you should be able to find some community where killing your adversaries, and trafficking in narcotics, and earning profit from prostitution, thereupon supporting cooperative political leaders, is just right for some, even if unacceptable to others. Thus, the expression goes: "To each his own." After all, values do vary from place to place. "No one has the last word on how I should live my life" most people would be prepared to say today. It's difficult enough for a person to find the right life for himself or herself, let alone dictating to the balance of the human race how it ought to conduct its collective life.

When one starts talking about a form of life that is "good," or "bad," or "virtuous," or "vicious," these are inevitably expressions of personal taste and preference, so the argument goes. They certainly aren't grounded in anything as firm and permanent as what the philosophers are prepared to call "the Truth." There might be truths of mathematics, the argument continues, but there are scarcely truths of ethics and morality. This is not the domain of objective knowledge; it's the domain of sentiment or belief, rank opinion—sometimes mere superstition.

Now, what we have here is the skeptic's orientation toward what is called "moral objectivity," and related aspects of moral philosophy. The Socratic/Platonic school must address this, and attempt to make out a case for the proposition that the problem of conduct is not to be solved at the level of merely personal desire. If there is a solution to the problem of how life should be lived, it is to be found with the use of the same argumentative and analytical methods that seem to be successful in addressing the problem of knowledge.

It was that approach that led to the conclusion that truth was, indeed, within reach, and there is no reason to assume that the same degree of certainty cannot be achieved in the moral realm, where the issue indeed is how life should be lived, what kind of life is right for beings such as ourselves. Nobody would argue, for example, that there are certain nutritional requirements that are right for beings such as ourselves, though different requirements for, let's say, bumblebees and sparrows.

It is not obviously counterintuitive, then, to say that just for a certain kind of being, there is a better form of life to be lived, and a worse form of life to be lived.

Now, this profound issue is addressed in any number of Plato's dialogues. The one I would choose for today's lecture is named after one of the central characters in the dialogue, the famous *Protagoras*, whom we've met before. The dialogue begins as a kind of theatre piece—many of the dialogues are theatre pieces—Socrates now in the house of Callias and telling his companion how young Hippocrates had awakened him early in the morning with the news that Protagoras was in Athens. Socrates then narrates what ensued. He's telling Callias how he was awakened by this youngster.

Now, he, Hippocrates here, is not the father of Greek medicine— more on that Hippocrates, of Kos, later. Hippocrates is a frequently enough occurring name in ancient Greece, not unlike Jack or Jill, so this is just young Hippocrates, who wants to get Socrates started on the day because something quite momentous is taking place—namely Protagoras is in town.

Now, Socrates is given an ironic line. He turns around and says to Hippocrates, who is so urgent about all this: "Why are you rousing me? Did he rob you?" Hippocrates then replies rather wisely: "Yes, of the wisdom he will not share with me."

Well, I should think very few things short of a fire would get Socrates out of bed more quickly than the news that a chap has arrived in town so wise as to be able to answer all our questions. I mean this is a form of baiting, if ever there was, so Socrates says: "Well, indeed, we had better go off and get these questions answered."

First, though, Socrates wants to be sure that this young man knows why he should be instructed by Protagoras in the first place, so he puts several questions to him.

"Why, for example, would you"—let's say he's talking to Hippocrates, now—"seek to be taught by, oh, let's say the other Hippocrates, Hippocrates of Kos?"

To this, young Hippocrates replies: "Why, to be a physician."

"Well, that makes sense. The great founder of Greek medical education—if you want to be a physician, study with him."

Next, Socrates asks what young Hippocrates would have as an aim, were he to study with Phidias or Polycleitus.

"Why," the answer comes back, "to excel as a sculptor, of course." Phidias, the great sculptor of the Acropolis.

Then, Socrates asks him what he seeks to become in turning his life over to Protagoras. You see it's going to make very good sense to say: "If you want to be a doctor, study with Hippocrates of Kos. If you want to be a sculptor, study with Phidias. Now, what is it that you are supposed to want to be for it to make sense for you to study with Protagoras?" Sensible question.

Well, Hippocrates is confused now, first saying only that Protagoras would make him a Sophist. Socrates has a bit of fun here, admonishing his young friend not to present himself to the Athenian people as a Sophist, but the point is made: Hippocrates really has not thought deeply enough on just what he should expect to derive from the teaching for which Protagoras is so famous. Would that today's students be paced through this kind of interrogative: "Why are you taking a course with So-and-So?" The usual answer is going to be: "Well, I'm planning to go to law school, and course 404 is required." Well, Socrates is a little more serious about the educations of Athenian and Bath youth.

After a time, the two go off to the house of Callias, entering the place where Protagoras is surrounded by the best and the brightest. After suitable introductions, Socrates stating that the youth Hippocrates requires Socrates himself to serve as a kind of proxy, the dialogue begins. Socrates, again, raises the sorts of questions he presented to Hippocrates: Just what is supposed to happen to Hippocrates? What is he supposed to become? How is he to be changed, just in case he is fortunate enough to become a pupil of Protagoras?

At this point, ever gracious and ever eloquent, Protagoras discourses at length on certain myths about how humanity received justice and wisdom, etc. He speaks of the central role of political virtue in the life of the person and of the state, making clear that it is thus that his teaching inculcates.

Socrates, so enthralled, he says—this is a comic piece, in parts—by the eloquence of Protagoras that he continues to hear his voice even after he has concluded his speech. He says: "The echo is still going on"—but then, he gathers himself. For the moment, and on the authority of Protagoras, he will accept that virtue can be taught, but first it will be necessary to establish just what it is. That is "I'll grant you it can be taught, if you'll tell me what it is." Once there is clarity on what virtue *is*, the question of if and how it is to be taught can be revisited. Well, can virtue be taught, and what is it?

Now, it's useful to recall that this dialogue features a still-young Socrates, in his 30s, facing one of the sages of the ancient world. Plato gives Socrates lines that make it clear early on Socrates is just getting his philosophical sea legs. He knows he's dealing with one of the most formidable intelligences in the ancient Greek world, and he wants to make sure that he, Socrates, is not going to get caught up in those very well-known sophistical devices that have you walking home wondering what hit you, so he gets Protagoras to commit himself to Socrates's own method, that dialectical method: "I will ask the questions, and your replies will be to the questions. Let's not engage in these mythical digressions and metaphors. Let's stay on target."

Protagoras, here, is really quite obliging, but when he begins to lapse into his own preferred mode of teaching, Socrates pulls him up short and says: "Look, I said what the ground rules were going to be; you agreed. And if you don't abide by them, I'm leaving," so that you get an almost petulant and, I think, rather nervous and defensive Socrates in this dialogue. This is a much-analyzed dialogue, and I surely don't think anyone would declare Socrates the clear winner by the time it ends—though, in the later dialogues, Socrates revisits the same issues and, I think, turns in a more consistent and confident performance, but that's the atmosphere of this dialogue, a young Socrates nervously taking on Pythagoras.

What are these questions going to be, then? Well, we can begin this way. Let's ask this question: "Suppose this Hippocrates, here, this young boy that I love as if he were my own son"—Socrates says repeatedly—"and you know I am very concerned about his future, etc. Suppose he wanted to excel in medicine. Now, with whom would you suggest he study?" These are the questions that Hippocrates had to consider before the two left for the meeting with Protagoras in the first place, and they prove to be illuminating questions when addressed to Protagoras himself.

Now, we all know why one would study with great physicians, sculptors, painters, musicians. Why would one study with the Sophist philosopher, and with Protagoras specifically? That is, what science or art will be thus cultivated? If study has a transforming effect, what is it that is to change as a result of this education? Again, I say, wouldn't it be something if today's undergraduates approach their colleges freshman year with just this question: "What is it that's going to change as a result of what I'm prepared to expose myself to here?"

"Look, what is it this young man would want to have to excel at for it to make any sense for him to study with you, Protagoras?"

Protagoras answers in a word. He would have to wish for moral excellence, for "virtue," for what in the Greek is *arête*. This, then, gives Socrates the interrogatives that actually dominate the dialogue. "Yes," he says, "but what is virtue, and can it be taught?"

Now, I want to parse these interrogatives lest they become little more than topics for a sort of "café-metaphysics." You know, "Ah, well, can virtue be taught?" he asked himself as he strolled down the street toward the setting sun." You know, the retreating lonely philosopher with resignation—"Can virtue be taught?"

That's not the burden of the question. This is a very serious question that is going to provide the context for a rigorous philosophical analysis on the nature of virtue itself and questions about what is teachable.

In his account of the myth of Zeus sending down to earth the virtues of justice, holiness, and temperance, Protagoras did not make clear, for example, whether these are separate virtues or parts of virtue as a whole. It makes a difference, for if separate, it should be possible for a person to be, say, virtuously just but intemperate, or holy but unjust, etc. When queried on this point, Protagoras answers that he intends these to be understood as "parts" of virtue.

Well, this introduces all manner of confusion. Now Socrates wants to know if these "parts" are like, for example, the nose, eyes, and mouth—the parts of a face, where "virtue" is akin to the face as a whole, but if virtue has these different parts—each of them different from the others and serving different functions—than virtue itself is not a "part" of any of these, and if justice is not in any way like temperance, then temperance must match up with what is not just, that is, with injustice! Ah! You begin to see that Socrates, though he's getting his philosophical sea legs, he's getting them very quickly, and he's got a head start on these issues.

There is then a long section of the dialogue devoted to a poem by Simonides, which contains the seeming "truism" according to which is called "It Is Hard to Be Good." Poets are allowed that form of philosophizing: "It is hard to be good."

Now, one issue arising from the poem has to do with how one retains goodness once it has been achieved. Let's say, for argument's sake, that in some sense, we've become good. How do we stay that way? The point is made that, as with ascending to the heights of a jagged rock, the journey is difficult but, once at the top, it is easy to stay there, but who would contend that once virtue has been attained, it is easy to remain in that state?

Consider now whether this elusive condition, or state, or property—call it "virtue" or "moral excellence"—is it teachable? Why would Socrates raise this question about the teachability of *arête*, this kind of excellence, this kind of virtue? Here, so many thoughts cloud the imagination as you become a participant in the dialogue, or if not a participant, a witness to it. You're standing there, and it's Athens in the 5th century B.C. Sparta has won this Peloponnesian War. Socrates and his friends are coming to grips with a certain political reality that is far from reassuring.

What do we know about Sparta? Well, we know this much: We know that Sparta had the laws of Lycurgus, but refused to reduce these laws to writing—whereas Athens, a century earlier, had a written law, Sparta does not reduce its laws to writing, because any man who learns his duty by reading about it can't be trusted. You get the picture here, don't you?

Here is battle-hardened Socrates, who already appreciates that there's something about moral excellence that defies merely academic exercises or pedagogical undertakings. There seems to be something in the being himself that reflects, generates, expresses virtue, moral excellence, *arête*. How can something of this nature be "taught"?

There is more to it than that. We don't find ourselves saying, you know, "Bill tends to be virtuous between 10 and 11 o'clock in the morning, and earlier and later than that, he's a felon, a bank robber, a child molester, but find him at the right time, and you've got a man of virtue."

Nobody thinks that. We tend to think that a person is virtuous when there is a quality about the person that expresses itself in just about every context, and for that to be the case, it must be because the actions of the person are guided by a principle or precept that is at once unified and universally applicable. It's not just that you do something at 11 o'clock or you do something on Thursdays. It's rather you make yourself into a certain kind of person, a person whose conduct is obedient to a principle.

Now, this obedience here is not blind. Socrates asks Protagoras if courage is a virtue, to which the reply is affirmative.

"Are the courageous also confident?"

"Yes," says Protagoras.

"Is this because they understand what it is that is called for, and are ready to do what is needed?"

"Yes, of course," says Protagoras.

"But what of those who are utterly ignorant? Would we say that, in doing the same thing, they too are courageous?"

"Surely not."

Thus, courage arises not from ignorance of what is involved, but with full knowledge of the risks, and it is so with all expressions of virtue: All expressions presuppose knowledge, the truth of things. Both will agree that there is nothing mightier than knowledge, and that this would remain so even for one whose aim was to choose a path leading to pleasure and away from pain. You'd still need knowledge

Now, if this is a *universal* principle—the need for knowledge if there is to be virtue; that is, there must be knowledge first, if there is to be virtue, and if it is a guide to life in all of the theatres of life and all of the stages of life, if it's a *universal* in that sense, well, alas, it is not accessible to the senses. Why is that?

The senses can only pick up particulars. They cannot pick up universals. So, if, in fact, behind the man of virtue—and it would be called "man of virtue" in that culture—behind persons of virtue, there stands a universal principle, an impelling principle, applicable in all contexts and known in some non-sensory way—this, again, is— we're hearkening to the *Meno* again. Do you see? This is very much like the Pythagorean theorem. It's true of all rectilinear triangles, not just that one or that one, and as it is universally the case, it is not accessible to the senses, because the senses pick up only what is particular, only a "this" and a "that."

Well, here's the bind. How do we teach anybody anything? Well, in most contexts, we teach people by saying: "This is a sheet of paper. This is a set of spectacles. This is a lectern. This is a shoe." That is, when we take a look at how parents teach children, they teach children by providing sensible, visible, or audible examples of what it is they are trying to convey. Teaching, as it's generally engaged in, at least early in life, is teaching by showing. It's defining things ostensibly. "This is a wall. That is a door. This is a person. This is a tie."

Now, teaching by showing—ah, well, anything that can be taught by showing cannot itself be universal. You can't point to that which is universal. You can't point to anything that is always the case. You can only point to a "this" and a "that."

Well, then, can virtue be taught? How could you possibly teach it? What is it you would show? What is it you would point to, to say: "There's virtue"?

Now, I want it to be understood that that's the burden of the question. The burden of the question is if we are dealing with something, if the something is to have this nature, a universal principle, universally operative, it can't be the subject of ostensive definitions. It can't possibly be something that you hold up or sound out, and if it can't be dealt with that way, well, then, for goodness' sake, how do you teach it? What do you point to?

This, then, is a serious question about what is teachable, and it's a serious question raised by one of the greatest teachers of all time, because you can quite understand that for someone like Socrates, if you can't teach virtue, then why bother teaching anything? I mean, what else would there be? Just a kind of training, as, "Now I'll show you how to weld, how to use the Bunsen burner, how to make nylon in the chemistry laboratory," exercises in what the Greeks would take to be arts and crafts, *techne*, as opposed to *sophia*, a kind of wisdom that should guide one all the days of one's life, and should prepare one's soul for an eternal life that is undertaken with the death of the body. No, virtue had better be teachable, because if virtue isn't teachable, Socrates is wasting his time. No one is going to take poison hemlock in order to defend his career as a teacher of welding.

Now, you might say: "Well, all right, can virtue be taught?" It's a central question, and it's made difficult by the fact that, defined in a certain way, virtue may refer to something that can't be held up or shown, but for goodness' sake, you can hold up and show rectilinear triangles. You can draw them on a piece of paper and say: "Here's a three-sided figure as best as I can do it. I've tried to make one of the angles 90 degrees, and that's what we mean by a right-angle triangle. Now, I'm going to teach you something about Euclidean geometry."

Ah, well, in other words, although you can't show the universal, you can show an instance of it, at least in a suggestive way.

Well, the turn the dialogue takes then is this turn: Perhaps we can't teach virtue in the empirical sense of pointing to virtue, but we certainly can point to virtuous acts. We can point to persons who act in a virtuous way. We can point to the morally excellent person, the person reflecting *arête*. We can point to that person.

Now, look, here's another problem. Suppose we take a one-year-old, and we sort of hold the one-year-old erect enough, there's the one-year-old wobbling around, and we take the one-year-old to Thermopylae during the Persian wars, and what we're going to show the one-year-old is the great General Leonidas at the pass, Leonidas knowing that he and all of his men are going to perish. They are sacrificing themselves for the liberty of the Hellenic world, one of the great heroic acts in military history, one of the great acts of bravery of all time—self-sacrificing, great courage, not heedlessness now but a principled act of courage that must end in one's own death and the death of one's brothers.

Okay, so now we've got the one-year-old looking at this. The one-year-old is not going to see anything by way of virtue at all. The one-year-old is going to be, as it were, looking at a game of some sort, probably enjoying the shiny helmets and the whinnying horses and the noise sent up by men in conflict, or the one-year-old may just take a few more sips of the bottle and go to sleep.

It isn't enough to say, then, that perhaps we can present a person of virtue, or someone behaving virtuously, and that's the way you teach it. Thus, Socrates argues to the conclusion that it cannot be "taught," as such, but just in case that in the end the necessary ingredient in all virtue—so much so as to be virtue itself—is wisdom, just in case the knowledge attained by philosophical reflection is the very grounding of virtue—well this, at any rate, is teachable.

However, as with the one-year-old, not all are ready for this, and many are never ready at any age. The students for this instruction must have already been prepared by the right sort of nature, at the right stage in life. Then, indeed, you might find within such persons something that will resonate when a virtuous act presents itself. You cannot teach the Pythagorean theorem to a one-year-old either, nor can you teach the Pythagorean theorem to an entity whose rational resources are simply not up to the task. And so, you cannot present, as the emblem of virtue, actions that are, indeed, understood to be virtuous actions but presented to a person whose soul has been so corrupted, or is so incompletely developed, so impoverished, as not to be able to resonate to, or in some way enter into a kind of sympathetic relationship with the exemplum.

Do you see the point here? The point is: This is a two-way street. It's not just a matter of holding up something. You've got to know who is on the witnessing side of this example—and if it's the wrong sort, no number of examples will get through to it. It would be like presenting a great musical symphony to a person who happens to be deaf.

Now, we have here, at once, the foundations of a kind of elitist position on who shall be virtuous. We're going to confront this again, famously in Plato's *Republic*, in which Socrates refers to the convenient fiction developed first in Hasid's writings, the convenient fiction of men of gold, men of silver, men of brass, and men of iron.

As I say, then, we already have the position being laid down now, according to which the life of virtue is not available to just anyone and everyone—it takes a certain kind of person. We also see the foundations here being laid for an essentially developmental theory. If you are ever going to be in a position where the lessons of virtue make some impact on you, it's going to be because from the earliest time in your childhood, your soul was conditioned in such a way as to be receptive to lessons of this kind, and again, in Plato's *Republic*, which is the subject of the next lecture, we begin to see what kind of preparation is necessary if one is ever to be accessible to instruction by the virtuous.

Now, Protagoras is mentioned centrally in another dialogue called the *Theaetetus*, in which that famous maxim of his is considered: "Man is the measure of all things." This gets back to the point that I raised at the very beginning of today's lecture—"Well, look, on this question of conduct, why not just say: 'I will act according to my caprice. I will do the things that please me, and the reason I'm going to pay any attention to you at all is because you might be in a position to undo me, etc., etc. I'll play the game in such a way as to keep you distracted, or keep you at arm's length, but I say, at the end of the day, it's my game that counts, and if that means you lose, so much the worse for you'?" After all, if man is the measure of all things, then that becomes one acceptable answer to the problem of conduct. The way we solve the problem of conduct is for everybody to solve it for himself.

Now, this is what, in the *Theaetetus*, Socrates says when he's asked: "Well, what do you have to say about Protagoras's position that, you know: 'Man is the measure of all things.' Tell us what you have to say about that."

Benjamin Jowett's translation has Socrates replying:

> I'm charmed with his doctrine…but I wonder that he does not begin his book with a declaration that a pig or dog-faced baboon or some yet stranger monster which has sensation is the measure of all things; then might he have shown a magnificent contempt for our opinion of him by informing us at the outset that while we were revering him like a god for his wisdom, he was no better than a tadpole.

In so many words, Socrates insists that we can't have it both ways. Protagoras can't stand there as the very paragon of philosophical wisdom and still contend that everybody has a right to his view on these things, and that no one has a greater authority than anyone else. At the end of the day, the problem of conduct is a problem of principle, and if the principle is right, the principle is universally right. It is not tarnished nor is it reduced to something else by the mere showing that large numbers of persons don't embrace it. Take it from me. "My opinion counts for nothing" is akin to the liar's paradox, which is: "Everything I say is false."

No, each man is not the measure of all things. There is a measure of things, and it is the task of the individual to come up with the means by which to understand that measure and apply it properly.

Lecture Ten

Plato's *Republic*—Man Writ Large

Scope:

This most famous of the dialogues begins with the metaphor—or the reality—of the *polis* as the enlarged version of the person. The fate of each is inextricably bound up with the fate of the other.

Plato's *Republic* is taken to be the foundational work in what we call "political science," but it is useful to recall that the dialogue begins with a quite different question—namely, what is it by which a man can be said to be "good"? In light of the complexity of the question, Socrates suggests that the subject of the inquiry be enlarged, made big enough so as to be seen more clearly. Thus, the question is transformed.

Outline

I. Plato's *Republic* is one of the most discussed philosophical tracts in history and the subject of both praise and condemnation. It is famous in political science—is, indeed, the origin of political science—but it also concerns itself with matters that are psychological: What makes a man good? What are the weaknesses of human nature?

II. Book I begins with a group assembling in the house of Cephalus, a wealthy and now old man whose son, Polemarchus, is among the group associating with Socrates. Cephalus and Socrates have an interesting conversation about reaching old age and the advantages of wealth.

   A. Cephalus asserts that as the end of life approaches, one begins to think increasingly about a time after death when one might be punished for moral failings. A rich man, having no need to cheat or defraud others, tends to have a clearer conscience and, thus, is less fearful of death.

   B. Socrates then mentions something he has learned—that what it means to be just is to pay one's debts. We are then plunged into an examination of justice. Before the end of Book I, the dialogue has raised the question of whether an unjust person can reach a state of happy and flourishing life.

C. Note that at least this far into Plato's *Republic*, there is no attention to political science or statecraft. The focus, instead, is on justice, and in seeking to establish what it is that qualifies a person as just, the dialogue begins to explore the motives and desires of people. Thus, it stands as a treatise on psychology.

III. In Book II, Glaucon forces Socrates to categorize justice into one of three distinct classes of "good things."

A. There are things that are good in and of themselves, independent of their usefulness, such as harmless pleasures. There are goods such as knowledge and health that are not only good in themselves but also for the consequences that arise from them. Finally, there are such goods as exemplified by money-making, which are, in and of themselves, disagreeable but are pursued for the sake of their results.

B. Socrates places justice in the highest category, where things are desired for their intrinsic value, not their consequences. This allows the debate to continue: What is it that makes a man good? Who exemplifies the ideal in a world that lusts after power and wealth?

C. Socrates is reminded that many seem just but are not and that the real determinants of conduct are not virtues, as such, but the fear of punishment and the expectation of reward. To make this abundantly clear, Glaucon refers to the mythical story of the ring of Gyges.

D. Glaucon asserts that if a just and an unjust man both wore rings that offered the power of invisibility, in time, their conduct would be alike; each would pursue his own desires fearlessly.

    1. Socrates takes on this assertion by tracing out the lives of the two, the just and the unjust. He desires, however, to make this question as large as possible so that it can be seen clearly.

2. Thus, the question is transformed into one regarding the good state, because in important respects, the person and the *polis* are reflections of each other.

IV. As the dialogue proceeds, Socrates places the origin of the state in small communities assembled to satisfy the most basic needs. Success enlarges the community. Specific needs are met by persons trained to perform specific functions. Greater success brings growth and prosperity and the need for defense, that is, guardians.

A. The excellent soldier must be trained, yet training will be useless unless the natural abilities of the potential soldier are substantial. To train guardians, the state must begin with youths of good background and establish a highly disciplined regime of early instruction. Further, to eliminate greed and resentment, there must be no money payments or property ownership in the community, and both wives and children must be possessed in common by the community itself.

B. Glaucon asks how the state will arrange to have a pool of suitable offspring to become guardians, and the scheme Socrates puts forth is pure eugenics, selective breeding for the purpose of acquiring those with the right natural endowments for the vital role of guardian.

C. Glaucon points out to Socrates that even good breeding may produce worthless offspring, and sometimes, mediocre parents have heroic children. Socrates says that undesirable infants are to be exposed. The state has no need for what it cannot use.

V. We now turn to the problem of knowledge as dealt with in Plato's *Republic*, where it figures centrally because Socrates must justify positions that seem to go against what most Athenians would take for granted.

A. The problem of knowledge is illustrated in *Republic* famously in the "allegory of the cave." In the cave, men are shackled and can see only a wall on which shadows are projected; they take the shadows for reality.

1. Being shackled is equivalent to being a material object, being tied to a body.
2. The shadows are taken for real, just as men take their own passions and points of view for the only truth, as Protagoras argues.
3. When one of the prisoners in the cave breaks his chains and climbs to the light, he sees what never before had been seen and begins to recognize that everything he had taken as true was just some shadowy illusion.
4. When this prisoner returns to the cave to inform his cohorts of his experience, they believe that he has been blinded by the light. In the allegory, the "light" is the guidance of the philosopher to universal truths.

B. We begin to recognize that the problem of knowledge is going to return always to a search for what is universally true, for a search for relationships, because it is the relationship that constitutes the true form.
1. The question "What is it that makes a government good?" must be answered in terms of certain relationships that obtain between the governing body and those governed, between the laws and those who are fit for the rule of law, and so on.
2. Justice, too, is understood as the harmonious relationship among the rational, the passionate, and the emotional dispositions of the soul.

C. The *Republic* offers a rigorously behavioristic theory of moral and civic development. Children must be protected, for example, against the corrupting influence of dithyrambic music. Children must also be trained in the disciplines of the good soldier.

D. To return to the story of Gyges, the point of the dialogue is not to examine what people will do if they were able to make themselves invisible. The point of philosophy is to determine how people ought to behave, not how they do behave.
1. Socrates recognizes that people are corporeal entities, inclined by pleasure and pain. He says that we might

regard ourselves as charioteers, pulled by both a good horse and a bad horse.

2. The metaphor of the chariot and the good and bad steed is also found in the Katha Upanishads: "Know now the soul [*atman*] as riding in a chariot. He who lacks understanding, whose mind is not constantly held firm, his sense is uncontrolled, like the vicious horses of a chariot driver."

3. We see from India to Athens this useful metaphor of the impulses of the body being like an untamed steed, pulling us in one direction. Socrates recognizes that we must have a will capable of resolving itself to follow the right course of action.

4. The will itself cannot determine the right course of action, and desire knows only one course of action—that by virtue of which it fulfills itself. How, then, do we discover the right course of action? The answer is through the supremacy of reason, which in turn, is a reflection of our recognition that mathematical proportion, harmony, and balance must be the guides and the goals of life.

Recommended Reading:

Plato. *The Republic* and *Protagoras*, in *The Dialogues of Plato*, 2 vols. B. Jowett, trans. Random House, 1937.

Annas, J. "Classical Greek Philosophy," in *The Oxford History of Greece and the Hellenistic World*. J. Boardman et al., eds. Oxford, 1991.

Questions to Consider:

1. Bertrand Russell, in his *History of Western Philosophy*, regarded the Plato of the *Republic* as a garden-variety fascist. Explain whether this is a sound reading of the dialogue.

2. Conclude whether there has ever been a "philosopher king." Marcus Aurelius comes to mind, and the record he compiled was rather mixed. Explain whether the special talents required for

each of these distinctive vocations is the same or even compatible.

3. Conclude whether virtue can be taught.

Lecture Ten—Transcript

Plato's *Republic*—Man Writ Large

Plato's *Republic* is surely one of the most discussed treatises in the whole history of philosophy, and it has been subjected to both praise and scorn almost without limit. No less a figure than Bertrand Russell—writing the first edition of his *History of Western Philosophy*, and writing this at a time when German bombs were falling on London—tells us that many people have attempted to revere Socrates without quite understanding him, but he, Bertrand Russell, will understand the Socratic program and will find in it nothing but a fascistic and imperious political scheme that freedom-loving people should reject out of hand.

Now, I don't think that was Russell's settled position on Plato's *Republic*, and I do think that the environment of the Second World War may have had something to do with a judgment like that, but, I say, Plato's *Republic* pulls no punches as regards the way states should be constituted, what the state's function is, what the entire purpose of political life is all about. It is thus an extremely influential and very revealing dialogue. Plato's *Republic* gives us any number of insights into the entire epistemological and ethical dimensions of Platonic thought.

It's said to be a foundational work in political science. You can ask any political scientist: "Where does the subject come from?" and the answer is likely to be: "Well, it begins with Plato's *Republic*." I think if you were to probe this a little further, you might come up with a rather different understanding of what the whole point of the dialogue is.

Well, political scientists can appropriate Plato's *Republic* as the foundational work without challenge, here. There is much on the nature of justice, and the character of the just, and well ordered states to be found in that dialogue, but tied to these very considerations is an examination of human nature, its weaknesses, its dominant motives, the features of it that must be controlled, and it is in these respects that Plato's *Republic* is as much a foundational work in psychology as it is in political science.

Book I begins with a group assembling in the house of Cephalus, a wealthy and now older person, an old man, whose son, Polemarchus, is among the group associating with Socrates. Cephalus is getting ready to leave, expressing regrets that he doesn't see Socrates much of late, and the two proceed to have a most interesting conversation about what it is like to reach old age and what the advantages of wealth are. Socrates says his conversations with the aged are useful, for in this way he can find out what awaits him; it's like speaking to those who have completed a voyage that one has yet to take.

Cephalus notes that when old people congregate, their conversations focus on aches and pains, and on the vigor of youth now so utterly spent. He recalls Sophocles having been asked in old age whether he has retained his sensual desires, and the great poet replying that they were gone and that it was as if he had been liberated from a madman, so you get the tone of the discussion between these two chaps.

As for wealth, Cephalus answers directly that as the end of life approaches, one begins to think increasingly of those stories about a time after death when one might be punished for moral failings. A rich man, having no need to cheat or defraud others, tends to have a clearer conscience and, thus, is less fearful of death. Clearly, though, Cephalus is no philosopher, and he seems eager to be on his way before the inevitable disputations commence, and commence they do.

It begins when Socrates tells Polemarchus what he learned from a lecture given by Simonides. He learned that what it means to be just is to pay one's debts. Thus, all are plunged into an examination of justice and what it means for a person to be just. Before the end of Book I, the dialogue has raised the question of whether an unjust person can reach a state of happy and flourishing life.

This is a fundamental question. We very often could pause and ask ourselves: "Well, why should I do anything that's good? Why should I aspire to justice? After all, the unjust seem to make great progress in the world at any time in the world's history."

Note, then, that at least this far into Plato's *Republic*, there is no attention to what we would call "political science" or "statecraft." The focus, instead, is on justice: whether it is a virtue, whether there can be happiness without it, what its defining character is. Now, in seeking to establish what it is that qualifies a person as just, the dialogue begins to explore the motives and desires of persons, and thus stands as a treatise on—what? Psychology, indeed, rather than one on political science.

Thrasymachus and Glaucon assert themselves in Book II, the latter by far the bolder of the two. It is Glaucon who insists that we can't regard justice as "good" until we agree on the sense of something being "good." After all, to say that justice is "good" or a virtue, we have to have some standard or scheme by which to accord goodness to some things, and not to other things.

He forces Socrates to accept three distinct classes of "good things." There are things that are good in and of themselves, independent of their usefulness, such as harmless pleasures. There is another class of good, such as knowledge and health, where what is possessed is not only good in itself but also for the consequences arising from such goods. Finally, there are such goods as exemplified by moneymaking—gymnastics, for example. These are goods that are, in and of themselves, sometimes-disagreeable activities—gymnastics can be fatiguing—but they are pursued for the sake of their results.

Now, in light of these distinctions, Glaucon asks where does Socrates place justice? Socrates will place it in the highest category, where things are desired for their intrinsic value, and not for their consequences, and this then permits the group to debate the point. At bottom, the question has to do with just what it is that makes a man good? Who exemplifies that *kalos anthropos*, that "good man," that Socrates seems to offer as an ideal in a world that lusts after power and wealth.

Glaucon and Thrasymachus remind Socrates that many seem just but are not just, that one might create an appearance to hide a reality and be all the better off for the deception. Further, that the real determinants of conduct are not virtues, as such, but the fear of punishment and the expectation of reward. To make this abundantly clear, Glaucon refers to the mythical story of The Ring of Gyges, and I shall also refer to the story of Gyges's ring.

Now, what is the myth of Gyges and his famous ring? This was a well-known myth at the time, and it has been copied in lore ever since, and there are earlier versions of it, too. Gyges is a shepherd in the service of the King of Lydia. An earthquake takes place, and results in the earth's splitting into a deep crevice. Peering into it, Gyges sees a large bronze horse inside of which is a god-like corpse wearing nothing but a golden ring. Gyges takes the ring, and then he runs from the site.

Assembling later with other shepherds preparing reports for the king, Gyges discovers that he can render himself invisible by twisting the ring. He can make himself appear or disappear at will, so what does he do? This is the question that Socrates is hit with. What does he do? What does Gyges do? He has himself appointed a messenger to the court and, once inside, he uses his new powers to seduce the queen, murder the king, and take command of the realm.

Moreover, Glaucon argues that if there were two such rings, one worn by the just and one worn by the unjust, in time, their conduct would be alike, in that each would pursue his own desires fearlessly. As he says, they would be "like a god among mortals." Just imagine this now: appear and disappear at will.

Following up on this, Adeimantus, Glaucon's brother, insists parents and tutors urge youngsters to be just not for the sake of justice, but for the sake of reputation. All told, then, Socrates's lovely notions about justice are simply unrealistic in the most damaging sense, Socrates here looking like a hopeless idealist.

Now, facing the challenge, Socrates agrees to trace out the life of the two, the just and the unjust, but as "justice" is a term applied both to persons and to states, Socrates suggests this: that the justice of the latter, the justice of states, be examined, for "the larger quantity of justice is more easily visible." If the question, then, is: "What is the nature and fate of the just person?" it is extremely difficult as a question. The subject has a certain obscurity about it—so, Socrates says: "Just as when we confront things in the visible world that are obscure, we sometimes get a much better reckoning by enlarging them. Accordingly, let's enlarge man as much as we can. Let's enlarge man to the size of the *polis* itself, the size of the political community itself, and let's ask ourselves: 'What makes a just and good *polis*?' Now, once we've come to grips with what it is that makes the state good, we'll have a clearer picture of what it is in the person that makes the person just and good."

I am only being playfully controversial when I refer to *Republic* as a foundational treatise in psychology. In fact, Plato would probably be the first to reject the claim that there can be a political science that is not fundamentally a psychological science. Indeed, the dialogues do reject that claim, insisting that you can make no progress with respect to politics, unless you understand the nature of human nature itself, and Aristotle will make the same claim and will defend it systematically.

As the dialogue proceeds, Socrates places the origin of the state in small communities assembled to satisfy the most basic needs. Their success enlarges the community. Specific needs are met by persons trained to perform specific functions—farmers, doctors, cobblers, and artisans. Greater success brings growth and prosperity and the need for defense. Thus, the successful state needs, what? It needs guardians; it needs a Department of Defense, so to speak.

Now, the excellent soldier does not just appear, but actually must be trained. Yet training will be useless unless the natural abilities are substantial, so how is this to be achieved? Well, you cannot get the guardians of the state simply by sampling randomly from the population. You've got to have good material to begin with. You must be able to produce offspring of comparably good material and then establish a highly disciplined regime of early instruction. Moreover, it is necessary to eliminate the major sources of dissention—greed, resentment. Thus, there is to be no money payment or property ownership in this community, and both wives and children are to be possessed in common by the community itself. You begin to see what bothered Bertrand Russell about all this.

Now, how do you get such persons? Glaucon asks: "How could you possibly manage such 'matings' as are likely to yield the best offspring?" A natural question.

"Well," says Socrates, "is not noble youth much like the well-bred dog?" Now, at this, it becomes clear that Socrates means to do what? He means to breed the guardians! Like the well-bred dog, the guardian must be able to sense who is a friend and who is an enemy, be gentle toward the one and fierce toward the other. "Indeed," says Socrates, "he who is to be a really good and noble guardian of the state will unite in himself philosophy, and spirit, and swiftness, and strength."

Glaucon says: "You actually mean we are going to breed these people?" and, indeed, the scheme that Socrates puts forth is pure eugenics, selective breeding for the purpose of acquiring those with the right natural endowments for the vital role of guardian.

Now, In Book V of the *Republic*, Socrates even sets down the strategy: At major festivals and banquets, with the participants somewhat distracted, perhaps softened by drink, the results of the marriage "lottery" are to be announced, but the desired male-female pairs actually have already been chosen. None the wiser, and committed to abide by the results of the lottery, the chosen "breeders" are now at liberty to live as mates.

You do get the picture, here. This is a kind of ruse that will be perpetrated on the unsuspecting. They believe that they are engaged in a purely "chance" kind of lottery. It just turns out that the matings have been set up in the back room, as we think Chicago politics operated for many years.

However, as is pointed out to Socrates, sometimes these good bondings produce worthless offspring, and sometimes, very mediocre parents have heroic children. In that case, says Socrates, the undesirable infants are to be—what? They are to be "exposed," which is to say, exposed to the elements. The state has no need for what it cannot use, and one, again, sees what Bertrand Russell would find so objectionable in this scheme.

I turn now to the problem of knowledge as dealt with in Plato's *Republic*, where it figures centrally, as Socrates must justify positions that seem to go against what most Athenians would take for granted.

The *Republic* is a late-middle dialogue. It's in the nature of these dialogues, as they develop chronologically, that they will take a step back and pick up a strand where they had previously left off, now with newer insights and more sustained discussions.

There is this definite sense in the dialogues being presented as forms of progressive knowledge—getting things better the more one deals with them, and the more obstacles they are required to overcome.

The problem of knowledge is illustrated in *Republic* famously in the "allegory of the cave," and, of course, every introductory philosophy student has to know all about the allegory of the cave. What is offered here, allegorically, is something quite akin to the daunting task that faced Theseus; there he is in the bowels of the labyrinth, but in the allegory of the cave, we actually have chaps who are in something like a labyrinth. They are down in a darkened cave, and they are shackled, so that they can't really turn around. There's no exit available to them. They're sort of locked in place. They are locked in place because their bodies are locked in place. They are tied to their bodies, and their bodies are tied, and there is a parapet, a kind of wall, in front of them—and from behind them, objects are being projected onto that wall: shadowy forms, things that seem to be real to them because they have no standard. The only standard available to them is that sort of Protagoras standard, "each man being the measure of all things."

Well, all right, what I see then is real. I have no standard external to, or superior to, the standard of my own puny experience, my own mere limited self-deceiving, materially bound sense organs; this whole segment is about being bound, do you see? Being arrested, being controlled, being out of self-control. So, for me in this situation, reality is whatever anybody projects on the wall. There isn't anything beyond that wall. There's nothing above it; there's nothing beneath it. All I will ever know—I'm like a puppet in this regard. I'm simply going to be worked in my knowledge claims by whatever the projectionist is doing.

Well, one of these unhappy figures actually breaks loose and starts the long climb up toward the light. Long and arduous is the journey, and there is no Ariadne here for guidance. Once the prisoner confronts the blinding light of day and finally adjusts to it, he begins to see what never before had been seen and begins to recognize that everything he had taken as true was, in fact, some shadowy illusion, some—what? Nearly hallucinatory experience, not unlike what a madman might experience, or a drunk.

Needless to say, his return to the cave, to inform his cohorts about all of these discoveries, must find him judged as having been what? Blinded by the light. "This poor fellow is pathetic. He doesn't realize that everything that's true is right there on the screen in front of his eyes. I wonder what must have happened to him when he climbed out of this reality."

There is so much conveyed by the allegory of the cave. First, being shackled, being tied down, because one is, at least in some sense, a material object. This creates vulnerabilities. It is the fact that gravity keeps our feet on the ground that limits the possibility of transcending the mere material facts of the world. It's being bound by our material selves.

Secondly, darkness and ignorance are the same thing. It's not seeing the truth. Ignorance is life in a cave. You can be in the Waldorf Towers or Buckingham Palace, but if blind to the truth, you are in a cave nonetheless. The actual physical surroundings are entirely irrelevant. You'll recall from the previous lecture my example of a one-year-old child brought to the Battle of Thermopylae, and looking at brave Leonidas, and seeing nothing great or brave because of not being in a position to see such things.

Well, one's surroundings count for nothing except insofar as one has become the sort of person who can see what is truly there, and can read through the purely delusional or distracting elements of the scene, penetrate through these clouds of shadowy and projected forms, and see behind them to the reality that is behind the appearance.

It isn't enough to be rich and famous, or in the right place at the right time if you're the wrong person. To be tone deaf at the Metropolitan Opera is not to hear *La Boheme*; it's to hear sound, and to hear *La Boheme* presupposes certain capacities that have been cultivated and have not atrophied from neglect.

You have, then, at once the shackling of a corporeal being, resisting the very possibility of transcendence, unable to rise above the plane of mere materiality. You've got ignorance as darkness, and you've got that special vulnerability suffered by those who believe whatever they see, and only what they see. Such persons are vulnerable to all of the artifices, the devices, the tricks of the trade—whether it be at the hands of a Sophist or the unscrupulous. Their situation is hopeless because the eyes and ears will never record the truth, and what they do pick up will never be parlayed into the truth—and so, what you've got is simply an experientialist, bumping into one wall and then the other, and regarding contact as proof of reality, all the while missing the very point of life, not even understanding that life has a point.

Now, what is the "light"? When the prisoner finally breaks loose and gets up out of the bowels of the cave and sees other things, well, the allegory here, the metaphor here, of light and knowledge is transparent. There are some things that can only be seen under the light of philosophical examination, under the light of the wise man's guidance.

Then, we begin to recognize that the problem of knowledge is going to get us back always to a search for what is universally true, for a search for relationships, because it is the relationship that constitutes the truth of the thing, the true form of the thing, and that when we are going to ask: "What is it that makes a government a good government?" it's going to be answered in terms of certain relationships that obtain between the governing body and those governed, between the laws and those who become fit for the rule of law, etc., etc.

It's going to be in that pattern of relationships, it's going to be a question of the right form of government, in terms of where authority is properly vested and for what purpose. Justice, too, is understood as the harmonious relationship among the rational, the passionate, and the emotional dispositions of the soul. Always relational. You hear the echo of Pythagoras in this, of course.

What we have here in *Republic* is also a rigorously—I would say, a ruthlessly—behavioristic theory of moral and civic development. Children must be protected against the corrupting influence of, for example, dithyrambic music—today's version being the thumping vulgarities featured in shopping malls and costly automobiles. Children must also be trained in the disciplines of the good soldier, and this requires exposure to martial music and other harmonious forms of sound.

What about Gyges? Well, as for Gyges, Socrates knows about as much about this myth as anyone else does, and would be very much inclined to have that story completed, because Gyges really does fall on horrible times, by the way, it's worth noting; if you're going to base your ethical theory, you probably should finish the thing. If you're going to use the myth, then, you might want to carry it through to its fated moral conclusion.

Well, the point of the dialogue, the point of the dialectical enterprise at large, is not to rediscover what people do. You see here's a moment of pause on this. You've got Glaucon and Adeimantus telling us what Gyges did, and what other people would do, and what Socrates wants to make clear is that you don't engage in the philosophical enterprise to recover the sorts of things people do. We don't need philosophy to discover what people would do if they were able to make themselves invisible. All you have to do to determine what people do is look at them.

The point of philosophy, at least at this juncture, is to determine how people ought to behave, not how they do behave. Thus, from what people do when they can render themselves invisible, nothing of ethical consequence follows. You might be right back in the cave again. You know, from the fact that if everybody in the world were in the cave, and everybody in the world declared that the only reality was the shadowy form being projected on the wall, it certainly would not follow that that's the only reality, and if it really were the case that if everybody in the world could make himself and herself disappear, they would all go off taking control of kingdoms and robbing banks and the like; it certainly would not follow that that is the right form of life. It would only follow that that's what persons of a certain kind do when they can get away with it. It really begs the question. It doesn't answer the question. The question remains, how should we behave? This is surely not answered by anybody who simply tells us how we do behave, so we're back to square one.

Now, in getting back to square one, Socrates says: "Look, Gyges is like all of us, at least in this sense." Of course, we are inclined by pleasure and pain. We are corporeal entities. People tend to do things that please them, and avoid things that cause them suffering. Sometimes, we are so driven by these sensual desires that, in fact, our rational powers are trumped. They are simply overcome; this is very risky. He says, in a sense, we might regard ourselves as charioteers; you know, we are standing in a chariot being pulled by two horses: a good one, and a horse that isn't a good horse.

I want to pursue this point, because here's a Platonic dialogue famously using the chariot driver being pulled by a good horse and one that isn't, and I want to return to the Katha Upanishads. You might recall the Upanishads from the very first lecture in this series, which finds us saying: "Know now the soul, know now the soul [atman] as riding in a chariot. He who lacks understanding, whose mind is not constantly held firm, his sense is uncontrolled, like the vicious horses of a chariot driver."

We see, then, from India to Athens this very useful metaphor of the impulses of the body being like an untamed steed, pulling us in one direction, and in the metaphor as it's used by Socrates, there is this other steed. Look, we do have to be pulled, don't we?

If we are going to do anything, there must be motives and desires, and we must have a will capable of resolving itself, resolving us, to follow the right course of action.

Now, the will itself cannot determine what the right course of action is, and desire knows only one course of action—that by virtue of which it fulfills itself; so, how, then, do we discover the right course of action? Through rational power. It has to be through the supremacy of reason, at least as regards determining what we ought to do.

The supremacy of reason is just a reflection of our recognition that mathematical proportion, harmony, and balance—these are the guides and goals of life. We must avoid excesses. We ought to find that central point, that point of proportionality—I'm inclined to say, that kind of Pythagorean numerological balance that just is the emblem of truth.

Lecture Eleven

Hippocrates and the Science of Life

Scope:

One of the signal achievements of the classical world of the Greeks was the *naturalization* of what had long been absorbed into mysticism, superstition, and magic. The perspective of the natural scientist is nowhere more evident, however, than in the commonsense approach of the Greek medical writers and practitioners whose teachings come down to us in the form of "Hippocratic" treatises. In other societies of the ancient world, medicine was regarded as a part of religion; even among the mass of Greeks, most consulted oracles and believed that disease was visited on the body by the gods in punishment for wrong done (the Christian era would take up this view again). But the Hippocratic *empirikoi*, or empirical practitioners, believed no disease was more divine than another; observation and clinical practice were of the essence; and health was a matter of balance, diet, and the right kind of life.

Outline

I. Hippocrates (469–399 B.C.) falls between Plato and Aristotle and should be dealt with between them, in part, because he and his school promoted a perspective on life that points to Aristotle: the perspective of naturalistic science.

   A. Unlike the civilizations of Persia and Egypt, Hellenism conferred on the priesthood no special insight into matters of a scientific, medical, or philosophical nature.

   B. In all other early societies, medicine was inseparable from magic and religion; in Hellenic society, which never had a religious establishment, it was not.

   1. The ancient Greek medical perspective is nothing short of amazing. The idea that the conditions of health and disease must be understood in a naturalistic, systematic, and scientific way is a great leap forward in the history of ideas.

2. Even in Homeric epics, one finds a matter-of-fact biology as a means by which to understand complex psychological processes: what drives us are conditions in our bodies.

3. The school of Pythagoras, who was, of all the early Greeks, most focused on the abstract and the divine, applied Pythagorean scientific precepts to medicine, treating the soul through the body by diet and a therapeutic regimen.

II. Hellenic society was singular in the ancient world for its tendency to objectify itself—its beliefs, its practices, its thoughts—for the purpose of scrutiny.

A. In doing so, it stands in vivid contrast to an understanding based on revelation or the canons of a religious faith. For the Hippocratic physician, there is no scriptural authority or divine voice to settle naturalistic questions.

B. Note that Hippocratic medicine comes to us in the form of "Hippocratic writing," treatises that were developed over a period of time and not necessarily written by Hippocrates himself.

C. According to these writings, the power of the gods can exert itself in any and all medical conditions; thus, there is no reason to regard any disorder as any more or less "divine" than any other. No disease (e.g., epilepsy) is any more "sacred" than any other.

D. This perspective is available only to those who have not accepted priestcraft as having *epistemological* authority. Whatever problems are to be addressed by oracles and priests, the problem of knowledge is not one of them, at least as this problem arises from the facts of the natural world.

1. If the chief knowledge claims of a society are religious in nature, progress is difficult.

2. Interpretations of reality are in the hands of the priests, and scholarship is confined to the analysis of divinely inspired texts.

E. The Greeks did not lack religious impulses even in their science and philosophy (*vide* Pythagoras), but inquiry was seen as an essential feature of rationality.

    1. The Hippocratic doctors were not skeptical about the gods but about their power in the body.

    2. This is part of the process of the secularization of knowledge that the Greeks would bequeath to philosophy and science.

III. The dominant school of Greek medicine as early as the 6th century B.C. is that practiced by the *empirikoi*, those who base their diagnoses and treatments on *observation* rather than theory and theology.

A. When the Hippocratics call themselves *empirikoi*, it is to distinguish themselves from those who consult oracles to discover the causes of disease and who think that disease—particularly mental and psychological disease—has been visited upon them for things they have done.

B. This attitude, rare in the following centuries, would be noticeable in Eastern Christianity, which was still in touch with Greek thought when Western Christianity considered epilepsy and madness punishment for sins.

IV. If one is to promote the health and well-being of the body, then one must raise the question of what it is that controls the affairs of the body. It is interesting to note how late in the game it was that naturalistic philosophy actually spoke of organs and systems in the body.

A. Even as recently as Aristotle—and Aristotle is one of the pioneering figures in the history of biology and natural science—we don't get the sense of the body as a collection of integrated systems.

B. The Hippocratics were quite correct, however, in identifying the brain as the part of the body in which sensory and rational processes are grounded. In contrast, Aristotle regarded the central mission of the brain to be the regulation of the temperature of the blood.

V. The naturalization of medicine was not singular in Greek culture; in politics and philosophy as well, naturalistic and scientific attitudes were cultivated by leading thinkers.

   A. These were not, however, the attitudes of most Greeks. The Greek man or woman in the street was a believer in magic and witchcraft, oracles and superstitions.

   B. Many Greeks were suspicious of philosophers. Aristophanes mocked them; the Athenians executed Socrates and forced Aristotle into exile.

   C. But there was also tolerance. Major figures gained and kept respect; for generations, the wealthy sent their children to be taught by men whom they saw not as wise so much as learned, men who knew useful arts of life.

   D. A perfectionist ideal spread widely through the population, resulting in support of all forms of excellence. Perfection was something to be prized, even when one didn't quite understand it or when one might find it dangerous.

   E. The statues of Phidias represent not the ordinary Greeks who looked up at them, but that ideal of humanity perfect in mind and body that the Greeks acknowledged. This legacy of perfectionism has come down to us today in such achievements as the space program, in which the integration of intelligence and courage, science and virtue, has resulted in humans reaching the moon.

Recommended Reading:

Hippocrates. "On the Wounds of the Head," in *Hippocrates*, W. Jones, trans. Putnam, 1923.

Lloyd, G., ed. *Hippocratic Writings*. Penguin, 1978.

Questions to Consider:

1. The Hippocratic physicians were successful, though they distinguished their efforts from those of magicians, sorcerers, and even philosophers. Summarize what their success says about the general attitudes prevailing in Athens circa 430–330 B.C.

2. Explain what the place of philosophy and religion should be in a therapeutic setting that is intended to be "holistic."

Lecture Eleven—Transcript

Hippocrates and the Science of Life

In this lecture, I want to pause, in a manner of speaking, between Plato and Aristotle for a separate lecture on Hippocrates and Greek medicine in general, and that, for several reasons, is worth recounting at the outset.

Chronologically, the dates for Hippocrates of Kos are just about the same as Socrates's own dates; approximately 469 B.C. for his birth—we're not quite sure when Hippocrates was born, but it must have been very close to 469—and, with more confidence, the date of his death being 399, so he overlaps nearly perfectly with Socrates.

Second, the movement from Plato and the Academy to Aristotle is a movement very much in the direction of natural science and a natural-science perspective on the nature of things, and Greek medicine had much to do with promoting that perspective.

Third, and as is well known, Aristotle's father was a physician, and I'm inclined to think that in all the subjects that Aristotle developed and mastered and invented, he was most at home with the biological disciplines, although he did not pursue a professional career in medicine.

Finally, the school of Hippocrates and Greek medicine in general provide us with a clearer picture of what it means to analyze, and secularize, and naturalize a subject that, in other cultures and civilizations, generally was subsumed under and even answerable to religion, priestcraft, magic, and superstition.

In this respect, I don't think one would be guilty of hyperbole in declaring the ancient Greek medical perspective almost a miracle of types. It is virtually without precedent when you examine the ancient medical writings on diseases and disorders. They are often astonishingly close to what we would take to be a contemporary view of things. The widest range of disorders—including epilepsy, seizures, bouts of madness, perceptual and motor deficits—is thoroughly bound up with conditions of the body, with diet, with hereditary predispositions, with traumatic injuries.

What is so remarkable about this is that if you look at any other age, even the great age of Egyptian medicine, medical views are inseparable from religious beliefs and customs, which is to say with what is—to put the matter in a descriptive but respectful way—mystical and even superstitious perspectives. In this light, we can say that one of the great ideas, as it were, in the history of ideas, is the idea that the conditions of health and disease—whatever form the diseases take—are to be understood in a naturalistic, systematic, scientific way. If that's not a great idea in philosophy, I want to see what is—philosophy in the broader sense.

Here, Greek medicine is tracking something that is already present in Hellenic thought. Indeed, it is already present in Homer. Homer, you will recall, tends to account for the behavior of the heroes in terms of conditions taking place in their bodies. The death scenes in *Iliad* are so graphic in describing precisely which organs fall out and when the sword has been removed—the graphic elements in *Iliad* are graphic to the point of being ghoulish, but more than simply reporting how death is attendant upon particular destruction of organs and systems within the body, there is also the psychobiological form of explanation that the Homeric epics provide, telling us why someone is driven or possessed; one is guided by *thumos*; or *epithumia*; by *lyssa*, the "wolf's rage," and these always have reference to something taking place—where? In the body. Thus, there is already, as early as the Homeric epics, a *naturalistic* tendency in the matter of how one is to explain significant human undertakings.

With Pythagoras, of course, we have a philosopher whose subject is nature, and for all of the transcendental elements of Pythagorean thought, there is a Pythagorean school of medicine, and there is great attention paid to the health of the body and to the bodily regimens, because, after all, the body is the house of the soul, and there is a communication between the two such that one can, in fact, corrupt one's spiritual element corporeally. This is what is behind the vegetarianism of the sect, its ritual performances, its therapeutic regimen. You treat the soul through musical harmonies, through the right dietary regimen, the right exercises—you treat the soul by treating the body. I say even with Pythagoras, then, who surely would be the most transcendental of the medical or quasi-medical practitioners of 6th-century B.C., there is this hefty dose of naturalistic thinking.

Now, I want to get behind the naturalism, to what I submit impels naturalism and a naturalistic outlook.

In a truly remarkable way, Hellenic civilization objectified itself. Hellenic civilization took itself—its central values, its core beliefs, its most committed desires and aspirations as a culture—both at the level of the *polis* and the level of the person, and externalized all of this, objectified it for the purpose of critical scrutiny.

This is not a natural sort of thing to do, which is probably why it took so long for it to happen at all, and here I return briefly to the question: "What is philosophy, and did the Greeks invent it?"

Think for a moment about how we go through life as subjects of our own experiences. The thoughts we have are the thoughts we have; there is not something external whispering to us about these thoughts. They are just thoughts, and desires, and motives. We do not stop in our tracks at a certain point and say: "Wait. I shall treat all this as if it were 'out there.' I'm going to take these desires, and thoughts, and beliefs, and convictions, and I'm going to undertake a critical examination of the entire process—and similarly with events arising in my own body."

I say, this is not the commonsense tendency or customary in any way across cultures. It is a process of objectification, and of the secularizing of knowledge. In this, it is in vivid contrast to such insights and understandings based on revelation, based on the wisdom of prophets, the canons of a religious faith. For the Hippocratic physician—as with his contemporaries in philosophy and contemporaries in mathematics and the natural sciences—there is no scriptural authority, no priestly hermeneutic, no divine voice that will settle matters once and for all. The view, instead, calls for us to externalize things, put them in the only world that is accessible to us, which is the natural world, and view them as facts to be explored.

Regarding the Hippocratic medicine—what comes down in the form of "Hippocratic writing"—the corpus of Hippocratic writing certainly was not put together by Hippocrates himself—these are treatises that were developed over a period of time. Whether he wrote any of them remains unsettled. However, that the writings, indeed, are richly indebted to Hippocrates's teachings, there is no doubt, so let me refer then to Hippocratic writings, rather than to what Hippocrates might have said or written.

Consider now how the Hippocratic physicians understood what their contemporaries referred to as "the sacred disease," for this is characteristic of the perspective and the achievements of the Hippocratic school. The Hippocratic physicians are not skeptical about religion and the gods—not at all. Rather, they're skeptical about understanding health and disease in the idiom of the sacred. Thus, when the question is taken up as to the nature of the so-called "sacred disease," the Hippocratic writers are not saying: "Well, there are no gods; therefore, there are no sacred diseases."

No, they are saying: "Well, look, religious teaching tells us that the gods are capable of producing anything and everything. Therefore, there is no one disease that is any more divine than any other"—so, in a manner of speaking, you can hold the religious account constant, because these will figure indifferently in everything. Therefore, there is no point in singling out one kind of disorder and saying: "Ah, the gods are the ones responsible for that," or, "That one is bequeathed directly or inflicted directly by the Olympians."

Now, this perspective becomes a perspective available only to those who have not accepted priestcraft as having *epistemological* authority. Whatever problems are to be addressed by oracles and priests, the problem of knowledge is not one of them, at least as this problem arises from the facts of the natural world, and I do want to underscore this. It is a point worth repeating.

Something momentous takes place when a culture takes the position that the problem of knowledge is essentially a religious problem, and invests its credulity in a denominated group of official interpreters whose judgments on matters of this kind are taken to be incorrigible. Here I do not presume to weigh the claims of religion and the claims of the secular world. My own guess is that for every secularly produced fact, there may be some profound religious truth on which it depends, but here, the complexity of the case and the shortness of life incline me, at any rate, to silence.

What I am testing, instead, are the implications that follow, depending on which of the positions is taken as a person or culture sets about to solve problems arising from life in the real world. Once one confers on a select and denominated group ultimate epistemological authority on core questions arising from the problem of knowledge, the nearly inevitable result is philosophical paralysis, and what is more likely to happen is positions will become quite hardened, and the only thing left for scholarship is to interpret the words of the wise; so, the entire debate now is not a debate about the nature of truth, but about how a text or holy maxim is to be understood. What the leaders of thought in the ancient Greek world might be inclined to say is that this may be the best way to get to heaven, but surely not to the moon.

The Hellenic world was scarcely—well, devoid—of religious influences on all aspects of thought and practice. No question about it. Religion is a central fact of ancient Greek life. Consider again Pythagoras, who was a man of great spiritual devotion, a man whose mathematics is seeking to rise to the level of the divine.

In Homer as well—whether it's *lyssa* or *thumos* or anything else invading the body—Homer leaves ample room for the realm of spirit to operate, and to operate powerfully, according to its own principles, these being obscure, powerful, and chthonic. I said in an earlier lecture that the ancient Greek world never had an official religion, but it was also never an entirely secular world, either. There is a remarkable integration of the secular and the religious in this robust and flourishing culture in the 5th and early 4th centuries B.C.

Nonetheless, the Hippocratics give us a particularly useful example of a science liberated from religious orthodoxies, an example matched by the productive scholarship of that same period in natural science, political science, psychology, and associated subjects. This is not to say that Hippocratic medicine was superior to what might have been found in Egypt even 500 or 1,000 years earlier, but it is to say that it was based on an entirely different set of presuppositions.

Now, throughout these lectures and in philosophy in general, there is a term that is quite commonly used to identify a particular approach to the problem of knowledge. The term is: "empirical." We often hear that one is engaged in "empirical research." We describe a philosopher as being "an empiricist." We say that science is an essentially "empirical enterprise."

Now, what do we mean when we use this word? "Empirical" is grounded in the ancient Greek word *empeiros*, which simply means "observation." Now, the Hippocratic physicians describe themselves as *empirikoi*, each one of them being an *emperikos*. In this, they meant to convey that their remedies were based on what had been observed, on what had been observed to be effective, not on some grand theory by which remedies were allegedly deducible. Now, today, if a physician is asked about how medical science approaches disease, the reply is likely to be something like: "Well, the approach of medical science is empirical," meaning based on clinical observations that tell us that when a particular condition is treated in a particular way, certain consequences follow. Those consequences that promote health are taken to be the right kind of therapy, and those consequences that don't do that, or make conditions worse, are then abandoned. Nowhere in the approach do we find overriding, overarching, non-scientific theories or beliefs driving the entire practice.

When Dr. Hippocrates says: "I am an *emperikos*," then, he's contrasting what he's doing with an approach that has one consulting oracles, or engaging in certain ritual acts, appealing to priests or holy men to intercede with the gods to relieve symptoms. Needless to say, one who believes that the symptoms themselves have been visited upon the victim presumably because of something the victim has done—there is little distinction between the concept of illness and that of a just dessert. After all, if the gods see fit to punish one directly by imposing some kind of disease on one because of something one has done—well, this almost looks like Olympian justice.

As for the notion of disease as evidence of sin, it would be perilous to believe that all this was left behind in remote antiquity. We don't want to exaggerate the richness of the Hippocratic view. Later in these lectures, I will consider the period 1400 to 1700, when the witch panics and the witch persecutions were common in Europe, and I will then return to some of the non-scientific, non-medical perspectives on why it is that certain people have certain disorders.

Let me just point out here, though, that the witch persecutions went on for not only 300 years, but primarily in periods we describe as a "Renaissance," then followed by the "great age of science." Witches are being executed in the age of Newton, and Galileo, and Descartes. This is not only a bleak chapter in social history, but a fairly recent chapter as well, and it draws attention, then, to the very size of that part of the Hellenic achievement, which I've referred to as the "objectification" of the self and the natural world.

Now, I want to go to yet another period, here, now, the first several centuries A.D., and particularly with respect to those forms of illness that we would describe as mental illness, madness, or forms of illness that seem to attack the spiritual or psychic side of life.

Of course, central among these was epilepsy. How do you account for someone falling to the ground and engaging in all sorts of fitful behavior? If anything looks like a visitation from powerful spirits, that does. Now, how a condition like that was understood in the early Christian period really depended on where in the Christian world you were, either Eastern or Western.

If in the East, where the influence was primarily the influence of the Hippocratics and Aristotelian science, a condition like epilepsy was understood the way we might regard a viral attack. "Well, it's something that happens to people, a condition of the body." Indeed, possession was understood the same way. Witches were understood in the same way. To be possessed was to have—I speak metaphorically here—to have a kind of bug. It was something that could pass with time, or maybe not. It could be a persistent bug.

If, however, you were positioned within Western Christianity during this early period—which is a much more theory-driven world, indeed, a world driven by highly rationalistic understandings of religion and the world itself—then all sorts of hypotheses come to be welded together, very much to the disadvantage of the sufferer, whose condition was likely to be understood as a kind of retribution for wickedness.

For example, consider the Salic Laws of the 7th century. One is permitted to dissolve his marriage if, after marriage, one's wife becomes insane—and how is this madness explained by the law, by Salic Law? She is mad—and I quote from the Salic Law—"because of her grave sins." Blaming the victim here is not a thoughtless act; it is a theory-driven act, according to which the body takes on conditions as a result of divine, spiritual, or unnatural influences.

Thus, I say again, the Hippocratic achievement is a central one in the history of ideas. It's part of the larger program of naturalizing the natural world and having us understand it in its own terms. This required uncommon intellectual integrity and discipline. There is a philosophy of medicine behind the Hippocratic medical teachings, and it is Greek philosophy—for at this time, there is no other.

Now if one is to promote the health and well-being of the body, then one has to raise the question of what it is that controls the affairs of the body. It might be of some interest to note how late in the game it was that naturalistic philosophy actually spoke out organs and systems in the body. There is much talk, as early as Homer, about certain fluids and humors, and things that flow around the body. There is talk about blood everywhere, except where the gods are concerned—for their immortal veins are filled with *ichor*—a distinct advantage, by the way.

However, even as recently as Aristotle—and Aristotle is one of the pioneering figures in the history of biology and natural science—we don't really have the sense of the body as a collection of integrated systems. He certainly knows about the organs of the body—he has actually done dissections—but we don't get accounts that by today's lights we would call "physiological" accounts: accounts of integrated systems functioning in a certain way. That actually comes later, and I should think one of the early leading figures in that whole line of thought would be Galen, in the 2nd century A.D., about whom more will be said later.

I don't want to gild the lily, then, and suggest that this naturalistic, Hippocratic perspective was utterly modern. Rather, it is a bridge to the modern. It's a bridge to science. It is a secularization of an enterprise that indeed should be secularized—namely, the natural functions of the body in health and disease.

The Hippocratics also were quite correct against even such formidable people as Aristotle in identifying the brain as the part of the body in which sensory and rational processes are grounded. The disordered, or destroyed, or traumatically insulted brain is the condition that reliably gives rise to events that today we would call pathological: sensory losses, the dragging of a leg, the paralyzed limb, blindness, deafness, unconsciousness.

In their clinical observations, the Hippocratics actually observed certain structure-function relationships tying the brain to specific sensory, motor, and cognitive abilities, and, of course, Aristotle, as we shall see, was finding some of this located more in the chest and the heart than in the brain. Aristotle famously regarded the mission of the brain to be the regulation of the temperature of the blood, so I sometimes say to students that Aristotle had a good head on his shoulders, though he tended to think of it as a kind of refrigerator. Today's leaders of thought tend to believe that the brain is essentially a computational device. Now, if I were forced to choose between the computer model and the refrigeration model, I am not quite sure which one I might find more suspect, but I will leave this for a lecture much later in this course of lectures.

Now, the ancient Greek medical writers and practitioners were not a breed apart. They were part of a community of thinkers, naturalistic in their orientation. Whether the topic was politics are ethics, the conduct of daily life, or the conduct of foreign affairs, there is a realism here, a kind of common-sense realism, that we find in the Hellenic world and that would be rare even today, and this leads me to an observation that can't be stressed enough: The celebrated figures of this age were in a conspicuous minority.

Let us recall that Socrates is not made philosopher-king, but is put to death. Aristotle, as it happens, leaves Athens just in time to avoid what probably would have been a similar fate. As Diogenes Laertes will say, when asked: "Why are you leaving?" Aristotle allegedly replied: "So that this city will not sin against philosophy a second time." The ancient Greek so-called "man in the street" is not to be confused with Hippocrates, Aristotle, Sophocles, Euripides, Plato, and the rest. We can satisfy ourselves that this would be an uncommon group in any age. The Athenian citizen is given to mystical beliefs, rank superstitions, prejudices, and ritualistic performances that surely would look almost preposterous by contemporary lights.

A deep suspicion toward philosophers was played upon by Aristophanes in plays like *Clouds*, where philosophers are found to be speculating either on what nobody can know, or speculating in a way that the man in the street, the so-called rider of the Clapham omnibus, would regard as simply ridiculous. Philosophers were very often held up to scorn. In the developed world of ancient Rome, subject to Greek tutors and Greek high culture, when things took a bad turn, who was exiled? The philosophers. The first thing the Romans did was to get the philosophers out of town, "the source of all our problems."

Thus, we want to say about this great age of Hellenic philosophy, art and architecture, medicine, and science, that it really was the work of the few. Now you might say, of course: "Well, inevitably it is the work of the few; how many Newtons are there?" However, it's not the work of the few, not in the sense that genius is rare, but in the sense that the perspective developed was not widely shared.

There is a leavening effect that I would also like to note in this connection. Notwithstanding the observations that I've just summarized, there was also an element of uncommon tolerance in the Hellenic world. Perhaps more positive than tolerance, there was a perfectionist ideal that did spread widely through the population, and that resulted in support of all forms of excellence—whether in sport, or in art, or in philosophy and science. Poets and dramatists competed for prizes and entered into contests in the Olympiads, which included recitations of literary works. The better families sent their children off to be instructed by philosophers, not judged so much to be wise men as to be learned: in the art and science, and in the science of the arts, in the art and the science of rhetoric, for example.

Aristotle tells us in his own treatise on the subject of rhetoric that of all the aspects of rhetoric that render it most effective, that which renders it most effective of all, is the perceived standing of the speaker himself, and this, I say, does finally get to the heart of the common-sense realism that surfaces and occasionally abounds in the ancient Greek world. When all is said and done, the ancient Greek is inclined to look at that which seems to approximate an ideal, a perfection ever more closely, as something to be prized, even when one doesn't quite understand it, and even when one might find in it something pernicious, or even dangerous.

Again, there is this perfectionist feature in ancient Greek thought and life, surfacing in the art and architecture of the period, but also in the science and the philosophy and mathematics of the period. We do have the picture of often poorly nourished, overworked, pimply, orthopedically disordered persons looking up at statues done by Polycleitus and Phidias and seeing the exemplification of divine perfection. They honor and revere it. These are not statues of the average Greek citizen, but intimations of the possibilities available to lives that aspire to perfection itself.

Perfectionism has worked its way through Western civilization, and even in its current and tarnished form is exemplified by achievements—it is always risky to single out an achievement, but by such achievements as the space program, for example, where you have to put together the greatest intelligences and technical sophistication in engineering, physics, and theoretical science, along with astronauts whose bodies have been conditioned for the task they confront.

This utter integration of confidence and science, medical examinations, gymnastics, and courage and virtue come together and result in—what? Mere *Homo sapiens* trotting upon the dust of the moon. This is as much a reflection of what Hellenism bequeathed as anything we can find today.

Lecture Twelve
Aristotle on the Knowable

Scope:

One of the greatest minds the world would host, Aristotle laid the foundations for most of the subjects to which science and scholarship have been devoted ever since. He was the greatest biologist, logician, political theorist, and ethicist of his age, and no one in any age could lay claim to so wide a range of original contributions.

Thus, he records his confidence in *empirical* approaches to the problem of knowledge. The son of a physician and himself keenly interested in the facts of the natural world, Aristotle was a tireless observer and classifier, his research covering all the sciences and especially the biological. A student in Plato's Academy for nearly 20 years, Aristotle was always deeply respectful of Platonic thought, but his own approach would depart in significant ways. Aristotle was the first to develop systematic definitions and methodologies applicable to the study of nature, of ethics and politics, and of psychology. Knowledge begins with the desire to know and with the exercise of our powers of observation, but developed knowledge goes beyond observation and arrives at universal laws.

Outline

I. Aristotle (384–322 B.C.) begins the *Metaphysics* with the observation: "All men by nature desire to know. An example is the delight we take in our senses. For even quite apart from their usefulness, they are loved for their own sake, and none more than the sense of sight."

   A. There is an essentially instinctive desire for knowledge common to all creatures, which is necessary if they are to survive. Aristotle is too much the natural scientist to dismiss the information gleaned by the senses.

   B. Nature does nothing by chance, and we have obviously been fitted out with senses in order to be guided by them.

C. As an opening statement, the first sentences of the *Metaphysics* are a vindication of knowledge gleaned by perception. That this is incomplete there is to be no doubt, but if we are to engage the problem of knowledge, perception—a sensory awareness of the world around us—must be our starting point.

   1. In his naturalistic works on animals, Aristotle assigns to perception many powers and functions we are inclined to subsume under such headings as "intelligence" or "cognition."

   2. In doing so, he grants to the animal kingdom rich perceptual powers that go well beyond elementary sensory functions, but he will then deny the animal kingdom that culminating and defining rational power reserved to the human psyche.

D. This leads us to Aristotle's understanding of the various powers that the animal kingdom comes equipped with and a scheme of classification that will distinguish between and among animal types in terms of these powers or faculties.

   1. Aristotle begins with the kind of question a scientist would ask when seeking a reasonable basis on which to divide the living from the inanimate realms. What is the fundamental power (*dynamis*) in virtue of which a living thing has life? What is it that the soul (*psyche*) of an entity must posses by way of animation such that life itself becomes possible?

   2. The basic powers are nutritive, reproductive, and locomotor (even some plants have the latter).

   3. Animals are differentiated by having the power of sensation: the power of perception, of acting consciously in response to events in the external world.

   4. These basic functions of nutrition, reproduction, locomotion, and sensation are all powers of the soul (*psyche*). As used by Aristotle, this word is a generic term for those processes that are life-giving and life-sustaining.

5. With more complex animal forms, to these powers of the soul is added some kind of intellectual or intelligent power: the power of problem solving. Aristotle grants this to much of the animal kingdom; they have that in common with us.

E. Aristotle reserves to human beings, however, a psychic power or faculty of a special kind. It is usually rendered in English as "reason," but the word he uses in his treatise *On the Soul* is *epistemonikon*, meaning the cognitive ability by which we comprehend universal propositions.

    1. *Epistemonikon* is a special feature of rationality, fitting us uniquely for, among other things, the rule of law itself. After all, what is the rule of law except the ability to apply some universal precept to an indefinitely large number of individual instances, each qualifying as, for example, "theft"?

    2. It is in virtue of this rationality that we become fit for a mode of political, social, and civic life that is unavailable to other "types" within the kingdom of life.

II. Given that we have these faculties and powers, how will Aristotle understand and approach the problem of knowledge? For Aristotle, to know something is essentially to know the cause of it; that is, to have a systematic, scientific understanding of things (*episteme*) is to know the causes by which things are brought about.

A. In effect, Aristotle says that a claim that someone knows that a right-angle triangle has 180 degrees can be understood in one of two ways.

    1. A person may know that a triangle has 180 degrees because she has measured the angles and sees that their sum is 180 degrees, or she may know that *by definition* a triangle has 180 degrees and, thus, knows this of all triangles without measuring any of them.

    2. What is the difference between the knowledge of one sort and the other? In one case, what is known is known by experience and does not rise to the level of *episteme*. In contrast, developed knowledge, such as could be gained by studying geometry, is a knowledge of the regulative principles and laws that govern the affairs of things, not simply factual knowledge of this or that.

B. Of course, to say that knowledge requires an understanding of the causes of things is to raise a question about just what a cause is. "Causation" can be understood in several senses.

    1. Every identifiable thing that exists is made of some particular material and could not exist except as a result of that material. The marble of which a statue is made is, thus, the *material* cause.

    2. Every such thing is recognizable as a given type or form of thing. This "form," then, must be present for the thing to be what it is. In this respect, the shape of the statue and its resemblance to an original is its *formal* cause.

    3. But form is imparted to matter by strokes and blows and other forms of mechanical influence. The shape of the statue is carved out of the stone by chisel and hammer; these are the *efficient* cause of the statue.

    4. The ultimate understanding of the object stems from the intelligent design that the object itself realizes. Aristotle refers to this as the *final* cause—that is, the final thing realized in time, although it is first in conception.

C. Truly developed knowledge embraces not only the material, efficient, and formal causes, but the *that for the sake of which* these causes were recruited. To understand x is to know *what x is for*, what its purpose or end, its *telos*, is. Thus does Aristotle seek *teleological* explanations as ultimate.

D. Questions of what things are *for* are also central to Aristotle's ethical and political thought. We have purposes and ends as the kinds of beings we are; how are those to be reached? How does the *polis* aid or hinder those ends?

    1. Our knowledge of ourselves must be grounded in a respect for just what our defining abilities achieve because these very abilities reveal the *that for the sake of which*....

2. The developed knowledge that we have leads us to an understanding that the things of the universe, including living things, instantiate a plan; they fit in. Nature does not do things without a purpose. The ultimate question for understanding, then, is: "How does this fit into things? What is it for? What purpose does it serve?"

3. We know at the outset that nothing with pattern and design comes about accidentally. As Aristotle says, "If the art of shipbuilding were in the wood, we would have ships by nature." Wood, however, is the material cause of the ship, and the workers who build the ship are its efficient cause.

4. The art of shipbuilding is finally in the ship's designer. It is the designer who knows what ships are for and how that purpose is served by the right materials, rightly assembled. To "know" in this sense is to comprehend far more than anything conveyed by the mere material composition of an object.

III. As a final point, we must note one other aspect of Aristotle's philosophy of explanation that is often misunderstood.

    A. Aristotle argues that a thoroughly scientific explanation is one that includes a universal principle of which the thing to be explained is an instance, something that is always the case. We do not fully understand any event unless we can show it to be an example of some universal principle of which it is an instance.

    B. When Aristotle writes on biological subjects, as well as psychological and social matters, he inserts a qualifier: *hos epi to polu*, which is best rendered as "for the most part," "by and large," or "in general."

    C. In other words, Aristotle teaches us to expect precision only to the extent that the subject at hand admits of it and to seek no more precision that what the subject at hand will admit of. When we examine complex social, political, and moral phenomena, we look for general precepts that are right by and large, in general, and for the most part.

Recommended Reading:

Barnes, J. ed. *The Complete Works of Aristotle*, 2 vols. Princeton, 1984, especially the treatises "Physics," "On the Soul," and Book I of *Metaphysics*.

Robinson, D. N. *Aristotle's Psychology*. Columbia, 1989.

Robinson, D. N. *An Intellectual History of Psychology*, 3rd ed. Wisconsin University Press, 1995, chapter 3.

Questions to Consider:

1. Evolutionary theory offers explanations that are "teleological." Explain how these differ from Aristotle's explanations.

2. Conclude whether the fitness of animals for the environments they confront establishes an intelligent or rational plan for the animal kingdom.

3. Modern science tends to limit explanations to those based on *efficient* causation. Conclude whether this really *explains* phenomena.

Lecture Twelve—Transcript

Aristotle on the Knowable

I've occasionally said to classes that if I had to single out any event as evidence of some civilization in a distant galaxy beyond the Milky Way taking pity on us for the slow progress of the human imagination in dealing with its problems, the evidence might well be the life of Aristotle and his accomplishments. It's almost as if such a distant galactic neighbor might have said: "For goodness' sake, those human beings don't seem to be getting on with it at all. Aristotle, why don't you go down there and get things going?"

There is so much in Aristotle that is original that, inevitably, much would be subject to criticism in subsequent centuries, but the sheer intellectual power of this man—expressing itself in biology, natural science, ethics, politics, metaphysics, and logic—is simply without parallel in the history of thought. There is almost no academic or scholarly subject commonly taught that does not bear the stamp of his influence, sometimes so utterly and durably that we had to get rid of the stamp in order to see further or more clearly, and perhaps progress beyond the point where Aristotle had left the subject.

No single lecture, then, or even a full course of lectures, can do justice to the breadth and depth of his accomplishments, but maybe a sketch will encourage further inquiries into the fuller picture. Aristotle was the son of a physician. In biology, we might guess, he had a particularly strong grounding, but surely in a far wider range of subjects. Though not an Athenian, he enters as a student in Plato's Academy, where he remains for nearly 20 years—and this, assuredly, is not because he was a slow learner.

He stays within the Platonic circle, where he would have surely been expected to compose dialogues, and there is evidence that his earliest writings were in the dialogue form. All of the students at the Academy had to do that. Those writings have not been found. In fact, such accounts as we can put together of what he did write, or at least notes taken on his lectures—the treatises that he actually is responsible for—indicate that we have only a small fraction of the total output of this fertile, searching intelligence.

Accordingly, one answer to the question: "What is Aristotle's position on x, or y, or z?" must be qualified to acknowledge that his firmest or final position might appear in works that we may never find.

I should begin with a few words about that treatise of Aristotle's that came to be called his *Metaphysics*. It is one of the greatest works in the history of philosophy. It has a feature, actually, that is sometimes overlooked. It is also the first treatise that serves as a critical history of philosophy, and it reflects a quite regular part of Aristotle's method: You begin a work by noting what others have had to say on the same subject, note what was either unexamined or poorly executed by earlier writers, and then, you begin to develop your own arguments. This is a standard approach in Aristotle.

In the *Metaphysics* especially, he sets down the teachings of a wide range of Socratic and pre-Socratic teachers. He tries to give a fair hearing to views we come to know are radically different from his own, and in this he is generally successful. He obviously has his own program and agenda, and this does color some of his presentation of competing views. Still, the *Metaphysics* remains the earliest systematic presentation of the ideas that were dominant in the several schools of pre-Socratic and Hellenic thought, in general.

However, the work opens, begins, on a new and different note, and I quoted part of this opening passage in a previous lecture. How does the *Metaphysics* begin, this utterly deep and penetrating inquiry? It begins this way:

> All men by nature desire to know. An example of this is the delight we take in our senses. For even apart from their usefulness, they are loved for their own sake, and none more than the sense of sight.

Here is the commencement of the *Metaphysics*: "All men by nature desire to know"—so he already accepts that there is an inexplicable impulse within us to acquire knowledge of the world, and then, in a nearly offhand way, he says straight out that the evidence for this universal inclination is, what? The delight we take in our senses. Thus, here at the outset, we discover that this long-term student of Plato's is not to offer a philosophy that depreciates the senses. Aristotle is too much the biologist, too much the natural scientist, too much the man with both feet on the ground, to be dismissive of the information gleaned by the senses.

Not only that, but famously Aristotle will argue that nature produces nothing without a purpose for it, that chance is not the operative principle in the universe, and that things are to be understood in terms of the purposes and ends they serve. Nature certainly would not have fitted out animals with sensory organs for the sole purpose of deceiving the entire animal kingdom, and, indeed, if that had been the design of nature—the senses as paths to deception—creatures would not be able to get from one side of the road to the other. Therefore, we already see in the very opening of the *Metaphysics* something of a commonsense, naturalistic perspective in a work that is otherwise probably the most subtle of Aristotle's philosophical writings.

As an opening statement, the first sentence of the *Metaphysics*—the opening sentences—are a veritable vindication of knowledge gleaned by perception. That this is incomplete there is no doubt, but if we are to engage the problem of knowledge with any hope of success, perception must be the starting point. The starting point for our journey toward the truth is a sensory awareness of the world around us. In fact, in other works, Aristotle will define the very essence of "animal" as such as "that which has sensation." The very power that establishes an entity as an animal is the capacity for sensation.

In his naturalistic works on the parts and the history of animals, Aristotle assigns to perception many powers and functions that we would be inclined to subsume under such headings as "intelligence" or "cognition," and in doing so, he grants to the animal kingdom rich perceptual powers that go well beyond elementary sensory functions, but he will then deny the animal kingdom that culminating and defining rational power that he regards as reserved to the human psyche alone.

Now, this is less Aristotle depreciating the animal kingdom, as elevating the role of perception in the affairs of life and in adaptation to the demands of the environment. Animals are not depreciated for want of rationality, because their perceptual resources include much that we would take to be rich, cognitive power and ability.

Now, because there is something joyous about perceptual experience itself and the knowledge thereby gained, Aristotle dilates on perceptual modes of knowledge. This all becomes possible because we are constituted biologically in such a way as to be able to pick up information from the external world. That's what the sense organs are all about, and this leads us to Aristotle's understanding of the various powers that the animal kingdom comes equipped with, and a scheme of classification that will distinguish between and among animal types in terms of these "powers" or "faculties." Now, "power" or "faculty" in the Greek is *dynamis*. We get the word "dynamic" from this. For example, "the power to walk" would be the *dynamis* for walking, and the English word "dynamic" is etymologically arising from that Greek word, and all variations of "dynamic," "dynamism," etc.

Now, if we are to have self-knowledge, or knowledge of other forms of life, we must have some basis on which to assign various forms of life to proper categories. Just where do human beings fit in the great scheme of things? What's so different about us versus rabbits?

Aristotle begins with the kind of question a scientist would ask when seeking a reasonable basis on which to divide the living from the inanimate realms. What is the fundamental power in virtue of which a living thing has life? There's the core question. How do you know you're in the realm of the living to begin with? What has to be there? That is, what is it that the soul, as it were, the *psyche* of an entity, must posses by way of, as it were, animation, such that life itself becomes possible? What *dynamis* must the soul have?

Now, at the most fundamental level, there must be a nutritive power. That's basic. There must be some means by which the creature can absorb nutritional elements from the environment, and, through that activity, grow and survive. All living things have this, which is essential for the survival of the individual creature.

Now, what about the survival of a whole class of creatures? For this, there must be a reproductive power—some means by which a given organism is capable of duplicating or bringing its kind about; so, again, at the most fundamental level of psychic power or psychic *dynamis*, the nutritive and reproductive functions are the essential properties of all living things.

Added to this, where living systems are more complex—and this includes plants, of course—there is also a locomotive power; the entity is now capable of some degree of movement. Aristotle notes there are plants that do this. The Venus flytrap, of course, is a common example. It will close over an insect caught in a sticky substance of the Venus flytrap—so, as we examine ever more complex specimens, we discover powers added to those of nutrition and reproduction. Here, now, we find locomotion, yet another *dynamis*.

However, inclusion in the animal kingdom requires something else—namely, sensation: the power of perception, the power of acting, as it were, knowingly, as we might say, consciously, reacting to events in the external world.

Now, at this point, we have creatures that are classified according to the basic functions of nutrition, reproduction, locomotion, and sensation—the last of these functions qualifying a living entity as "animal."

These are all powers of the soul. When Aristotle in his treatise *On the Soul* offers what he takes to be a precise definition of the soul, the psyche—in the Greek, *psyche*—he says: "By soul, I mean, by *psyche*, I mean the *Archezoa*, the first principle of living things; the principle according to which a thing, if it is alive, comes to have life." He is not treating the soul as a "thing" capable of existing outside a material entity. Rather, "soul" is a generic term for those processes that are life giving, life sustaining, endowing entities with such powers and faculties as movement and sensation. The "psychic" here refers to a set of processes or powers.

With more complex animal forms, to these powers of the soul is added some kind of intellectual or intelligent power: the power of problem solving. Aristotle grants this to much of the animal kingdom; they have that in common with us. Combined with perception—which, on Aristotle's account, has a very versatile and cognitive dimension to it—the intellectual faculty of more complex animals provides them with formidable psychological resources for learning and memory.

Nonetheless, Aristotle reserves to human beings a psychic power or faculty of a very special kind. It is usually rendered in English as "reason," but the word he uses in the treatise *On the Soul*—at least the word he employs the first time he refers to this power—is not the Greek *nous* or the *logos* for "reason," rather, it is *epistemonikon*. Now, let me not be tedious in trying to define some of these ancient words, but by *epistemonikon* one would ordinarily be referring to the means, or the power, the cognitive ability by which we comprehend universal propositions.

That is, a young child exercising the faculties of perception and intelligence might be said to learn many things about a "this" or a "that," but at too young an age, the child could not possibly comprehend a reference to "all things," or "all of that." The child can learn that Uncle Jack and Aunt Mary have died, but it would be very difficult for a three-year-old to know that "all men are mortal."

Now, that capacity to comprehend universal propositions is what *epistemonikon* is intended to convey. It's a special feature of rationality. It fits us out uniquely for, among other things, the rule of law itself. After all, what is the rule of law except the ability to apply some universal precept to what is an indefinitely large number of individual instances, each qualifying as, for example, "theft"? It is in virtue of this rationality that we become fit for a mode of political, social, and civic life that is otherwise unavailable to other "types" within the kingdom of life, types lacking this rational power.

Now, given that we have these faculties and powers, how is Aristotle going to understand and approach the problem of knowledge? Well, for Aristotle, to know something is essentially to know the cause of it. "Happy is the man who knows the causes of things" is the ancient maxim. To possess this is to possess what, in the Greek, is called *episteme*. To have that kind of systematic, scientific understanding of things is to know the causes by which things like that are brought about.

Aristotle on this subject returns ever so briefly, without ever mentioning the dialogue, to the problem Socrates faces in *Meno*. The difference between Aristotle's and Plato's approach is fundamental. Aristotle says, in words to this effect, that when we claim that someone knows that a right-angle triangle has 180 degrees, this can be understood in one of two ways. Someone may know that a triangle has 180 degrees because he's actually got some sort of measuring instrument, has measured the angles, and sees that the sum of the angles in a triangle comes to 180 degrees, but someone may know that *by definition*, a triangle has 180 degrees and, thus, knows that this is true of all triangles without measuring any of them.

Now, what is the difference between the knowledge of one sort and that of the other? Well, in one case, what is known is known by experience, such knowledge not rising to the level of *episteme*. Let's say that it is Mr. Smith who has the measuring device and whose knowledge is limited to what the device reads out when applied to a given triangle, and let's say that Mr. Jones has studied geometry. Jones has a genuine *episteme* with respect to triangles. Jones really knows what the triangle is, in and of itself, and essentially. Smith just happens to know something about a given triangle. So, on Aristotle's account, developed knowledge is a knowledge of the regulative principles and laws that govern the affairs of things, and not simply factual knowledge about this or that.

However, of course, to say that knowledge requires an understanding of the causes of things is to raise a question about just what a cause is. The Greek word *aitia* is used indifferently across cases, but as Aristotle is quick to point out in the *Metaphysics* and in his treatise on physics, "cause" is not a univocal term. It actually has rather different senses.

This is a point that can be easily confused. Let me take, as an example, some statue, or bust, or work of sculpture, something that all tourists will know about. Now, everyone traveling to Rome—well, surely, all Americans, when they go to Rome, generally head first for the Piazza Navona to buy very, very expensive coffee, and then treat themselves to Bernini's "Fountain of the Rivers." It's a great work of sculpture, and at least you can go home and say you saw Bernini's "Fountain of the Rivers."

Now, suppose you came from Mars, you landed in the Piazza Navona right in front of the "Fountain of the Rivers" and then you were to ask tourists: "What's the cause of that?" Let's say you pointed to the "Fountain of the Rivers" and said: "What caused that?" You ask some knowing person to account for it.

Well, understand that many entirely correct answers can be given to that question. One answer might be this: "Look, to have anything like this, you've got to have some kind of material that will retain shape. You can't get something like this if the universe consisted only of air, or fluids. If what you mean, then, by a cause is that which, in the absence of which, something else could not be, then surely one of the causes of the 'Fountain of the Rivers' is the material of which it is made." Absent that kind of matter, you couldn't have that kind of thing. Now, this answer reaches what Aristotle means by the *material* cause of something.

Of course, the Martian at that point might say, "Well, look, lots of things can be worked into a shape of some sort. This looks like something special." "Well," you might go on to say, "Not only do you need something that is able to take on a certain shape, but in order for it to be this kind of thing, it has to take on a recognizable shape. It has to have a 'form' that reveals the fact that, indeed, it is the representation of something; it stands for something. It's a something of a certain kind." Thus, you can't have a "that" unless it formally incorporates some special feature constitutive of things "like it." Now, such formal features ground what Aristotle meant by the *formal* cause of something.

Now, of course, a pile of bricks is not a house, so what you've got to do to make a house is to start piling up the bricks, putting cement between them, and so forth, and when it comes to the "Fountain of the Rivers," someone, or some group, had to stand there with hammer and chisel and start working the material into an identifiable shape, each blow of the hammer on the chisel having some definite effect on the matter, and thus giving shape and form to the block itself. Blow by blow, the material is being changed, and each one of those interactions, each blow, now is part of the *efficient* cause of what ultimately appears as the "Fountain of the Rivers." It's the billiard ball colliding, hitting another billiard ball, and the second one

197

moving: The impact of the first on the second is the efficient cause of the motion of the second.

Now at that point, if the Martian were an inquisitive chap, he might say: "Well, how do you know where to hit this material?" Well, at that point, Aristotle would be inclined to say: "You don't know where to hit this block of matter unless you already have in mind, as it were, what it is you're trying to bring about." That is, unless you've got Bernini there with this end, or goal, or aim in mind, this goal, in the Greek, this *telos*—the "Fountain of the Rivers" simply isn't going to take place. Only when the matter is worked according to a plan or goal, thus the ultimate understanding of the cause of the object, the ultimate explanation of the "Fountain of the Rivers" is just that intelligent design, and aim, and objective that was Bernini's.

This is what Aristotle means by the *final* cause. What he means by the final cause is that which is the final thing resulting in time, though it is the first in conception. Do you see? Initially conceived first, the final cause is the end as it is actually brought about.

Unless you have the intelligent plan to begin with, none of the rest of these causal modalities will operate to any effect at all; so, all of the other causal modalities—choosing the right material, giving it a certain shape, striking blows, all of these are done—what? For the sake of something, and what they are done for the sake of is the original plan, or design, or pattern, or goal.

A causal explanation that includes these considerations is called, after the Greek *telos,* a *teleological* explanation. You explain an object or event by uncovering or identifying the purposes, plans, designs, and goals that the object or event realizes or instantiates when finally brought about.

Now, teleological explanations do not have to presuppose some actually intelligent, divine being with a plan. Evolutionary theory is teleological in that certain characteristics or phenotypic properties of organisms are what they are because they serve certain purposes integral to the life of the organism, and you understand fins, and wings, and plumage, and mating behavior, and the like in terms of survivalistic considerations. These are teleological explanations nonetheless, though they are not what might be called agentically teleological; they don't require the operation of a super-entity with a *telos* in mind, somehow bringing all of this about for the sake of this ultimate creature called a "swan" or a "bird."

In any case, on Aristotle's account, we do not understand anything fully. We do not have *episteme* with respect to something unless we are able to comprehend all four causal modalities. To understand what a thing is, is centrally to know what it is *for*, to know its purpose. The number of things we can know is based on the number of questions we can ask, he says, of which there are the following: "Does a thing exist? If it exists, to what degree does it exist? In what relation does it stand to other things, and what is it for?"

Now, this is a central part of the Aristotelian program, whether in the domain of knowledge or in the domain of ethics or politics. In the domain of politics, the question would be: "What's the *polis* for?" In the domain of ethics it's going to be: "What kind of being am I?" and in light of that, "How do the actions of mine either realize what is potential within me, or stultify what is potential within me?" These potentialities are, in a manner of speaking, "What I am here for," and "How do I live my life in such a way as to honor that central fact of my being?"

Now, the developed knowledge that we have leads us to an understanding that the things of the universe, including the living things of the universe, do instantiate a design feature, a plan; they fit in. Nature does not do things without a purpose, so when you find a reliably occurring phenomenon, the ultimate question you are asking at the epistemic level, after you have satisfied yourself that it's made of stone, or it's made of marble, or it's made of wood—the ultimate question is: "How does this fit into things? What is it for? What purpose does it serve? What is its function?"

The explanations ought to be functionalist explanations, but functionalist in a rather enlarged sense. You do know at the outset that nothing with pattern and design is going to come about accidentally. As Aristotle says in his treatise on physics: "If the art of shipbuilding were in the wood, we would have ships by nature."

Let me repeat that; it's a statement made in the *Physics*, and, in fact, it really grounds Aristotle's notion of final causes very aptly. If the art of shipbuilding were in the wood, there would just be something about wood, such that if you left it around long enough, a great ancient Greek trireme would develop—sails there, and oars, and oarsmen. Do you see? Leather sails and all of that. "No," says Aristotle, "you do not get ships that way." Leave wood out for a very long time, and you get rotten wood.

The art of shipbuilding is not in something intrinsic to wood. You may need wood to make ships, but wood just enters in as the material cause of the ship. You need all sorts of workmen to know where to put the dowels and the sails and rudder, but they serve here as modes of efficient causation—as instruments serving some purpose of which they might well be ignorant. The art of shipbuilding is finally in the ship's designer. It is the designer who knows what ships are for and how that purpose is served by the right materials, rightly assembled. To "know" in this sense is to comprehend far more than anything conveyed by the mere material composition of an object.

This is an almost offhand reply to Democritus and the atomistic theory of reality. It's not enough to say that the ultimate constituents of reality are atomic particles. That provides no more than an account of the materiality of the universe, but that surely is a very pared-down form of knowledge, and certainly nothing that rises to the level of *episteme*. Truly developed knowledge embraces not only the material, efficient, and formal causes, but the *that for the sake of which* these causes were recruited in the first instance: the *that for the sake of which*.

Now, there is something else in Aristotle's philosophy of explanation, his philosophy of science, worth noting, because I think Aristotle on this count is sometimes misunderstood. Aristotle does argue that a thoroughly scientific explanation is one that includes a universal principle of which the thing to be explained is an instance. What he's getting at is the notion that we do not fully understand an event unless, in fact, we can articulate the general law that it is an example of, but when Aristotle is writing on biological subjects, as opposed to purely physical ones, when he's writing on biological and particularly on psychological and social matters, he inserts a qualifier—almost like a place mark. The expression in Greek is: *hos epi to polu*, which is best rendered as "for the most part," "by and large," or "in general."

One should not go away, then, with the view that Aristotle's model of explanation requires an explanation that it is always expressed to the *n*th place after the decimal, covered by an unswerving deterministic physical law. Obviously, if there is variability in the phenomenon itself, the best explanation will not hide from it. Aristotle teaches us to expect precision only to the extent that a subject allows it, and to seek no more precision than what the subject at hand will admit of.

We do not ask for probable reasoning from a mathematician, nor do we ask for certainty from a shoe cobbler—so, when it comes to those phenomena, those complex social, political, and moral events, understandings, dispositions, and characteristics overwhelmed by the complexities of life, by the ambiguities inherent in the case, what we look for are general precepts that are right by and large, in general, and for the most part. *Hos epi to polu*. Read in a certain light, it is a rather liberating conception in relation to the teachings of the Academy.

Timeline

800–600 B.C.E. .... Morality tales, such as the Hindu Upanishads, appear in many settled communities.

~750 B.C.E. .... Homer composes *The Iliad* and *The Odyssey*.

700 B.C.E. .... Colonization of Sicily, the east coast of Italy, and islands off the coast of Asia Minor begins, primarily to grow produce that can be sent back to mainland Greece.

6th century B.C.E..................... Schools of critical inquiry emerge in ancient Greece. Parmenides and other pre-Socratic philosophers emerge. *Empirkoi*, or empirical practitioners who followed Hippocrates's philosophy, make up the dominant school of Greek medicine.

570 B.C.E. .... Birth of Pythagoras.

551 B.C.E. .... Birth of Confucius.

4th century B.C.E..................... Isocrates composes the *Panegyricus*, a work that raises the question of whether philosophy is something that just the Greeks do.

479 B.C.E. .... Death of Confucius.

469 B.C.E. .... Birth of Hippocrates.

469 B.C.E. .... Birth of Socrates.

446 B.C.E. .... Birth of Isocrates.

427 B.C.E. .... Birth of Plato.

399 B.C.E. .... Death of Hippocrates.

399 B.C.E.	Death of Socrates.
384 B.C.E.	Birth of Aristotle.
360 B.C.E.	Plato writes his dialogue *The Republic*, generally considered to be the foundational work in political science. It addresses the question of how a man's virtue may be measured.
347 B.C.E.	Death of Plato.
338 B.C.E.	Death of Isocrates.
322 B.C.E.	Death of Aristotle.
300 B.C.E.	Stoic philosophy develops.
106 B.C.E.	Birth of Marcus Tullius Cicero.
43 B.C.E.	Death of Marcus Tullius Cicero.
1st century C.E.	"Hellenized" Jews build Christianity.
354 C.E.	Birth of St. Augustine.
397 C.E.	St. Augustine publishes *The Confessions*, a personal, introspective work of psychology.
430 C.E.	Death of St. Augustine.
476 C.E.	Fall of Rome.
632 C.E.	According to the teachings of Islam, the Prophet Muhammad had revealed to him a divine message that would be faithfully recorded in the Koran.
650–850 C.E.	The Dark Ages.
1150–1300.	Medieval period.
13th century	Advent of a "renaissance" of scholarly thought, with Roger Bacon

and others recovering the spirit of experimental modes of inquiry.

1214	Birth of Roger Bacon.
1225	Birth of Thomas Aquinas.
1274	Death of Thomas Aquinas.
1294	Death of Roger Bacon.
1304	Birth of Francesco Petrarch.
1374	Death of Francesco Petrarch.
15th century	The Italian Renaissance.
1452	Birth of Leonardo da Vinci.
1483	Birth of Martin Luther.
1497	Savonarola burns the vanities.
1517	Martin Luther protests aspects of the Catholic Church.
1519	Death of Leonardo da Vinci.
1546	Death of Martin Luther.
1546–1648	The Protestant Reformation, launched by Martin Luther's 1517 protest against aspects of the Catholic Church.
1561	Birth of Francis Bacon.
1588	Birth of Thomas Hobbes.
1596	Birth of René Descartes.
1626	Death of Francis Bacon.
1632	Birth of John Locke.
1633	Galileo is called before the Inquisition.
1642	Birth of Isaac Newton

1646	Birth of Gottfried Wilhelm von Leibniz.
1650	Death of René Descartes.
1660	The Royal Society becomes the center of a growing culture of science.
1660	Thomas Hobbes publishes *Leviathan*.
1679	Death of Thomas Hobbes.
1685	Birth of George Berkeley.
1694	Birth of François Marie Arouet, who wrote under the name Voltaire.
1699	Lord Shaftesbury publishes *An Inquiry Concerning Virtue or Merit*, offering an explanation of moral conduct based on the notion of natural dispositions and affections.
1704	Death of John Locke.
1705	Gottfried Wilhelm von Leibniz offers a significant critique of the Lockean view in *New Essays on Human Understanding*.
1709	Birth of Julien Offray de La Mettrie.
1710	George Berkeley publishes his critique of the Lockean view, *A Theory Concerning the Principles of Human Knowledge*.
1710	Birth of Thomas Reid.
1711	Birth of David Hume.
1712	Birth of Jean-Jacques Rousseau.

1715.. Birth of the French philosopher Claude Adrien Helvetius.

1715.. Birth of Etienne Condillac, John Locke's translator in France.

1716.. Death of Gottfried Wilhelm von Leibniz.

1724.. Birth of Immanuel Kant.

1729.. Birth of Edmund Burke.

1734.. Voltaire writes his *Letters on the English*.

1739.. David Hume publishes *An Enquiry Concerning Human Understanding*, which aimed to defeat Skepticism by putting philosophy on a firmer footing, grounding morality, science, and politics in the realm of experience.

1743.. Birth of Condorcet.

1748.. La Mettrie publishes the banned book *Man—A Machine*, which extends the materialistic drift of Descartes's psychology.

Mid-18th century .... The "Scottish Enlightenment."

1751.. Death of La Mettrie.

1757.. Birth of Pierre Cabanis.

1758.. Birth of Franz Joseph Gall.

1764.. Thomas Reid publishes *An Inquiry into the Human Mind*.

1770.. Birth of Georg Wilhelm Friedrich Hegel.

1771.. Death of Claude Adrien Helvetius.

1772	Helvetius's *A Treatise on Man*, which maintains that human essence does not precede our existence and experiences in the world, published posthumously.
1773	John Locke's *Two Treatises* is published in colonial America.
1776	Death of David Hume.
1778	Death of Jean-Jacques Rousseau.
1778	Death of François Marie Arouet (Voltaire).
1780	Death of Etienne Condillac.
1781	Immanuel Kant publishes his *Critique of Pure Reason*, which credits David Hume with awakening Kant from his "dogmatic slumber."
1783	Death of George Berkeley.
1787	The U.S. Constitution is forged in Philadelphia. During the subsequent ratification period, Alexander Hamilton, James Madison, and John Jay write essays in the New York newspapers addressing and countering the various arguments that had been advanced against the Constitution and the federal model of governance. These essays became known as *The Federalist Papers*.
1794	Death of Condorcet.
1794	Death of Pierre Flourens.
1795	Condorcet's *Sketch for a Historical Picture of the Progress*

of the Human Mind published posthumously.

1796... Death of Thomas Reid.

1797... Death of Edmund Burke.

1804... Death of Immanuel Kant.

1806... Birth of John Stuart Mill.

1808... Death of Pierre Cabanis.

1809... Birth of Charles Darwin.

1818... Birth of Karl Marx.

1822... Birth of Francis Galton.

1828... Death of Franz Joseph Gall.

1830... Auguste Comte publishes his *Course of Positive Philosophy*, which reflected on the achievements of the Enlightenment and concluded that human thought passes through distinct stages.

1830s .... The British Reform Act ends British participation in the slave trade and extends political rights to those long denied the franchise, including those not members of the Church of England.

1831... Death of Georg Wilhelm Friedrich Hegel.

1833... Charles Lyell publishes his *Principles of Geology*, which provided a time frame compatible with the requirements of Charles Darwin's theory of evolution by natural selection.

1842... Birth of William James.

1844	Birth of Friedrich Nietzsche.
Mid–late 19th century	The Aesthetic movement.
1856	Birth of Sigmund Freud.
1859	John Stuart Mill publishes *On Liberty*.
1862	In November of this year, Hermann von Helmholtz gives a lecture on conservation of energy at Heidelberg, where he addresses, among other issues, the relatively new division between leading scientists and philosophers.
1867	Death of Pierre Flourens.
1869	Francis Galton, cousin of Charles Darwin, publishes his studies of hereditary genius, which conclude that natural selection yields a very few exceptional human types, but general human flourishing disproportionately depends on their merits.
1871	Charles Darwin publishes *Descent of Man*, which puts forth his theory of natural selection.
1872	Friedrich Nietzsche publishes his first notable work, *The Birth of Tragedy and the Spirit of Music*.
1873	Death of John Stuart Mill.
1875	Birth of Carl Gustav Jung.
1882	Death of Charles Darwin.
1883	Death of Karl Marx.
1889	Birth of Ludwig Wittgenstein.

1890.. William James publishes *The Principles of Psychology*.

1896.. Sigmund Freud and Josef Breuer publish *Studies of Hysteria*, in which the theory is advanced that hysterical symptoms are the outcome of repression.

1900.. Death of Friedrich Nietzsche.

1910.. Death of William James.

1911.. Death of Francis Galton.

1912.. Birth of Alan Turing.

1938.. Death of Sigmund Freud.

1950.. Alan Turing publishes his Computing Machinery and Intelligence.

1951.. Death of Ludwig Wittgenstein.

1954.. Death of Alan Turing.

1961.. Death of Carl Gustav Jung.

Glossary

Apatheia: Freedom from pathos and suffering.

Atman: The soul, or core reality of the human individual. Hindu.

Brahma: The "creator" within the Hindu divine triad—Brahma, Vishnu, Shiva.

Categorical imperative: Driver for one alternative action over another made on principles whose moral authority takes precedence over any merely hypothetical imperative. Categorical imperatives derive from the intelligible realm governed by "the laws of freedom," rather than the natural realm of physical determination. Unlike hypothetical imperatives, they must be universally applicable. That is, they do not depend on a calculation of utility or on any calculation of possible consequences in particular circumstances.

Chthonic religion: Earth-centered religion, in which women or female deities are central figures because of their procreative power. Common in matriarchal societies.

Common sense: Scottish school of thought from the 18th and early 19th centuries, holding that in the perception of the average, unsophisticated person, sensations are not mere ideas or subjective impressions but carry with them the belief in corresponding qualities as belonging to external objects.

Contiguity: Similarity in time or place.

Ecstasis: Greek; "ecstasy." Stepping outside oneself or being removed from oneself.

Ego: According to Sigmund Freud's theory of psychoanalysis, one of the three parts that make up the self. The ego is purported to stand between the id and the superego to balance our primitive needs and our moral/ethical beliefs.

Eidola: "Phantoms," or atomic emanations from material objects that have some access to the organs of sense. Concept proposed by ancient atomists to explain hallucinations, dreams, religious visions, and so on.

Empiricism: The philosophical view that all human knowledge is derived from experience and that which cannot be confirmed via experience is not naturally known.

Enlightenment: Eighteenth-century European intellectual movement that rejected the presumptive authority of the past in favor of a reliance on experience and reason/science.

Enthousiasmos: Greek; "enthusiasm." Presenting oneself in such a way that the gods can enter the self.

Ephistemonikon: Abstract and universal statements.

Episteme: Scientific knowledge.

Epistemology: The study of how we know what we know and whether the way we go about knowing is defensible, one of the central questions in the study of metaphysics. Examines the question of knowledge and attempts to characterize the nature of truth and science.

Eudaimonia: The doing of something for its own sake, as the gods do. "Happiness."

Experimenta fructifera: One of two types of experiments described in Francis Bacon's *Novum Organum*; these consequential experiments are designed to allow the observer to choose between competing accounts of facts on hand.

Experimenta lucifera: One of two types of experiments described in Francis Bacon's *Novum Organum*; these "light-shedding" experiments alert the observer to factors operative in the causal matrix that brings things about. Such studies are essentially exercises in fact gathering.

Fallibilism: View that there is always *more* to the account than any current version *can* include, because other experiences, beliefs, and needs are always in existence.

Fatalism: The belief that every event is bound to happen as it does no matter what we do about it. Fatalism is the most extreme form of causal determinism, because it denies that human actions have any causal efficacy.

Functionalism: The view that consciousness is not a material entity attached to the brain, but a process, a stream of experiences knitted together as they flow by a supernumerary intelligence.

Hedonism: Doctrine holding that pleasure is the highest good.

Hypothetical imperative: Driver for one alternative action over another made to attain a specific end. Hypothetical imperatives are contingent; they are tied to a particular context and to the needs and desires of natural creatures under the press of the needs to survive, to avoid pain, and to gain pleasure. Decisions thus grounded are non-moral, because they arise from our natures as merely human beings, not as rational beings; that is, they are essentially reactions.

Id: According to Sigmund Freud's theory of psychoanalysis, one of the three parts that make up the self. The id is purported to represent primary process thinking—our most primitive need-gratification thoughts.

Intuition: An instinctive knowing, or impression that something might be the case, without the use of rational processes.

Ius civile: Expression of local values and interests, which differs from place to place and people to people.

Ius gentium: Universally adopted precepts of those who live under any rule of law, such as the idea that harm done to another without cause is wrong, as is the taking of what clearly belongs to another.

Jainism: Ethical school based on the Pythagorean teachings, which emphasizes the celebration of all that lives.

Labor theory of value: The concept that property is worth only as much as the labor invested in it; the surplus is profit, which accumulates as capital.

Logos: The aims and goals generated by the rational intelligence behind the order of the cosmos.

Lyssa: "Wolf's rage"; extreme anger in the heat of battle.

Malleus maleficarum: A coherent theory of witchcraft, a set of tests to determine witchcraft, and a list of appropriate punishments used during the witch hunts from 1400 to 1700 and beyond.

Marxism: A form of communism based on the writings of Karl Marx, who theorized that actions and human institutions are economically determined, that the class struggle is the basic agency of historical change, and that capitalism will ultimately be superseded by communism.

Metaphysics: Concept referring to two distinguishable but interconnected sets of questions: first, the question of what really exists and, second, the question of how we know such things and whether the way we go about knowing is defensible or defective. The term is derived from the writings of Aristotle.

Mimesis: The imitative representation of nature or human behavior.

Mythos: The complex of beliefs, values, and attitudes characteristic of a specific group or society.

Naturalism: The meta-ethical thesis that moral properties are reducible to natural ones or that ethical judgments may be derived from non-ethical ones. Also, a scientific account of the world in terms of causes and natural forces that rejects all spiritual, supernatural, or teleological explanations.

Natural law: An ethical belief or system of beliefs supposed to be inherent in human nature and discoverable by reason rather than revelation. Also, the philosophical doctrine that the authority of the legal system or of certain laws derives from their justifiability by reason and, indeed, that a legal system that cannot be so justified has no authority.

Natural rights: Rights inherent in a being because of its nature as a being of a certain sort.

Nomological: The mode of causation employed by God, according to the Stoics; immutable laws control the affairs of the cosmos.

Nomos: Prevailing social expectations and requirements, or "the law of the land."

Noumena/Phenomena: According to Immanuel Kant, knowledge arises from experience; therefore, it must be knowledge of *phenomena*, that is, of things and events as these are delivered by the senses. From the evidence at the phenomenal level, we can reason to the fact that there is a *noumenal* realm of being. Thus, we can know *that* it is but cannot know *what* it is. Ultimately, our knowledge claims must be utterly bounded by the pure intuitions of time and space and the pure categories of the understanding.

Ontology: The study of what really exists, one of the key questions central to the concept of metaphysics.

Philosophy: The rational pursuit of truths deemed to be answers to perennial questions, as well as a historical study of intractable problems; literally, the love of wisdom.

Phrenology: A Victorian-era science of character divination, faculty psychology, and brain theory derived from the Viennese physician Franz Joseph Gall's system, which held that the surface of the skull could be read as an accurate index of an individual's psychological aptitudes and tendencies.

Phronesis: Greek term for practical wisdom or prudence; the application of good judgment to human conduct, in contrast with the more theoretical inquiry leading to *sophia*, or wisdom generally.

Phusis: Greek, "nature."

Physiognomy: The study of the shape and configuration of a person's face to determine his or her character and intelligence.

Pluralism: The philosophical doctrine that reality consists of several basic substances or elements.

Polis: Life within a settled community, in which one participates and from which one draws lessons for life.

Positivism: A form of empiricism that bases all knowledge on perceptual experience, rather than on intuition or revelation.

Pragmatism: The doctrine that practical consequences are the criteria of knowledge, meaning, and value.

Providential: The mode of causation employed by God, according to Hellenistic philosophy. The cosmos is created and ordered by a perfect rational entity, whose knowledge is also perfect. The creative entity takes an interest in its creation.

Pyrrhonism: An early Greek form of Skepticism.

Pythagorean theorem: One of the earliest theorems known to ancient civilizations; named for the Greek mathematician and philosopher Pythagoras. The Pythagorean theorem states: "The area of the square built upon the hypotenuse of a right triangle is equal to the sum of the areas of the squares upon the remaining sides."

Res cogitans/res extensa: The metaphysical dualism on which the Cartesian philosophical system rests. *Res cogitans* is God and the human soul; *res extensa* is the corporeal world.

Revelation: An enlightening or astonishing disclosure. Also, communication of knowledge to man by a divine or supernatural agency.

Romanticism: A movement in literature, art, and intellectual thought during the late 18th and early 19th centuries that celebrated nature rather than civilization and valued imagination and emotion over rationality.

Sophia: Greek, "wisdom."

Sophists: Greek philosophers who showed complete indifference to the problems of the world of matter and centered their efforts on man. But man can be an object of study in his sense knowledge, as well as in the more profound world of reason. The Sophists stopped at the data of experience—at empirical, not rational, knowledge—and from this point of view, they wished to judge the world of reality.

Stoics: Greek philosophers whose worldview was one of a rationally governed universe of material entities, each answering to its controlling principle and, thus, participating in the overall cosmic *logos*. In its most developed form, Stoicism takes the lawfulness of the cosmos as the model on which human life is to proceed. The rule of law is the defining mark of our humanity, according to this philosophy.

Sturm und Drang: German; "storm and stress." Romanticism perceived this evolutionary struggle that produces new and better things not predictable in a mechanistic view.

Superego: According to Sigmund Freud's theory of psychoanalysis, one of the three parts that make up the self. The superego is purported to represent our conscience and counteract the id with moral and ethical thoughts.

Tabula rasa: A blank slate. In the Lockean view, the condition of the human mind at birth.

Teleia philia: Perfected or completed friendship, the aims of which do not go outside the friendship itself.

Teleology: The philosophical study of purpose; a doctrine that assumes the phenomena of organic life, particularly those of evolution, are explicable only by purposive causes and that they in no way admit of a mechanical explanation or one based entirely on biological science.

Tetraktys: In Pythagorean philosophy, the sacred integers: 1, 2, 3, and 4.

Thomistic theory of law: Philosophical approach predicated on what is taken to be good for man, given the character of human nature. As "an ordinance of reason," law gives and honors good reasons for certain actions and good reasons for forbearing to act in certain ways. An action is good when it is in accord with the basic goods. A desire is bad when its fulfillment is in defiance of good reasons for action.

Turing machine: An algorithm—not a machine as such—that translates any input signal into a determinate output.

Ubermensch: Friedrich Nietzsche's concept of the "superman," an exemplar of self-creation who is free from the influence of the general populace.

Unconscious motivation: Concept central to Sigmund Freud's theories of human behavior; the idea that the subconscious portion of the mind plays a larger role in determining behavior than does the conscious portion.

Upanishads: Pre-philosophical Hindu morality tales that address questions of knowledge, conduct, and governance.

Biographical Notes

Aeschylus (525–456 B.C.): Earliest of the three greatest Greek tragedians, the others being Sophocles and Euripides; known for his masterpiece, *The Oresteia* trilogy. Aeschylus's greatest contribution to the theater was the addition of a second actor to his scenes. Previously, the action took place between a single actor and the Greek chorus.

Anaximenes (585–525 B.C.): Pre-Socratic Greek philosopher who held that the air, with its variety of contents, its universal presence, and its vague associations in popular fancy with the phenomena of life and growth, is the source of all that exists.

Thomas Aquinas (1225–1274): Dominican priest and scholastic philosopher whose "natural law" theory defined law as an ordinance of reason, promulgated by one who is responsible for the good of the community. His treatises on law would form the foundation of critical inquiry in jurisprudence for centuries, integrating classical and Christian thought.

Aristotle (384–322 B.C.): Greek philosopher who, along with Plato, is often considered to be one of the two most influential philosophers in Western thought. Aristotle most valued knowledge gained from the senses and would correspondingly be classed among modern empiricists. Thus, Aristotle set the stage for what would eventually develop into the scientific method centuries later.

St. Augustine (354–430 C.E.): Roman Catholic bishop and Christian Neo-Platonist who was a leader in the widespread merging of the Greek philosophical tradition and Judeo-Christian religious and scriptural traditions.

Avicenna (980–1037): Inspired by Aristotle's *Metaphysics*, articulated a mode of philosophical reasoning that would virtually define medieval thought and scholasticism. Put Arab scholarship and Islamic thought at the center of naturalistic and scientific thinking.

Francis Bacon (1561–1626): Generally considered the "prophet" of Newton and the father once removed of the authority of experimental science. Known for his groundbreaking *Novum Organum* ("*New Method*"), which established the authority of observation in discovering the nature of the external world and the authority of the experimental method as the way to select the correct from competing theories of causation.

Roger Bacon (1214–1294): Thirteenth-century English scholar who stated the basic program of experimental science. Known for his *Opus Maius*, considered one of the foundational works in the modern scientific movement.

George Berkeley (1685–1783): Bishop of Cloyne in Ireland and a scientist. Offered a critique of the Lockean view in his *A Theory Concerning the Principles of Human Knowledge*, which attempts to defeat materialism and the skepticism it spawns by establishing the essentially mental preconditions for a material world to exist at all.

Josef Breuer (1842–1925): Viennese neurologist who worked with Sigmund Freud on the theory of repression.

Ernst Brucke (1819–1892): One of Sigmund Freud's teachers, along with Hermann von Helmholtz, Karl Ludwig, and DuBois-Reymond.

Edmund Burke (1729–1797): British political writer and statesman. Burke's essay on the sublime, written in the period of the Enlightenment, prefigures the Hegelian worldview, defining the *sublime* as that which strikes awe and terror in the heart.

Pierre Cabanis (1757–1808): One of the leaders of thought in the French materialist tradition, known for his series of essays on the relationship between the psychological and physical dimensions of human life.

Marcus Tullius Cicero (106–43 B.C.): Roman orator, lawyer, politician, and philosopher who considered philosophical study most valuable as the means to more effective political action.

Auguste Comte (1798–1857): French writer whose works—a series of essays published collectively under the title *A Course of Positive Philosophy*—influenced John Stuart Mill. One of the fathers of a version of positivism.

Etienne Condillac (1715–1780): Locke's translator in France, who offers the model of the "sentient statue" whose character, knowledge, and conduct are carved into it by a ceaselessly impinging environment.

Condorcet (1743–1794): French philosopher whose *Sketch for a Historical Picture of the Progress of the Human Mind*, written while he was hiding from France's new "liberators" during the Reign of Terror, delivers the idea of progress in one of its most summoning forms. The mind has progressed from murky superstition and timidity toward the light of reason in stages, each stage requiring the abandonment of ancestral ignorance. The advent of the scientific worldview now abets this progress.

Confucius (551–479 B.C.): Chinese philosopher who maintained that adherence to traditional values of virtue is necessary to achieve a state of orderliness and peace.

Charles Darwin (1809–1882): British naturalist who developed the theory of evolutionary selection, which holds that variation within species occurs randomly and that the survival or extinction of each organism is determined by that organism's ability to adapt to its environment.

Democritus (460–370 B.C.): Pre-Socratic Greek philosopher who taught an atomic theory of reality, that all things are made of atoms and void.

René Descartes (1596–1650): Discovered analytical geometry, was an important contributor to the physical sciences, and was, perhaps, the most important figure in that branch of philosophy called *philosophy of mind*. Known for his proof of existence: "I think, therefore I am."

Denis Diderot (1713–1784): Most prominent of the French Encyclopedists. In the circle of the leaders of the Enlightenment, Diderot's name became known especially by his *Lettre sur les aveugles* (London, 1749), which supported Locke's theory of knowledge.

Diogenes (4th century B.C.): Leading philosopher of the pre-Socratic school of Cynicism. Diogenes practiced self-control and a rigid abstinence, exposing himself to extremes of heat and cold and living on the simplest diet.

Erasmus (1469–1536): Fifteenth-century humanist. His best known work is *Praise of Folly*, a pamphlet mainly directed against the behavior of ruling classes and church dignitaries while exposing the irony of mankind's vanities.

Euripides (480–406 B.C.): Greek playwright best known for the tragedy *Medea*.

Pierre Flourens (1794–1867): French physiologist who—along with François Magendie and Xavier Bichat—surgically destroyed selective regions of animals' brains and observed the behavior of the survivors. Through this technique, Flourens discovered that the areas of the brain that Franz Joseph Gall had identified with certain specific functions were not connected with those specific functions.

Sigmund Freud (1856–1938): The father of psychoanalysis. Freud, in collaboration with Joseph Breuer, articulated and refined the concepts of the unconscious, infantile sexuality, and repression and proposed a tripartite account of the mind's structure, all as part of a then–radically new conceptual and therapeutic frame of reference for the understanding of human psychological development and the treatment of abnormal mental conditions.

Franz Joseph Gall (1758–1828): Leading neuroanatomist of his time; propounded the "science" of phrenology, a theory that brain structures are related to brain functions, which became dominant in the scientific thinking of the 19th century and thereafter.

Francis Galton (1822–1911): Cousin of Charles Darwin. Published his studies of hereditary genius in 1869, stating that natural selection yields a very few exceptional human types, but general human flourishing disproportionately depends on their merits.

Johann Wolfgang von Goethe (1749–1832): Eighteenth-century writer best known for *Faust*.

Georg Wilhelm Friedrich Hegel (1770–1831): German philosopher who merged and synthesized many of the strongest tendencies in Romantic thought. First is the idea of progressive and evolving reality—not the staid mechanical repetitiousness of mere causality, but an active principle at work in the natural world. Second, there is the criticism of science as not being up to the task of comprehending this world, tied as it is to reductive schemes.

Hermann von Helmholtz (1821–1894): Nineteenth-century physicist and physiologist; one of Sigmund Freud's teachers. In a November 1862 lecture at Heidelberg, Helmholtz tried to clarify why leading scientists visibly shunned philosophers, when previously, the natural philosopher was the natural scientist.

Claude Adrien Helvetius (1715–1771): French philosopher who, in his *A Treatise on Man*, puts forth a radical environmentalism, which holds that our essence does not precede our existence and experiences in the world; rather, it is a record of those experiences.

Herodotus (5th century B.C.): Greek scholar said to be the first historian in the modern accepted sense of the term; the "father of historical scholarship." Known for his treatise *The Persian Wars*.

Hippocrates (469–399 B.C.): Greek physician considered to be the father of modern medicine.

Thomas Hobbes (1588–1679): British philosopher who rejected Cartesian dualism and believed in the mortality of the soul; rejected free will in favor of a determinism that treats freedom as being able to do what one desires; and rejected Aristotelian and scholastic philosophy in favor of the "new" philosophy of Galileo and Gassendi, which largely treats the world as matter in motion. Hobbes is perhaps most famous for his political philosophy, which maintained that men in a state of nature, without civil government, are in a war of all against all in which life is hardly worth living. The way out of this desperate state is to make a social contract and establish the state to keep peace and order.

Homer (~ 750/800 B.C.): Blind Greek poet who wrote about the Trojan War, considered a defining moment in Greek history and presumed to have concluded a half-millennium earlier. Best known for his two epic poems *The Iliad* and *The Odyssey*.

David Hume (1711–1776): One of the most influential philosophers to have written in the English language, Hume offered an experiential theory of knowledge, morality, and religion. He made more credible the notion that a bona fide *science of the mind* was within reach.

T. H. Huxley (1825–1895): British physician and surgeon who was one of the first adherents to Charles Darwin's theory of evolution by natural selection; Huxley did more than anyone else to advance the theory's acceptance among scientists and the public alike.

Isocrates (446–338 B.C.): Greek philosopher who lived and wrote in the same cultural situation as Plato. Isocrates held that reality is immediate human experience and metaphysical speculation is a waste of time and energy. He also said that all knowledge is tentative and values are relative. Composed the *Panegyricus*, a work that raises the question of whether philosophy is something that just the Greeks do.

William James (1842–1910): American psychologist and philosopher who maintained that every idea belongs to someone, that mental life is not an empty container filled with experiences agglomerating with one another. Thus, the external world is chosen for the content that will be experienced and associated.

Carl Gustav Jung (1875–1961): A younger colleague of Sigmund Freud, Jung divided the psyche into three parts: the ego, or conscious mind; the personal unconscious, which includes anything that is not currently conscious but can be; and finally, the collective unconscious, or reservoir of our experiences as a species, a kind of knowledge with which we are all born but are never directly conscious of. The contents of the collective unconscious are called *archetypes*, unlearned tendencies to experience things in a certain way. The archetype has no form of its own, but it acts as an "organizing principle" on the things we see or do.

Immanuel Kant (1724–1804): Kant's most original contribution to philosophy is his Copernican Revolution that the representation makes the object possible, rather than the object making the representation possible. This introduced the human mind as an active originator of experience, rather than a passive recipient of perception.

Julien Offray de La Mettrie (1709–1751): French philosopher whose naturalism tends toward materialism. His *Man—A Machine* extends to its logical conclusion the materialistic drift of Descartes's own psychology.

Gottfried Wilhelm von Leibniz (1646–1716): Offered a significant critique of the Lockean view in his *New Essays on Human Understanding*, which concluded that an organizing and rationally functioning mind must be present for there to be coherent experience and that nothing in the operation of the biological senses can constitute a thought or an idea.

Leonardo da Vinci (1452–1519): Italian painter, architect, engineer, mathematician, and philosopher who is widely considered to represent the Renaissance ideal.

John Locke (1632–1704): Physician and one of the "fathers" of British empiricism. Locke set out in *An Essay Concerning Human Understanding* (1690) to defend a naturalistic account of mental life and a reductionistic strategy for studying and explaining that life. Accordingly, both knowledge and self-knowledge are derived from experiences and the memory of them. One's very personal identity is but that collection of entities in consciousness entering by way of experience.

Martin Luther (1483–1546): Began the Protestant Reformation with his protests against aspects of the Catholic Church.

Ernst Mach (1838–1916): German physicist who formulated a positivist creed in science that John Stuart Mill would develop. Mach said that we recognize our work as science to the extent that it is *not* metaphysics and that physical laws are only systematic descriptions of sense data that need no metaphysical description or underpinning.

Karl Marx (1818–1883): Philosopher, social scientist, historian, and revolutionary who developed a socialist system that came to be used as the basis for many regimes around the world.

John Stuart Mill (1806–1873): Known for his *System of Logic*, published in 1843, which analyzed inductive proof. Mill provided the empirical sciences with a set of formulas and criteria to serve the same purpose for them as the timeworn formula of the syllogism had served for arguments that proceeded from general principles. Mill's work is not merely a logic in the limited sense of that term, but also a theory of knowledge such as Locke and Hume provide.

Friedrich Nietzsche (1844–1900): German philosopher who sharply criticized traditional philosophy and religion as both erroneous and harmful for human life, arguing that they enervate and degrade our native capacity for achievement. Best known for developing the concept of the *Ubermensch*, or "superman," a rare, superior individual that can rise above all moral distinctions to achieve a heroic life of truly human worth.

Francesco Petrarch (1304–1374): Father of humanism. An Italian scholar and poet who is credited with having given the Renaissance its name.

Plato (427–347 B.C.): Greek philosopher and student of Socrates whose writings convey the spirit of his master's teachings on the theory of forms, the problem of knowledge, cosmological speculations, and the treatment of government.

Protagoras (490–420 B.C.): Pre-Socratic Greek philosopher. A leading figure in Sophist thought, he proposed that "Man is the measure of all things."

Pyrrhon of Elis (360–272 B.C.): Greek philosopher known as one of the great fathers of Skeptical thought.

Pythagoras (c. 580-500 B.C.): Greek philosopher who maintained that the ultimate reality was abstract and relational, depending on numbers. His harmonic view of the universe provided one of the foundations for Platonic philosophy. The first person to demonstrate the theorem that with any right triangle, the sum of the squares of each of the two sides is equal to the square of the hypotenuse.

Thomas Reid (1710–1796): Father of the Scottish Common Sense School. Scottish philosopher who laid the foundations for a "common sense" psychology based on the natural endowments by which we (and the animals) understand the world and act in it. His influence was broad and deep, reaching the leaders of thought at the American founding. Reid was the leading figure in a group of scholars and scientists at Aberdeen committed to the larger Newtonian perspective. He also was David Hume's most successful critic.

Jean-Jacques Rousseau (1712–1778): Swiss-French philosopher, author, and political theorist whose work largely decried the harmful effects of modern civilization.

Girolamo Savonarola (1452–1498): Italian religious reformer best known for his attempt to reform Renaissance Florence society and the Catholic Church from the vices of modern life as he knew them.

Friedrich von Schiller (1759–1805): German historian, philosopher, and dramatist; his *Letters on the Aesthetic Education of Man* maintained that it is freedom that creates, determinism that limits and kills. Friend of Johann Wolfgang von Goethe.

Socrates (c. 469–399 B.C.): Greek philosopher committed to objectifying the self and holding it up to scrutiny in order to examine human nature. Developed the Socratic method, which tests every assumption for its grounding and implications.

Sophocles (496–406 B.C.): One of the great playwrights of the Greek golden age; known for his tragedy *Antigone*.

Herbert Spencer (1820–1903): British philosopher and sociologist who supplied the phrase "survival of the fittest" and gave Darwinism its most portentous set of social implications.

Alan Turing (1912–1954): Mathematician and cryptographer who developed the concept of the computable algorithm.

Voltaire (1694 –1778): French Enlightenment writer and philosopher who maintained that our experience is the key to understanding human nature and the nature of the world around us. His real name was François Marie Arouet.

Alfred Russel Wallace (1823–1913): Worked with Charles Darwin to develop the theory of evolution by natural selection. Wallace concluded that he could not see natural selection at work in three domains: (1) abstract thought, which seems to serve no evolutionary purpose; (2) art, in which resources are willingly squandered in the service of the merely beautiful; and (3) moral thought and ethics, where we sacrifice our own most cherished interests in the service of others.

Ludwig Wittgenstein (1889–1951): Austrian philosopher whose *The Tractatus* stated that the world consists entirely of independent, simple facts out of which complex ones are constructed. Language has as its purpose the stating of facts by picturing these facts.

Bibliography

Essential Reading:

Barnes, Jonathan. *Early Greek Philosophy*. New York: Penguin Books, 1987. A concise and authoritative introduction to the pre-Socratic world of Greek philosophy.

Berkeley, George. *A Treatise Concerning the Principles of Human Knowledge*. New York: Oxford University Press, 1997. Berkeley's systematic critique of materialistic theories and his alternative "immaterialist" thesis.

Brock, Dan. *Life and Death*. New York: Cambridge University Press, 1993. A thoughtful review of the ethical aspects of those "life-and-death" issues arising from modern medicine.

Darwin, Charles. *The Expression of the Emotions in Man and Animals*. New York: Oxford University Press, 1998. Evidence and argument according to which the emotional dimension of human life is on the same continuum as that which includes non-human emotional expression. The utter "naturalization" of human sentiments and their origins in natural selection.

Descartes, René. *Selected Philosophical Writings*. New York: Cambridge University Press, 1988. Excellent selections from the *Discourse on Method* and related works.

Hume, David. *An Enquiry Concerning Human Understanding*. New York: Oxford University Press, 1999. One of the most influential philosophical works in the English language, and one of the most consistent defenses of empiricism.

James, William. *The Will to Believe*. Cambridge: Harvard University Press, 1979. In this work, James analyzes the psychological and philosophical grounds of belief and answers challenges coming from scientific critics.

Kant, Immanuel. *Critique of Practical Reason*. Cambridge: Cambridge University Press, 1997. A difficult work but Kant's fullest development of his moral theory.

Locke, John. *An Essay Concerning Human Understanding*. Amherst, NY: Prometheus Books, 1995. Perhaps the classic statement of the empiricist theory of mind and mental life.

Mackie, J.L. *Ethics: Inventing Right and Wrong*. New York: Penguin, 1977. Among the best of the modern "skeptical" critiques of moral realism.

Plato. *The Dialogues of Plato*. New York: Random House, 1937. The works to which, on Whitehead's account, all subsequent philosophy is but a footnote.

Reid, Thomas. *An Inquiry into the Human Mind*. University Park, PA: Penn State University Press, 1997. The most incisive criticism of Hume's philosophy written in Hume's lifetime; a trenchant analysis of the proper methods of philosophizing.

Robinson, D. N. *Praise and Blame: Moral Realism and Its Application*. Princeton, NJ: Princeton University Press, 2002. A defense of moral realism and appraisal of anti-realist critiques of realism.

Van Fraassen, Bas. *The Scientific Image*. New York: Oxford University Press, 1980. One of the more influential "anti-realist" works in contemporary philosophy of science.

Supplementary Reading:

Annas, Julia. *Platonic Ethics, Old and New*. Ithaca: Cornell University Press, 1999.

―――. "Classical Greek Philosophy." In *The Oxford History of Greece and the Hellenistic World*. J. Boardman et al, eds. Oxford: Oxford University Press, 1991.

Aristotle. *The Complete Works of Aristotle: The Revised Oxford Translation*. J. Barnes, ed. Princeton, NJ: Princeton University Press, 1984. Now the standard source of Aristotle's extant works.

―――. *Metaphysics*. W. D. Ross, trans. (downloadable). A useful Internet version of Aristotle's pioneering work in metaphysics.

Arnold, Matthew. *Culture and Anarchy*. New Haven, CT: Yale University Press, 1994. The "classic" defense of the humanistic perspective and the basis on which civilized life depends.

Augustine. *Confessions*. New York: Oxford University Press, 1992. A groundbreaking work in introspective and "depth" psychology and an early analysis of various psychological processes associated with cognition and memory, emotion and motivation.

————. *On Free choice of Will*. T. Williams, trans. Cambridge: Cambridge University Press, 1993. Augustine was among the first to examine in detail the theory of moral freedom against the claims of determinism. His locating the issue within the Christian canon deprives his analysis of none of its philosophical power.

————. *The City of God* (downloadable). An Internet source of Augustine's moral and political philosophy.

Bacon, Francis. *Novum Organum*. P.Urbach and J. Gibson, eds. Chicago: Open Court, 1994. Here is the "Baconian" revolution, designed to create an empirical science of discovery as a counter to traditional authority in science.

Barker, S. and T. Beauchamp, eds. *Thomas Reid: Critical Interpretations (Philosophical Monographs)*. Vol. 3. Philadelphia: University of Science Center, 1976.

Barnes, J. ed. *The Complete Works of Aristotle: The Revised Oxford Translation*. Princeton, NJ: Princeton University Press, 1984. Now the standard source of Aristotle's extant works.

Bate, W. *From Classic to Romantic*. Cambridge: Harvard University Press, 1946.

Bede. *A History of the English Church and People*. London: Penguin, 1968. Here the "Venerable Bede" presents a record of the early Church in the English speaking world, rich in detail and often astonishing in its claims.

Birks, Peter, ed. *Justinian's Institutes*. Ithaca, NY: Cornell University Press, 1987. The laws codified and promulgated by the Emperor Justinian.

Boardman, John et al., eds. *The Oxford History of Greece and the Hellenistic World*. Oxford: Oxford University Press, 1991. A fine source text edited by distinguished scholars.

Borst, C.V., ed. *Mind/Brain Identity Theory*. New York: St. Martin's Press, 1970. Old but not "dated," the essays in this collection more or less exhaust the candidate "solutions" to this most vexing of issues.

Brown, P. *The Body and Society*. New York: Columbia University Press, 1988. Peter Brown's study of the patristic and early medieval cultures of faith are illuminating at every level of detail. The special significance of man's corporeal nature is examined closely.

Budd, Malcolm. *Wittgenstein's Philosophy of Psychology*. London: Routledge, 1989. The Wittgensteinian "discursive turn" is featured, as the grammatical confusions in psychology are noted.

Burke, Edmund. *Philosophical Enquiry into the Origin of Our Ideas of the Sublime and Beautiful*. New York: Columbia University Press, 1958. Here is one of the earliest contributions to aesthetics and its psychological grounding, presented by a young Burke, already a master of English prose.

Careri, Giovanni Bernini. *Flights of Love: The Art of Devotion*. Linda Lappin, trans. Chicago: University of Chicago Press, 1994. Bernini's philosophy of aesthetics and defense of the Baroque.

Cassell, E. *The Nature of Suffering and the Goals of Medicine*. New York: Oxford University Press, 1991. A balanced and thoughtful treatise in medical ethics.

Cassirer, Ernst. *The Renaissance Philosophy of Man*. Chicago: University of Chicago Press, 1967. An informed summary of major philosophical perspectives in the Renaissance.

Churchland, Patricia Smith. *Neurophilosophy: Toward a Unified Science of Mind-Brain*. Cambridge, MA: MIT Press, 1986. Philosophy of mind can get no more "materialistic" than this.

Clark, Kenneth. *The Romantic Rebellion: Romantic versus Classic Art*. London: J. Murray, 1973. The claims of genius against those of science, the claims of the imagination against those of measurement.

Cohen, J.B. *Revolution in Science*. Cambridge: Harvard University Press, 1994. The author offers a sensible evaluation of the idea of scientific "revolutions" and their relation to the larger intellectual context.

Collingwood, R. G. *The Idea of History*. New York: Oxford University Press, 1994. Essays on the nature of historical scholarship and explanation.

Condorcet. *Selected Writings*. K. Baker, ed. Indianapolis: Bobbs Merrill Publishing Co., 1976. Condorcet was the most scientifically acute of the "philosophes." The subtle and appealing character of his thought comes across vividly in this collection.

Cottingham, J., et al., eds. *The Philosophical Writings of Descartes*. 2 vols. Cambridge: Cambridge University Press, 1988. This is the most accessible collection of Descartes's major philosophical works.

Dane, N., and J. Ambrose, eds. *Greek Attitudes*. New York: Charles Scribners Sons, 1974. The editors select wisely from the literary, political, philosophical and aesthetic offerings of the Classical age of Greece.

de Bruyne, Edgar. *The Esthetics of the Middle Ages*. trans. Eileen B. Hennesey. New York: F. Unger Publishing Co., 1969. A close and informing study of the conceptual and religious grounding of medieval art.

Dworkin, R. *Taking Rights Seriously*. Cambridge: Harvard University Press, 1977. An argument for the liberal state and a defense of "judge-made" law.

Epictetus. *The Discourses*. C. Hill, ed. London: Everyman, 1995. The classic Stoic position on the widest range of social, political, and individual issues.

Erasmus, Desiderius. *Ten Colloquies*. New York: Liberal Arts Press, 1957. More an "op ed" set of essays on the state of the world at the close of the 15th century; a quintessential "humanistic" work.

Fairfield, Roy, ed. *The Federalist Papers*. Garden City, NY: Anchor Books, 1966. All 85, with their analysis of the essential nature and aims of politics and a realistic perspective on the odds for success; the most incisive set of political essays struck at a single time, ever.

Ferruolo, S. *The Origins of the University*. California: Stanford University Press, 1985. The modern university is indebted to the Scholastic age of scholarship and analysis, its commitment to a broadly based curriculum and its major modes of instruction and examination.

Fideler, D. ed. *The Pythagorean Sourcebook and Library*. York Beach, Maine: Phanes Press, 1987. Pythagoras and his disciples did not record their beliefs and discoveries, but here we have a set of maxims and fragments with which to construct a fuller picture of the teachings of the sect.

Findlay, J. *Hegel: A Reexamination*. London: Allen & Unwin, 1958. The ever elusive Hegel comes to life in this treatise, as attention is drawn to the background and to the influences of Hegelian thought.

Finnis, J. *Natural Law and Natural Rights*. New York: Oxford University Press, 1980. A modern and authoritative defense of natural law theory.

Flanagan, O. *Consciousness Reconsidered*. Cambridge, MA: MIT Press, 1992. Useful as a critical review of current thinking on the nature of consciousness; a respect for the complexity of the issues associated with the phenomenon of consciousness.

Fodor, J. *The Modularity of Mind*. Cambridge, MA: MIT Press, 1983. A standard defense of the view that mental phenomena as such are composites of functions performed in modular fashion.

Foster, J. *The Immaterial Self: A Defence of the Cartesian Dualist Conception of Mind*. London: Routledge, 1996. One of the most thoughtful of current attempts to defend dualism against the usual lines of criticism.

Freud, Sigmund. *The Interpretation of Dreams*. New York: Penguin, 2003. Here is the essential work in "depth psychology," a treatise that Freud regarded as pointing to the "royal road" to the unconscious.

Galton, Francis. *Hereditary Genius: An Inquiry into Its Laws and Consequences*. New York: St. Martin's Press, 1978. Nativism, unadulterated!

Garland, Robert. *The Greek Way of Life: From Conception to Old Age*. Ithaca, NY: Cornell University Press, 1990. A fine introduction to the social, political, and daily life that was "the Greek way."

George, Robert, ed. *Natural Law Theory: Contemporary Essays*. New York: Oxford University Press, 1992. Arguments for and against versions of natural law theory and on philosophy of law in general.

Guthrie, Kenneth. *The Pythagorean Sourcebook and Library: An Anthology of Ancient Writings*. Grand Rapids, MI: Phanes Press, 1987. The elusive thought of the Pythagoreans captured here in "snapshots."

Hamilton, Alexander, James Madison and John Jay. *The Federalist Papers*. London: Penguin Books, 1987. Perhaps the most detailed and thoughtful set of disquisitions on the nature of politics to appear in one volume.

Hare, R. M. *Moral Thinking*. New York: Oxford University Press, 1981. A classic statement of the universalist and prescriptivist criteria of morals.

Hart, H. L. A. *The Concept of Law*. New York: Oxford University Press, 1961. The most influential defense of legal positivism.

Haskins, C. *The Renaissance of the Twelfth Century*. Cambridge: Harvard University Press, 1927. This is a "classic," drawing attention to the centuries preceding that famous Italian Renaissance, and alerting the reader to the truly original scholarship and science developed in this "Middle" Age.

Hempel, Carl *Aspects of Scientific Explanation*. New York: Free Press, 1965. Hempel's deductive-nomological model defended and defined; one influential approach to the entire nature of science written in the past century.

Herodotus. *The Persian Wars*. G. Rawlinson, trans. New York: Random House, 1942. HISTORY 101, as its inventor intended it.

Hippocrates. Works of various authors, all presumably in the "Hippocratic" tradition, revealing the essentials of Hippocratic medicine.

———. "On the Wounds of the Head," in *Hippocrates*, W. Jones, trans. New York: Putnam, 1923. The Hippocratic understanding of brain-based disorders is a remarkable achievement given its date and the method then available.

Hobbes, Thomas. *Leviathan*. New York: Cambridge University Press, 1996. Here is the "mechanistic" and scientific approach to statecraft by one of the architects of modern thought on the nature of law and society.

Hodges, Andrew. *Alan Turing: The Enigma*. New York: Simon and Schuster, 1983. An interesting account of Turing's background, his approach to the problem of decidability, and his achievements in code-breaking.

Hollingdale, R. J. *Nietzsche: The Man and His Philosophy*. Baton Rouge: Louisiana State University Press, 1965. An accessible account of an elusive and, indeed, troubled mind, as revealed in selections from his major works.

Homer. *The Iliad*. Chicago: University of Chicago Press, 1951. The "Genesis" of Hellenism.

Honore, A. *Emperors and Lawyers*. New York: Oxford University Press, 1994. An authoritative and non-technical introduction to Roman law and to the part taken in its development by a number of emperors.

Hume, David. "Of the Standard of Taste." In *Essays Moral, Political and Literary*. Eugene Miller, ed. Indianapolis: Liberty Fund, 1985. Eugene Miller has collected the most important of Hume's briefer works, including essays that Hume withdrew from publication.

Hume, Robert, trans. *The Thirteen Principal Upanishads*. New York: Oxford University Press, 1971. Snippets that convey the elusive but elevating abstractions of Hindu thought.

Hussey, E. *The Presocratic Philosophers*. Cambridge: Cambridge University Press, 1983. This is a fine collection of the sparse record that remains of this fertile philosophical tradition.

Irwin, T.H. *Plato's Ethics*. Oxford: Oxford University Press, 1995.

Isocrates. *Panegyricus*. George Norlen, trans. Cambridge: Harvard University Press, Loeb Classical Library, 2000. In this work one hears the rhetoric of Isocrates as he attempts to persuade Hellenes to locate their true enemy (Persia) and to cease fighting with each other. In this same place, he identifies the "Hellene" as one committed to a conception of culture.

James, William. *Essays in Radical Empiricism and a Pluralistic Universe*. Chicago: Phoenix Books, 1977. Empiricism with the courage of its convictions, liberated from all forms of the "block universe."

Kant, I. *Groundwork of the Metaphysics of Morals*. Cambridge: Cambridge University Press, 1998. In this work, Kant labors to make clearer what is rather ponderously developed in his *Critique of Practical Reason*. It is, of course, one of the classic works in moral philosophy.

————. *Critique of Pure Reason*. N.K. Smith, trans. New York: St. Martin's Press, 1965. One of the more difficult treatises in all of philosophy; the most systematic of epistemologies and of attempts to determine the nature and limits of rational comprehension.

————. *The Moral Law*. New York: Hutchinson's University Library, 1948. An abbreviated version of the second critique and rather more accessible.

Kaufmann, W. *The Portable Nietzsche*. New York: Viking Press, 1961. Carefully chosen by a leading scholar, this handy volume samples the full range of Nietzsche's critical perspective on life and thought.

Keen, M. *Chivalry*. New Haven: Yale University Press, 1984. This is the best study of an often misunderstood social institution; the one that conveyed to European civilization much that is "civilizing" in human conduct.

Kim, J. *Mind in a Physical World*. Cambridge: MIT Press, 1998. Another approach to the mind/body problem.

Larner, Christina. *Witchcraft and Religion: The Politics of Popular Belief*. New York: Blackwell, 1984. A most interesting analysis of the "witch" theory and the "science" surrounding it.

Leibniz, Gottfried Wilhelm. *The Monadology and Other Philosophical Essays*. Robert Latta, trans. Oxford: Oxford University Press, 1981. These short and numbered passages convey significant features of Leibniz's philosophy of mind.

Lerner, R., and Mahdi, M., eds. *Medieval Political Philosophy*. Ithaca: Cornell University Press, 1963. The selections leave no doubt but that the medieval age was rich and subtle in its political theories and its recognition of the challenges to ordered liberty.

Levack, Brian. *The Witch-Hunt in Early Modern Europe*. New York: Longman, 1995. Data, trials, theories and informing commentary on a woeful chapter in political history.

Lichtheim, G. *Marxism: An Historical and Critical Study*. New York: Praeger, 1961. This is a readable overview of Marxism and its philosophical underpinnings.

Long, A. A. *Hellenistic Philosophy: Stoics, Epicureans, Skeptics*. Berkeley: University of California Press, 1986. A standard work, featuring informing essays on the major figures in these schools of philosophy.

Loux, Michael. *Metaphysics: A Contemporary Introduction*. London: Routledge, 2002. The book to read before reading Aristotle on the same subject.

Lloyd, G. ed. *Hippocratic Writings*. London: Penguin Books, 1978. Works of various authors, all presumably in the "Hippocratic" tradition, revealing the essentials of Hippocratic medicine.

Luce, A. A. *Berkeley's Immaterialism*. New York: Russell and Russell, 1968. Berkeley explained!

Marx, Karl. *Selected Writings*. Indianapolis: Hackett, 1994. Useful selections for those attempting to extract a philosophical position from Marx's critiques of society.

McDonald, Forrest. *Novus Ordo Seclorum: The Intellectual Origins of the Constitution*. Lawrence: University Press of Kansas, 1985. Surely one of the best works on the American founding, its constitutional jurisprudence, and background philosophies on which major proposals were based.

Mill, John Stuart. *Autobiography*. London: Penguin Books, 1989. Very informative, showing the progress of Mill's thought to and then past Comte and Bentham.

————. *On Liberty*. Upper Saddle River, NJ: Prentice Hall, 1996. The "classic" statement of political liberalism.

Moore, G. E. *Principia Ethica (1903)*. New York: Prometheus Books, 1988. A common sense and intuitionist theory of morals.

Nietzsche, Friedrich. *The Portable Nietzsche*. Walter Kaufmann, ed. New York: Penguin Books, 1976. Choice nuggets from the deeply thinking critique of modernity.

Oates, W., ed. *The Stoic and Epicurean Philosophers*. New York: Random House, 1940. Here is a good sample of the works and wisdom of philosophical schools arising after the period in which Plato and Aristotle were most influential.

O'Daly, Gerard. *Augustine's Philosophy of Mind*. Berkeley: University of California Press, 1987. The book to read before reading Augustine's *Confessions*.

Paine, Thomas. *The Rights of Man* (downloadable). The reader today will probably be moved as irresistibly as were those reading the work in the 18th century.

Perry, Ralph Barton. *The Thought and Character of William James*. Nashville, TN: Vanderbilt University Press, 1996. Still the standard biography.

Plantinga, A. *God, Freedom and Evil*. New York: Eardmann, 1974. One attempt to reconcile the traditional conception of God and the problem of evil.

Quinton, A. *Francis Bacon*. London: Hill and Wang, 1980. A most readable general account of Bacon's life and scientific project.

Robinson, D. *An Intellectual History of Psychology* (3rd ed.). Madison: University of Wisconsin Press, 1995. Brief review of major intellectual and scientific developments associated with the emergence of psychology as an independent discipline.

———. *Aristotle's Psychology*. New York: Columbia University Press, 1983, chapter 1. This chapter outlines the "Socratic context" of Aristotle's philosophical development, pointing to differences between the two approaches in method and perspective.

Robinson, D. N. *Philosophy of Psychology*. New York: Columbia University Press, 1982. Review of standard problems of explanation, models of mind, the mind/body problem.

———. *The Enlightened Machine*. New York: Columbia University Press, 1980. A general review of the history and major concepts of the brain sciences, intended for the non-specialist.

———. *Toward a Science of Human Nature: Essays on the Psychologies of Mill, Hegel, Wundt, and James*. New York: Columbia University Press, 1982. Summaries and appraisals of four who dominated 19th-century thought on the nature of mind and mental life.

———. *Wild Beasts and Idle Humours*. Cambridge, MA: Harvard University Press, 1996. Historical review of the legal conception of mental competence from remote antiquity to modern times, with emphasis on the insanity defense.

Rorty, A., ed. *Essays in Aristotle's Ethics*. Berkeley: University of California Press, 1980. Fine interpretive essays are offered, illuminating the often subtle aspects of Aristotle's ethical theory.

Rossiter, C. *The Federalist Papers*. Garden City, NY: Anchor, 1963.

Rousseau, Jean-Jacques. *The Social Contract and Discourses*. London: Dent, 1993. The history of the law's conception of mind in health and disease.

Ruskin, J. *The Stones of Venice*. Vol. 1. London: Smith, Eldeer & Co., 1853. This work did much to restore interest in and admiration for the "Gothic"; a work by the leading aesthete of Victorian England and one of the greatest of prose writers.

Stace, Walter Terence. *The Philosophy of Hegel: A Systematic Exposition*. New York: Dover, 1955. This is not a Hegel for beginners, but it is a good introduction to Hegel's phenomenology.

Sulloway, F. *Freud: Biologist of the Mind*. New York: Basic Books, 1979. By far the best study of Freud as scientist, as aspiring scientific theorist.

Swinburne, R. *Providence and the Problem of Evil*. New York: Oxford University Press, 1998. How is the problem of evil to be understood? The author sees "evil" as permitted on the grounds that it improves all who must contend with it.

Turing, A. "Computing Machinery and Intelligence." In *Mind*, 1950. Vol. 59.

Vernant, Jean Pierre, ed. *The Greeks*. Chicago: University of Chicago Press, 1995. Scholars specializing in different aspects of ancient Greek thought offer rich interpretive essays on the major aspects of that culture.

Voltaire. *Philosophical Letters* (downloadable at www.classicsnetwork.com). Voltaire's comparisons of English and French culture, custom, and science were powerfully influential.

Walzer, Michael. *Just and Unjust Wars*. New York: Basic Books, 2000. Major theories of "just war" are considered and appraised.

Walzer, Richard. *Greek into Arabic: Essays on Islamic Philosophy*. Columbia: University of South Carolina Press, 1970. Islamic philosophy, replete with its Greek inspirations.

Westfall, Richard. *Never at Rest: A Biography of Isaac Newton.* New York: Cambridge University Press, 1994. The authoritative biography of a universal genius.

Wittgenstein, Ludwig. *Philosophical Investigations.* Cambridge, MA: Blackwell, 1997. For all "flies" seeking an exit from the bottle!

Xenophon. *Memorabilia.* Ithaca, NY: Cornell University Press, 1994. Socrates as known by a friend and neighbor.

Yates, Frances. *Giordano Bruno and the Hermetic Tradition.* Chicago: University of Chicago Press, 1964. Renaissance science and its shifting movements away from and back toward mysticism.

Yolton, John. *Thinking Matter: Materialism in Eighteenth-Century Britain.* Minneapolis: University of Minnesota Press, 1983. The arguments of Locke, Priestley, Hartley et al. toward a materialist theory of mind.

Young, R. *Mind, Brain and Adaptation in the Nineteenth Century.* Oxford: Oxford University Press, 1970. The author locates the brain sciences within the larger Darwinian context of the second half of the nineteenth century, but with close attention to anticipations.

Internet Resources:

www.Epistemelinks.com. Best source for basic materials in philosophy.

http://lxserver.uniba.it/lei/suber/philinks.htm. Guide to philosophy on the Internet.